A Journal of Faraway Lands

Trình Quang Phú

Translated from Vietnamese into English by Tuyết Mai
Edited the English version by Kim Hương

Ukiyoto Publishing

All global publishing rights are held by

Ukiyoto Publishing

Published in 2022

Content Copyright © Trình Quang Phú

ISBN 9789360161750

All rights reserved.
No part of this publication may be reproduced, transmitted, or stored in a retrieval system, in any form by any means, electronic, mechanical, photocopying, recording or otherwise, without the prior permission of the publisher.

The moral rights of the author have been asserted.
This book is sold subject to the condition that it shall not by way of trade or otherwise, be lent, resold, hired out or otherwise circulated, without the publisher's prior consent, in any form of binding or cover other than that in which it is published.

www.ukiyoto.com

Foreword

A FEW THOUGHTS ABOUT "A JOURNAL OF THE FARWAY LANDS" BY Trình Quang Phú [1]

The writer NGUYEN TRUONG
(Director, Editor-in-Chief of Thanh Nien Publishing House)

In the 63-year of Thanh Nien Publishing House, author Trinh Quang Phu is one of our closest collaborators. His publication "The Red River Girl" published in 1962 had significant impression. Since then, more than 40 books have been published by him, many of which have been reprinted 16 times.

"A Journal of the Farway lands" that are in the hands of readers is his latest work at his "rare" matured age, but his pen is still strong, and his flow of writing is still powerful.

Journal is Trinh Quang Phu's forte. His writing is simply natural, yet thoroughly and deeply. We see the glimpse of Paustovsky when the writer describes the beautiful scenery of Moscow in the golden autumn then the birch forest was in its changing season "a bright yellow 3-dimensional space as if to lift up the human soul ", or the scene". And the beauty of Mount Fuji of the land of cherry blossoms is as if in the painting of Levitan, appearing in front of the reader.

We see Nguyen Tuan's style in Trinh Quang Phu's writing which is illustrated through his thoroughness in researching documents and writing with his thorough thoughtfulness and understanding. The author visits many countries but not neglected, he has read, listened, exploited and took photos so that his writing is thorough description and clearly describes all the aspects of history, geography and culture of every country. Therefore, reading his journal is interesting and attractive; while enjoying the smooth writing of illustrating beautiful

---

[1] The introduction to the 1st publication of "A Journal of the Faraway lands" – Thanh Nien Publishing House 2017

scenery, readers deeply understand about the country that they have never been to and contemplating about the world.

The author once worked as the diplomat in the National Front for the Liberation of South Vietnam which was the Provisional Revolutionary Government of the South Vietnam in 1969, he was immersed in the heroic atmosphere of that times, when Vietnam was "standing on the top" of the battle against colonialism and imperialist aggression. So, wherever the delegation visited, they were warmly welcomed and even promoted as heroes. Would Vietnam ever be admired and welcomed by the world as so?!

The author has great luck and opportunity to travel from the East to the West, from the South to the North, from vast countries such as the Soviet Union, China, and the United States to small countries with only few hundred thousands of people and an area of few kilometers such as the Principality of Monaco, Andorra, Liechtenstein ... Thoroughly understanding each country and discovering the wonders of each land, he and his readers will realize the truth and the way to support our country to be equal to these countries and surpass them...

Understanding people through his writing, Trinh Quang Phu has lived a life of experience, he has traveled a lot, understood and immersed himself in the most heroic times of the nation. As a result, it explains why he has written a lot about Uncle Ho, about the country's political and spiritual life and the revolutionary heroism... He loves this regime from the bottom of his heart and turns his love into powerful writing.

Contents

Impressive Singapore	1
Remembering Uncle Ho,	8
On A Visit To Quang Chau	8
A Moment Of Bali	15
Legend Of Langkawi	22
Phuket – Jade Island	29
Cambodia – The Land Of Smiles	39
Feeling The Land Of Cherry Blossom	51
From Seoul To Busan	62
Jeju Island, The Wonder Of The World	76
Taiwan – The Pearl Island	85
Visiting Algeria	96
In Memory Of France	106
Russia-The Autumn	134
Moscow, The Golden Autumn	140
The Bridge Of Love	149
Saint Petersburg - Leningrad And The White Nights	151
The Land Of Roses	158
Profound Berlin	171
Visiting Musical Genius W. A. Mozart	179
The Western Corners	183
From Copenhagen To Bodensee	195
Venice – A Honeymoon Destination	201
Verona, The City Of Love	204
Ten Days In Cali	211
From Sydney To Gold Coast	223
About the Author	*230*

Impressive Singapore

Known as an island nation, Singapore has an area of less than 700 km² which includes 54 islands, in which 34 small islands are uninhabited; the national population is about 5 million people and it has a developed economy.

In the past, this island area was once called Temasek (which means "sea" in Malaysian) and had a very prosperous development period. In the 16th century, Temasek belonged to the Kingdom of Johor (today Johor is a land of Malaysia, sharing its border with Singapore).

According to a legend, Prince Nila Utama of Johor dynasty in 11th century, in a hunt in Temasek region, encountered lions, so he named the region Singa (which in Malaysian means "lion") and called it Singa Pura ("pura" means "city" in Malaysian). In 1819, Mr. Thomas Stamford Raffles, a member of the board of directors of the East India Company from Great Britain, negotiated with the Kingdom of Johor and, together, they eventually signed an agreement that would grant his company the rights to exploit the Singapura as a commercial port, which he renamed as Singapore. Singapore quickly developed from an old fishing wharf to a British colonial trading port. Today it is the urban center of Singapore and, at the bustling waterfront, stands a statue of Raffles who discovered Singapore.

In 1959, Singapore was split into a separate country, but continued to belong to the Federation of Malaya, along with the autonomous states of Sabah and Sarawak. It was not until the 9 of August 1965 that, due to disagreements with the Federation government, Singapore declared its independence and became the Republic of Singapore with Mr. Lee Kuan Yew as Prime Minister. The Singapore flag with a crescent moon embracing 5 small stars symbolized a rising Singapore on a white background of purity. The five small stars represent Singapore's five goals: democracy, equality, development, justice, and peace.

After becoming an independent republic, Singapore faced many difficulties such as poor natural resources, especially clean water; low intellectual level among the population; high unemployment rate, and lack of housing. To tackle these problems, Lee Kuan Yew enlisted the support of the country's allies and rallied its people in resolute efforts to build infrastructure, roads, electricity and water supply and, especially, public housing. He immediately built two North-South roads across the Tebrau channel that would connect to Johor Bahru, Malaysia's second largest city located in close proximity to Singapore, breaking the isolation of the island nation. Lee Kuan Yew gradually adopted a consistent policy to get rid of poverty by ways of export and services development. Industrial zones were constructed to attract investors. He went on to create mechanism of free trade zone and free market and then expanded the nation's seaport, building it into a free port. The result was that, two years after the declaration of independence, there were 1,000 factories owned by Singaporeans and 100 factories from many countries, with an average of 3,000 people in one factory, mostly concentrated in the northern area bordering Johor. In the following years, with the most favorable tax regime and banking services, thousands of foreign companies set up branches in Singapore for their worldwide business. Singapore became an industrial country; the port of Singapore became an international transshipment port.

Since those early days, planning and mechanisms have always been prioritized. Along with economic development, Singapore has been always determined to turn itself into the most beautiful green city in the world.

The environmental protection for Singapore is carried out not only by the state, but by the whole population as well, in a highly conscious way. No one cut down trees; planning trees become the common sense for everyone. Couples contribute S$ 200 to plant a tree of happiness on their wedding day. Businessmen contribute to plant trees for prosperity. Singapore has the program of "Every park is my garden". All people, from the youth to the old, from the households to the whole community as a whole, love green, plant trees and keep the city clean. Laws which prohibit cutting down trees, littering, creating graffiti on walls, and leaving cigarette butts, are voluntarily obeyed by the people. The clean streets of Singapore have made the green color even more impressive. Green is a message not only for this island nation but for all of humanity: Keeping green is keeping the earth alive.

After a half-century struggle, Singapore has become a developed country with a GDP per capita of above 61,000 USD. Singapore is determined to strive for becoming a world's leading prosperous city, the central point of the global intellectual economy network.

***

Singapore is a very narrow and small country that has constantly grown by human hands. Mountain soil, coastal sand, and coastal sand from other countries are used for land reclamation. In this way, Singapore has been able expand from a total territory of 581 km² as of 1960 to 700 km² as it is today and is striving for another 100 km² in the next 15 years. New massive tourist facilities have been built on these great reclaimed lands.

One thing that deeply impressed us is the development of tourism and services in Singapore. It seems that the whole city of Singapore is a great resort due to its crowded high-class hotels along with commercial areas and supermarkets all close together. Green trees and flowers can be seen everywhere in the whole city. Flowers in the airport, flowers running along the boulevards, flowers on the bridge overpasses, all are brilliant. It is said that Singapore Prime Minister Lee Kuan Yew, on his visits to other countries, has frequently brought new varieties of plants back to Singapore. Big old trees covering whole streets, and tropical forests with their abundant shrubs and vines, all look like a great jungle right in the middle of the city, next to the 5-star Mandarin hotel. The rivers, canals and lakes are embellished. The authorities paid meticulous attention to planning. The Planning Department under the government has been gathering many talented architects, who carefully calculate every square meter of land with a view to ensure good ventilation for all households and respect the environment. Thus, newly built houses never huddle together or cover previously ones.

Amusement parks, such as Jurong Zoo, Night Safari, Orchid Garden, Ecological Garden, Sentosa Island, are attractive destinations of this island nation for many years. During my many visits to Singapore, I have been to these places - Jurong Zoo, Night Safari and the like. Of those, I really liked Sentosa Island, which is, in my opinion, a great model of green tourism. That's why I call Singapore as a great resort. Great care for ecology can be seen everywhere. Walking in the middle of Singapore's main road, Orchard Avenue with ancient tamarind trees 30-40 m high running along both of its sides, their branches covering the entire road, listening to birds singing, cicadas chirping, you feel like walking in the middle of a forest. Great care for ecology can be witnessed in every hotel, while public services and public transport are readily for comfortable use.

***

In the inauguration speech as Prime Minister, Mr. Lee Hsien Loong (son of Mr. Lee Kuan Yew) said: *"We have had success, great success. But we cannot stand still. Because the world is changing, the people are changing, Singapore must also change", "We must get rid of what is no longer relevant, create new ones, develop new strengths and new strategies to thrive in a different world".*

As the Prime Minister of Singapore has said, Singapore is not satisfied with what it has, never stops, but always makes breakthroughs. In the early years of the 21st century, many new projects have been launched and even the already impressive ones have been changed to be more impressive, more beautiful, more civilized.

The Prime Minister and the officials of the National Assembly and the Government have long rejected casinos projects, but then opened two world-class casinos at once. And in the first year, those attracted two million visitors from other countries to visit Singapore, and what followed was a planned investment in amusement parks and large-scale ecological areas that have strong attraction to foreign tourists.

I would like to mention here a new destination *"in a different world"* of Singapore, by the words of the Prime Minister of Singapore himself, which is Marina Bay Sands. A complex of entertainment, shopping, casino and resort, it is located on the beautiful Marina Bay. Five years ago, it was just an ordinary park. Now, the sight of Marina Bay as from the bridge overlooking it on the left is simply mesmerizing. As I was moving from the airport and crossing this bridge on my way to the center of Singapore, the whole landscape struck me as the most beautiful city in the world. Three 55-storey towers rise to the sky, close to each together. A casino, a 6-star hotel with 2,600 rooms, an exhibition area, an international conference center, a shopping mall with 300 shops and famous restaurants, all are housed in these three towers. With an area of only 15.5 hectares, Las Vegas Stands Group has invested 6 billion USD to create a modern and ecological new world. Located on the top of three 55-storey towers is 10,000 m² Sky Park, designed in the shape of a great green boat located on a 400 m high floor. Amid the sky and among floating clouds, there are beautifully manicured gardens, completed with trees and flowers. A swimming pool where visitors can have the feeling of swimming in the clouds. In the Sky Park, there is a Spa area, and a restaurant with famous chefs. This is one of the five top-class restaurants of Marina Bay Sands Sky Park that can accommodate up to 4,000 guests at the same time. Only by walking in Sky Park, can we fully feel the rising of Singapore to new heights. Also in Marina Bay there is a financial district with skyscrapers reflecting on the bay and, within 5-minute walk, there are three gardens: South Bay, East Bay, and Central Bay. The 101-hectare garden containing more than 250,000 species of rare and precious plants in the world is a unique, modern and perhaps unmatched park in the world.

The largest garden is South Bay with giant trees that give you a profound impression with the help of the play of lights at night. The garden is located in a 16-storey greenhouse where rainwater is stored, and electricity is fuelled by solar energy. A bridge connecting two of the giant trees makes it possible for pedestrians to admire the whole garden from above. During the day, you are lost in the land of green forests, while at night the green forest becomes truly magical with the outdoor light show at the OCBC Garden Rhapsody. There is an African garden with dates, Algerian Néples, and the typical hot Mediterranean climate. There is an air-conditioned, greenhouse garden for Northern plants and flowers. All of these are located on the shore of the bay and make Marina Bay an extremely beautiful and unique princess. This complex won an award at the 2012 International Architecture Festival.

Singapore has always been a green city, a city of trees and flowers. Now, with Garden by the Bay, it becomes even greener, more ecological, more civilized, and more attractive.

My friend David Koh also introduced me to a unique project called River Safari – called by the Vietnamese 'a wild river park'. It symbolizes eight major rivers of the world with the presence of 5,000 animal species and 300 aquatic species. The Mississippi River in the Americas, the Nile in Africa, and the Mekong in Asia, all can be seen here. This is Asia's first large-scale wildlife park.

***

I return to Sentosa Island where I have been many times. And right from the first time, standing on the escalator and watching hundreds of types of fish in the underwater world made a deep impression on me. I secretly think that a tourism model like Sentosa is perfect and needs to be multiplied. Back to Sentosa this time, I saw clearly the will of this nation, just like the image of the crescent moon on the national flag. The new moon will become the full moon - Sentosa has grown unimaginably. In just a decade, Sentosa Island became a tourist paradise worthy of its name, the Island of Tranquility (Sentosa in Malay means Peace). Genting Group (Malaysia) is famous for its exploration and transformation of the Genting hills into a casino with full services that attracts a lot of international visitors. Genting Group won the bid for this North Sentosa and invested US$ 5.38 billion in the Resort World Sentosa complex.

Resort World Sentosa and Marina Bay Sands are two of the largest investment tourism complexes in the world.

Resorts World Sentosa is a large-scale resort complex with 6 adjacent 5-star hotels. The entire northern cluster of the island is a high-class Resort World with entertainment and sports areas such as a modern casino, two high-class golf courses, and a movie studio. Universal Studios was the first Hollywood movie park in the area. Young people who like thrills can experience a 4-D journey in the world's first Far Far Away castle. The world-class entertainment is very impressive with world's largest robot technology shows, musical performances, and circus performances. It also has a unique Crane Dance, a musical performed by top stars. Resorts World Sentosa is also a shopping place, with many luxury shopping stores designed by famous designer Michael Graves, author of very modern and attractive works. Many Asian-European, Japanese, and Korean restaurants are located on Festival Walk, serving guests all night.

I can not help but express here my admiration for Marine Life Park, a new aquarium, even bigger and more modern. The largest marine aquarium in the world with all kinds of big and small fish including the rare dugong. The giant rays soar like 'flying fortresses' in the ocean. Marine Park, with over half a kilometer long tropical river together with the Maritime Museum offers visitors the most satisfying knowledge about oceanography. In earlier times, visiting Sentosa could be a one-day trip. Today, if you want to experience all of Sentosa, you may have to stay here for at least 3 to 5 days. It makes sense to call Sentosa a new world, a paradise of tourism. I still like tropical forests with multiple layers of trees and vines. Many modern, magnificent constructions are being built, and yet 70 per cent of the island is set apart for ecology. David told me that Sentosa was formerly called a dead island with a poor fishing village, but today Sentosa is a tourist paradise with millions of visitors every year.

Sentosa Butterfly Park has up to 2,500 butterflies from 50 butterfly species from all over the world. There is an area where the entire lighting is supplied by 5,000 fireflies, an ingenious way to attract guests. Walking through the Sentosa amid the singing of birds and the colorful butterflies fluttering their wings as if to welcome me, I feel myself elevated. Alone among thousands of butterflies as if lost in a fairyland, I pondered about Singapore, the way in which its government has been ruling the nation, the numerous policies set out to attract talented people, and how Singaporeans have been resolutely striving forward. Singapore has no lions. A thousand years ago, Prince Nila Utama must have mistakenly seen an animal resembling a lion, so he called it Singa. However, the use of "lion" as a symbol for Singapore is absolutely true. Singapore has been always rising with the strength of a Singa - lion. That strength is the combined result of the determination, consensus, policies, mechanisms, and institutions with which Singapore moves forward to the top ranks of the world.

October 2014

Remembering Uncle Ho, On A Visit To Quang Chau

I have been to China many times, on different business trips that took me to a number of different places, from Beijing, Shanghai, Tianjin, to the Great Wall and Yihe Yuan, and Zhongnanhai. The area that left the strongest impressions in me, however, is Guangzhou, the capital of Guangdong province, one of the three largest cities in China.

The most profound impression to me is the fact that Guangdong known as the first capital city of the first legitimate dynasty of Vietnam established by Emperor Trieu Da (Trieu Vu De) and his beloved wife, Queen Trinh Thi Lan Nuong. We are proud to learn that a daughter of our Trinh clan became the queen of the first dynasty of Nam Viet over 2,200 years ago. Traditionally, our historians have once failed to have a right understanding about Trieu Da, and yet, but at the beginning of our national revolution, Uncle Ho, in his speech "History of our country", said: *"Trieu Da is the wise king / Nam Viet the dynasty that passed down through five kings"*. Nguyen Trai, in his "Binh Ngo Dai Cao" also mentioned the Trieu Dynasty in the following, *"Trieu, Dinh, Ly, Tran succeeded in founding the country / With Han, Tang, Song, Nguyen claiming to be emperors"*. The temple of Trieu Da and Queen Trinh Thi Lan Nuong was built and worshipped by kings of dynasties in Xuan Quan (Van Giang, Hung Yen province) and in Dong Xam (Thai Binh province). On returning to Dong Xam, we saw the statues of King Trieu Da and Queen Trinh Thi Lan Nuong. The bustling festival is organized annually. Queen Trinh Thi Lan Nuong was a beautiful and talent woman. She was known as the person who established the Chèo village and the Ca Trù village. I wonder whether she was the founder of the art of Chèo as it is today. During my research, I learned more about the origin of Trieu Da. He was formerly known under the name Nguyen Than, born in Van Noi, Thanh Oai, Hanoi. His father was Hung Duc Cong, the younger brother of the 18th Hung King. His mother was Tran Thi Quy. Nguyen Than lived in Chem (Hanoi) during his childhood with his parents. When Thuc Phan An Duong Vuong captured Van Lang, he was exiled to Guangxi. A mandarin of Guangdong province noticed his health and good appearance and adopted him, then changed his name to Trieu Da; Trieu Da could speak both Vietnamese and Chinese. After his decease, Trieu Da's grave was moved to Binh Phan, Thanh Oai, Hanoi. Therefore, Trieu Da was Vietnamese, founder of the country Nam Viet which included the Guangdong and Guangxi provinces of present-day China including its capital of Panyu, known as Guangzhou city. The independence of the country was kept intact during the reign of the five kings of the Trieu Dynasty, which lasted 97 years.

I've been rambling a bit about history because I could never expect such a beautiful story that, several thousands of years ago, our ancestors from our Trinh family had produced a queen who lived happily with Trieu Da and gave birth to Trong Thuy (whom later married My Chau), also in this land of Guangzhou.

I have been to Guangzhou since this area was still in poverty. In those days, the roads were very cramped and narrow, the houses in poor condition, and life greatly difficult. Today, Cantonese people still have a dish which is porridge served with salted radish, a dish from the years of poverty.

Today, Guangzhou is one of the busiest and fast-growing cities of China with sustainable development planning. Its 3-4 tier transport infrastructure connects the expressway to a lot of different directions. Guangzhou connects to Shenzhen, Foshan, and Dongguan to become a megacity with a population of nearly 14 million people, of which immigrants account for 40 percent, and the city is known as a " Global City". Guangzhou's Baiyun Airport used to be very small with only two telescopic tubes. Today, it is a modern airport ranked among the top 20 largest airports in the world, serving approximately 45 million passengers annually. In Guangzhou, motorbikes have been banned for more than a decade, to be replaced by eight subway lines transporting millions of people every day. Guangzhou's growth rate has always been around 7% and its GDP per capita is over 24,000 USD, a number that speaks for itself. Its people, who used to live on nothing more than porridge, dumplings and salted radish, now have an average income per capita ten times higher than that in the big cities of Vietnam. At night, seen from the window of a 5-star hotel overlooking Guangzhou, the city looked like a brilliant sky with endless colorful lights; perhaps only few cities in the world have such colorful and brilliant night lights. The Canton Tower is 600 meters high, the second highest in the world just after the Tokyo TV Tower, and is symmetrical with the Canton West Tower, also known as the International Financial Center of Guangzhou with 103 storeys (over 438 meters high).

Canton Tower is not only a TV tower, but also a tourist attraction. Guests can go up to the top of tower for a panoramic view of the city and enjoy their lunch in the middle of clouds or have a cup of coffee while overlooking Guangzhou at night. In particular, the Canton Tower is equipped with a unique lighting system with changing colors wherever a light show takes place. Standing on the banks of the Zhu Jiang River, you can look up to marvel at the sight of the tower rising to the sky with its endless play of lights and reflecting itself on the shimmering and fanciful Zhu Jiang River.

As for the Guangzhou West Tower, it looks like a pillar city, with a height of 438 meters and 250,000 square meters of floor area. The first sixty floors are for offices and services; whereas all the remaining floors, from the 69th up to the 98th one, are occupied by the Four Seasons Hotel. Assuming the average of over ten square meters for each person, the tower has a capacity of over 20,000 people.

This city is abundant in tourist attractions and landscapes. I would like, however, to dedicate the remaining part of this article to the recollection of Uncle Ho's activities during his years in Guangzhou.

Twelve years after leaving Nha Rong Port and traveling to France, America, and England, Uncle Ho came to the Soviet Union where he worked in the Communist International; thanks to which he learned a lot about Marxism, about the revolution needed to liberate the nation from foreign oppression, and about Communism. Now equipped with an enormous knowledge with which to save his country, he decided to return. Considering the situation his native country was in, however, he had to decide the place he should go first. Should it be Thailand, Cambodia, Laos, or Singapore?

Uncle Ho determined that revolution, first of all, is about the people, the leadership, and the organization. Guangzhou is nearby to Vietnam and various groups of young Vietnamese patriotic people were gathering together in Guangzhou, including Phan Boi Chau and his comrades, and

Tâm Tâm Xã, a revolutionary organization of young Vietnamese patriots like Ho Tung Mau, Le Hong Son, Pham Hong Thai, Le Hong Phong. Out of those, the one who left the most powerful impact to him was Pham Hong Thai, who attempted to assassinate the Governor General of Indochina Henri Merlin who passed by Guangzhou on his way from Japan to Vietnam. Pham Hong Thai, with the support of Le Hong Son, entered the ballroom disguised as a journalist. Two grenades were hidden in the camera. In those days, the camera was vet big, not convenient to carry by hands and often covered with a black cloth. Pham Hong Thai threw both grenades into the middle of the dining table but only one of these exploded, and Governor General Merlin was injured in the leg... Police arrested Pham Hong Thai. The 28-year-old man bravely overcame the encirclement of enemies and rushed towards the bank of *Zhu Jiang* River. Being chased, he missed the rendezvous with his team. Pham Hong Thai sacrificed his life so as not to fall into the hands of the enemies. The event, called "The Bomb Sa Diện", and the sacrifice of Pham Hong Thai urged Uncle Ho even more. He saw clearly that Guangzhou could be the international base for the revolution in the home country. Uncle Ho officially asked the Communist International to let him return to Guangzhou with a view to build Vietnam's revolutionary forces. However, "because of many reasons, one after another, week after week, month after month" his proposal was not responded ("Ho Chi Minh Chronicle", National Politics Publishing House). Uncle Ho had to ask for help from his French communist comrades from the Communist International. Finally, at the end of September 1924, the Communist International made the decision to officially send Uncle Ho to Guangzhou in order to establish a communist organization in Indochina under the fund of the Oriental Committee of the Communist International. It was arranged by the Communist International that Uncle Ho arrived at Guangzhou under the guise of a reporter from the Russian news agency Rosta with the pseudonym O. Lus. On November 11, 1924, the ship under the Soviet Union flag, with Uncle Ho on board, began its journey up the *Zhu Jiang* River in the direction of Guangzhou. At that time, M. Borodin, an acquaintance of Uncle Ho in the Soviet Union, was Head of the Soviet Union's advisory delegation to the Government of Sun Yat-sen. Uncle Ho, under the name Ly Thuy, was assigned as translator for Borodin's delegation. In a discussion with me, Professor Hoang Tranh, a Chinese scientist who had studied Ho Chi Minh all his life, stated: In

1924, Sun Yat-sen had just established the Revolutionary Government with the slogan "Associating with the Soviet Union and the Communism, Supporting the Workers and Farmers". The revolutionary movement was so vibrant. Ho Chi Minh's Chinese friends who knew him since the 1920s back in France, including as Zhou En-lai, Li Fuchun, Zhang Tailei, as well as numerous Vietnamese journalists and patriots, were all in Guangzhou. Guangzhou was then known as the "Moscow of the East", with the Soviet advisory delegation to the Sun Yat-sen Government. Those were the advantages that President Ho Chi Minh discovered, so he decided to go to Guangzhou in order to build the foundation for the Communist Party of Vietnam and for the Vietnamese revolution.

In the first days after arrival to Guangzhou, Uncle Ho stayed in the headquarters of the Soviet advisory delegation. After being able to contact the Vietnamese journalists and youths, however, Uncle Ho moved in and lived with them under the name Vuong Bac; he founded the Communist Union and then the "Vietnam Revolutionary Youth Association" located at 13 and 13.1 (13B) Van Minh street, (presently 248-250), a 3-storey house located on quiet small road running along the Chau Giang river. This location was also where Uncle Ho opened three training courses for nearly 30 key persons of the Vietnamese revolution. It can be said that this was the "training cradle" of the first revolutionary leaders of Vietnam including Tran Phu, Le Hong Phong, Pham Van Dong, Nguyen Luong Bang, Phan Trong Binh, Le Thiet Hung…

From here, the Vietnam Youth Revolutionary Association began to expand its operation to Vietnam, built its bases throughout the three regions of Central, South, and North of Vietnam, and even among the Vietnamese-Thai population in Thailand. The association had contact with the Communist Party of China, the French Communist Party, and the Communist International. Uncle Ho also selected elite members to send to the Eastern Soviet Union University and to the Huangpu Military School (directed by Zhou Enlai and Ye Jianying) for training with a view to prepare them as the core force of the Party and, later on, the revolutionary military activities. These people included, among others, Tran Phu, Le Hong Phong, Bui Cong Trung, Phung Chi Kien, Nguyen Son, Le Quang Dat, Le Thiet Hung... Also here, Uncle Ho founded the roneo-printed weekly "The Youth" with a pentagram on the front page next to the headline in both Vietnamese and Chinese.

The first issue of "The Youth" was published on June 21, 1925 and the weekly had a total of 88 issues throughout its existence. "The Youth" is the first publication of the Vietnamese revolutionary press. June 21 was later designated as the Vietnamese Press Day.

On the other hand, Uncle Ho gathered a number lectures initially designed for the revolutionary classes and, after an amount of careful editing, he made them into the first revolutionary book called "The Revolutionary Road". In 1927, the book was officially published. Also, in Guangzhou, he campaigned for the establishment of the Union of Oppressed Countries including Vietnam, China, Korea, India, Indonesia and Myanmar. Uncle Ho wrote the manifesto of independence including the famous sentence: "We should unite soon and join forces to claim our rights and freedoms! Let's join forces to save our people." It was these activities that urged Uncle Ho decide to unite the various party organizations in Vietnam, an act that led to the establishment of the Communist Party of Vietnam on February 3, 1930 (January 6 according to the lunar calendar), the first official political party of Vietnam revolution.

Guangzhou is the cradle of the Vietnamese Revolution, the land where Uncle Ho had planted the seeds for the Communist Party of Vietnam. The Chinese professor Hoang Tranh also said: "China has 33 provinces. Uncle Ho has lived and worked in 21 provinces during 10 years. But Guangzhou was the first place where he was most active and left the most memories. Here he not only made the decisive preparations for the Vietnamese revolution, but also took part in the movement to develop the Chinese Communist Party. Uncle Ho himself wrote: "I had the honor to work in the Communist Party of China during two periods. Arriving in Guangzhou in 1924-1927, I was observing the revolutionary movement in our country while participating in the tasks assigned by the Communist Party of China".

Uncle Ho had been to and stayed at many other places in Guangzhou as well, such as the second campus on Hung Nhan Street, and Dong Cao, Mr. Bao's restaurant at Dong Hieu Square, where Uncle Ho stayed for a long time after his sojourn at N.13 on Van Minh Street.

Ninety-five years having passed, the house at 13 Van Minh Street, the training school for Vietnamese revolutionaries in those days is still there, recognized by China as a national revolutionary relic, and a destination for tourists.

I spent the whole morning visiting Hoang Hoa Cuong Park where the grave of Pham Hong Thai is located, and also the burial ground for 71 Chinese martyrs who died in the Tan Hoi revolution next to Pham Hong Thai's grave. Uncle Ho came here with his Vietnamese comrades to pay to the brave patriot.

I have visited the house at 13 Van Minh Street. The house is still as it was 100 years ago, with the tables and chairs, and the meeting room of the Vietnamese Revolutionary Youth Association. Uncle Ho used to stand there to give lectures or sit at the middle chair to run the meetings. Here, receiving the envoy of the Communist International Jacques Doriot, Uncle Ho ordered the outstanding young man Pham Van Dong (later Prime Minister of Vietnam) to give the welcome speech in French. The house next door was where the students lived and Uncle Ho also lived with them. In order to earn money, Uncle Ho had to work overtime as interpreter, typist, sometimes selling newspapers and cigarettes on the streets of Guangzhou.

I stood on the windy bank of Chau Giang River at sunset, looking at the cable-stayed bridges and watching the cruise ships with glowing lights bringing tourists leisurely down the river, and suddenly thought of the Soviet ship that landed in Guangzhou with Uncle Ho onboard ninety-five years ago, on the 11 of May. I felt like Pham Hong Thai still here, and wondered how our Uncle might have spent many nights walking along the bank of river from the house in Van Minh street, thinking about the future of the country. I wonder if there was a girlfriend accompanying him on this riverside. Or was he thinking about his first love at Nha Rong Port 13 years ago... That's right, the love of a 35-year-old person was fulfilling him, becoming the great love for his homeland and for the country. That love was the fire that spread to young people attending the class of the Revolutionary Youth to later become leaders and key personnel of our Party and country. Everything is changeable, but the memories of Uncle Ho and the friendship between the two countries Vietnam and China are eternal.

May 2019

A Moment Of Bali

I have been to Indonesia several times, once as a member of the delegation of the National Front for the Liberation of South Viet Nam, led by Madame Nguyen Thi Binh, crossing the Tan A pass and flew to Bandung to attend a conference. Another time, I came at the invitation of the Chairman of the Ciputra Group to visit Jakarta and 10 Ciputra projects.

Consisting of 17,508 islands of all sizes, Indonesia is the fourth largest country in the world in terms of population, and also the world's largest Muslim community. But for Bali, widely known as a Southeast Asian Eden, this was my first encounter.

I had a younger but close friend, Professor Thai Quang Trung, a French Vietnamese who had been residing in Singapore for several decades and whose footprints were all over ASEAN countries. He was a dedicated person whose life-long goal and concern was to introduce and promote green economy and green tourism in his motherland.

He often told me stories about green tourism models in ASEAN, and this time he invited Daniel Popo, an award-winning architect who participated in the planning of the island, to be our Bali tour guide.

Daniel was a sturdy, dark-skinned man with a gentle and friendly smile. I shook his hand, "Delighted to meet you, planner of a paradise." He smiled humbly, "A token of love for my hometown."

As night came, we drank Singaporean coffee and chatted. I asked him what was his first priority when he devised the blue print for this island. He explained it slowly, as a way to familiarize us with Bali.

Bali is a chicken-shaped island whose head faces the south, and whose beak are its two ports, Cekik and Gilimanuk. The comb is made up by the Pragat Agung peninsula and the smaller, westernmost islands. With more than three million residents, this is one of the most densely populated islands in the world. This sacred land is home to more than 20,000 temples, large and small, old and new. Each town, each village, each workshop has its own temple, and the whole island is consequently immersed in a profound spiritual atmosphere. Mountains are sacred, lakes are sacred, and forests are also sacred. There is an active volcano in Bali, also Indonesia's highest mountain at 3000 meters, the Gunung Agung. Balinese believe that it is the home of many gods.

Originally a mountainous area, Bali features many waterfalls and lakes, is surrounded by the blue ocean and endowed with beautiful beaches and wild bays.

Hinduism arrived in Bali as early as the first century CE. Balinese culture is rich and unique in its combination of localized Hinduism and Indonesian Islam.

Returning to my question, Daniel said, "My planning, it was such a difficult task, because it had to be built upon the sacred but rather primitive local Hindu culture, where people mostly lived by agriculture, fishery, and handicrafts. On the other hand it was also an advantage for the planner. I think it was essential to preserve the indigenous culture and the gifts of nature, and to enhance their beauty. Tourism is all about enjoying, not just good housing and good food, but also about imbuing yourself in the local quintessential, with culture at it core. Spirituality can be both a selling point and a way to foster kindness and empathy in people's hearts and minds.

***

Our first night in Bali, Popo arranged for us to stay in a luxury seaside resort. I had never been to a resort of this type. The bungalows were of ancient architecture, the garden was dimly lit, barely enough for you to find your path, which were lined with statues of god. Those lifelike figures startled us quite often on our way back from dinner. The rooms were luxurious but offered no modern facilities, no television or telephone, all softly lit by coconut-oil lamps. "Let's return to primitive life for one night," Thai Quang Trung and Daniel both laughed. "A true vacation is where you are cut off from the daily noise of life," Daniel added. It was a unique concept much appreciated by Westerners, which made up a fair share of guest here.

After spending one night in that unique resort, we seemed to be fully recharged, thanks to a deep sleep in full isolation from the bustle of modern life. Daniel took us on a Bali tour. We spent two days sweeping that corner of the island, visting resorts, beaches and several temples.

Balinese culture is the essence of Daniel's mindset. I loved his talks about the jungle culture, which I shared and fully agreed. Human originated from the jungle, they first inhabited the caves and fed on the jungle, before migrating to the riverside and following the creeks and rivers to the sea. Balinese jungle houses spiritual mysteries. The most famous one, Ubud, even had a palace inside it. Balinese call Ubud the land of sauntering gods. Statues were placed everywhere in the jungle, giving it a sacred and spiritual ambience. Ubud is also the sanctuary for hundreds of long-tailed macaque, who are fearless of human and often naughty enough to steal food from visitors.

Luxury resorts and villas are also permitted in the spiritual Ubud. I had been to a cliffhanging villa with an infinity pool which gave you an ethereal, eco-friendly experience. Jump into this pool and you would immerse yourself in the vast white clouds above and the 70-meter deep gorge below. An European visitor said to me, "I really love this, having a world of your own, an exclusive space full of cloud and mountain's fragrance. The road that runs through Ubud jungle is only wide enough for two lanes of car. The town of Ubud is situated on a steep slope and is just a wall away from the jungle. Every cottage is neatly hedged. The terraced rice fields features a marvelous countryside painting, where the steps of brilliant yellow rice resembles a Balinese's stairway to heaven. Wood carving is a local specialty. Ubud is home to the renowned female writer Elizabeth Chandler and the inspiration for her best-seller "Eat, Pray, Love." It was the novel and its movie adaption that brought Bali to the wider world.

There is a poem about the forest of Ubud, about the forest of Bali which is roughly translated as follows: "Smooth River / immense terraced fields / towering mountains / deep mountains / tranquil pristine lake / deep caves /wild and spiritual forest". Balinese has a great love for jungle and mountain, they treasure them as a vital part of their lives.

The mountain of Gunung Agung looms large over Bali and can be seen from anywhere in the island. Balinese legend has it that Agung was created when the Hindu God Pasupati split Mount Meru and formed Mount Agung with a fragment. Along the slopes of the Gunung Agung, at the altitude of one thousand meters, scatter twenty two temples over three kilometers, with Pura Besakih at the center. It occupies such a scenic spot, everlastingly reflected by the mirror-like lake nearby. Its high-rise gate looks like an entrance to the spiritual world.

Being more than two thousand years old, this is the largest, oldest and most sacred temple, which carries, in its quietude and serenity, the ancient history of Bali. Bali is definitely number one when it comes to temple. The island of 3 million people has more than 20,000 temples of all sizes, which means in average there is a temple for every 150 locals. Many of them are renowned for their sacredness and mystique, as well as for their beauty. That includes the Gunung Kawi, built in the 11th century in the green valley of Lushest, the Uluwatu which worships the sea goddess Dewi Danu, standing on a high cliff overlooking the awe-inspiring blue sea. Then there's the Tanah Lot, one of the seven seaside temples, which is located on a small island just a few hundred feet from the shore. At high tide, the temple becomes an island, its yard covered with waves. At low tide, it reconnects with mainland. The looming temple serenely overlooks the sea, producing such a tranquil and sacred scene. In Balinese Tanah Lot means "temple on the sea." Balinese has strong faith in their gods, they believe that gods reside on the mountains and in the jungles, they travel to villages at night to grant their blessings. Therefore each evening they put white champaca, jasmine, plumeria in trays folded by lotus or banana leaves and place them on the doorsteps. They say the gods always drop by before sunrise, and the flowers are meant to be their tributes. And they go to bed with their heads towards Gunung Agung, where they believe is the sanctuary of the high gods and also their ancestors. Many solemn rituals are conducted every year.

Local ceremonies are always accompanied by music and dances in colorful and extravagant costumes, reminding me of the traditional opera in Middle Viet Nam. Every day there is always a ceremony in one temple or another. Dances are Balinese way of expressing their will and conveying their messages: praying for good luck, banishing the evil… Barong and Yudapati are two among the most famous Balinese dances. This year in Thailand, Barong was featured by Daniel at the ASEAN Art Festival sponsored by ASEAN Secretary General Surin Pitsuwan, where it was widely praised.

It can be said that Balinese culture is an indigenous polytheistic culture which combined original Hinduism with the island's distinct rituals, customs and arts. This easternmost region of Asia has produced a diverse art scene which includes Asian, Middle Eastern, and modern

Western culture. However, it takes a keen eye to realize that the essence of Balinese culture remains Hinduism, which is practiced by 90 percent of the island's population. Dance is the language of Bali. Each year there are numerous festivities, some even last a whole week, such as Nusadua, the five-day Samurai on Sanut beach, the aqua sports festival, the food festival, the festival of ethnic dances, and the Bali kite-flying festival, where the Denpasar sky is filled with thousands of kites in all sizes, shapes and colors.

The most special of all is the New Year Festival, also known as Nyepi, held in July. Nyepi means silence in Balinese. Three days before the ceremony, there is a big march to carry the statues of the gods to the river or the sea for a spiritual bath, before returning them to the temples. The team of ritual maidens wearing lace kebaya and colorful waist-belts head-carried their trays of offerings into the temple at noon. It includes flowers, fruits, cakes, and effigies which symbolize the sacrifice. This is when the whole village stands still and silence befalls. After the hour of silence, the crowned girls in colorful short-sleeved and glittered dress joined the muscular men in dances.

The evening started with a huge parade in the beat of gongs and drums and other musical instrument, accompanied by the mob's singing that shook the whole village. A huge monster effigy at 10 meters height was carried on a bamboo frame by forty nine persons in 7x7 formation. The relentless music signified the villagers' fierce desire to banish the evil spirits out of their land.

In the afternoon we visited Kuta, a curving coast with the cliffs closing on the sea here and there, forming beautiful beaches. Kuta is located at the southern part of the island, together with Sanut, Nusadua, Jimbaran. This is also home to the top resorts, with many world-famous names such as Intercontinental, Accor, Marriott, Shangri La, Sofitel, Novotel...

We stayed at a resort with, according to Popo, the most beautiful pool in Bali. Overlooking the sea, it was flanked by two rows of statues of charming Balinese fairies. And beyond its were villas scattering on the hillside.

At sunset, the sky turned red. Sunrise and sunset always moved our hearts. Sunset was so different here. The sun was much rounder and bigger, probably because Bali is nearer to the equator than Viet Nam. The sun was red but its light not too harsh. The clouds were bustling in many shapes, from sauntering elephants to galloping horses and flying dragons. The sunset painted the sea pink and intensified the beauty of the waves, the water, and the white sand of Kuta. Popo took us to the beach to have dinner outdoor, in a seaside restaurant. Rows of simple but neat tables lined along the beach, and restaurants are separated only by narrow footpaths that all led to the sea.

The dishes were mostly seafood: shrimp, crab, clams, oysters, and a wide range of fish, either steamed, grilled or fried. After some freshly-caught crabs, Popo ordered a Balinese specialty, sate lilit. It was unique: minced boneless seafood was seasoned with pepper, chili and garlic, then added some lemongrass, honey and mixed coconut milk. This pulp was then stuffed into an emptied half of wild lemon, and grilled on charcoal. They said coconut charcoal grilling was the only way to give it that unique aroma. It was a great experience eating sate lilit, savoring Indonesian Bintang beer, and watching the sunset. The restaurant owner said he had made it less spicy to suit our taste. It was such a memorable mixture of sweetness and sourness and spiciness.

The sun had already set but the horizon remained rosy. Popo gave us a brief introduction of the southern beaches. Bali had more then 1200 hotel, i.e. one per every 2,600 locals. If a hotel offered on average 100 rooms, it is one room per 26 persons. Yet Bali was still fully booked in high season. The first hotel was built by the Americans in 1936, it did not see tourism development until the 1960s.

Nowadays Kuta is full of luxury hotels and resorts, chosen by the tourists for their marvelous sunset view. Kuta offered one of the best sunsets in Bali. Balinese had been preserving the ecology and holding the forest and sea sacred, properties of the gods, in the belief that human bear the responsibility to conserve them, protect them and make them even more beautiful.

Now that the sun had disappeared, the strings of electric bulbs emitted barely enough light to create a soothing atmosphere for the beach. The owner exchanged some whisper with Popo, then presented another Balinese specialty called *bebek betuta*, or deep-fried duck stew. In Viet Nam it is either deep-fry or stew, but here it was the combination of both. The owner said he must select a six month old duck and stewed it for ten hours until the bones became tender but the meat did not turn mushy. Then he seasoned it with honey, curry and chili before a deep-frying. The result was a golden duck, crispy from bone to flesh and skin.

The duck was served with a special wine which contain infused wild Ubud flowers, known by local as fragrance gifted by the gods. As we enjoyed the duck and the magic wine we felt energized by the joy of discovery. It was culinary culture that enriched Bali and made it a more attractive destination.

***

My last night in Bali, I wandered on the Kuta beach reflecting on this tourism wonderland. When culture is celebrated and fostered, tourism will reach a new height. No matter how many luxury resorts are established and how many large swimming pools are built, without the connection to and exploration of culture, ranging from arts to cuisine, from forest to spiritual values, they will simply be another resting place and will leave no profound impression on the visitors. When nature and culture are incorporated, it will definitely be a great tourism destination.

March 2019.

Legend Of Langkawi

Langkawi is an archipelago of 104 islands, but five are only above water level at low tide. So it is often said that Langkawi has 99 large and small islands.

"The legends of Langkawi" by Tun Mohamed Zahir clearly states that in ancient Indian sound, the word **Langka** means beautiful, **wi** means infinity, so Langkawi means extreme beauty. But according to another interpretation based on the ancient Malay language, **Lang**, in the word helang, means eagle. This island in the past was the land of Eagles; today in the northern region bordering Thailand, there are still many eagles, so they explain Langkawi as an eagle, an island of eagles. No matter what you call it, we can understand Langkawi as eagle island, a gorgeous island. However, I still prefer the interpretation Langkawi as an extreme beauty.

Langkawi is nearly 500 square kilometers. The main island is home to over 50,000 people with a length of 25 km, covering an area of 60% of the archipelago's total area. Langkawi appeared in Malaysian history 1,500 years ago as the first home of Malaysian residents; the Machinchang range has a mountain up to 890 meters high with primeval forest surrounding the giant freshwater lake Tasik Dayang Bunting.

In 2007, UNESCO recognized three ecological conservation areas of Langkawi as a World Geopark, including Machinchang Cambrian Mountain, Kilim Eco Park, and Tasik Dayang Bunting freshwater lake.

Langkawi is located in Kedah state, home of Mahathir Mohamad, the former Prime Minister of Malaysia. During his 12 years as Prime Minister, Mahathir was the architect of the rapid modernization of the country, and he paid particular attention to his hometown. Since 1981, he had planned to develop the island while preserving its ecological beauty and constructing infrastructure, roads, and airports. He created a tax-free mechanism to attract investors and tourists. A handicraft center was built to encourage production. Since then, 2,500 products made by the islanders have contributed to the increase in their income because many unique indigenous products are attractive to tourists.

Investors rushed to the island; sandy beaches were exploited; hotels, resorts, tourist areas, and amusement parks were built along the coastline.

One can get to the island by air, but other transportations are also available such as modern marinas and ports connecting to the mainland. To the north is Kuah port with ferries and speedboats to bring guests to Satim in the Southern Thailand and to the mainland of North Malaysia such as Payar, Pinang, Kuala Kedah... To the west of Langkawi is Awana port with high-class 5-star ship transporting passengers from Malaysia to the island and other ships visiting Langkawi by sea.

An archipelago of just over 50,000 people welcomes up to 5 million international visitors each year, an average of 100 guests per resident. The number itself speaks volumes, the number that proves **the legend of Langkawi**.

*

* *

The Langkawi Islands are close to Thailand, not far from the northwest coast of Malaysia. The large and small islands standing still, looking down at the calm sea like the models on giant green glass. Looking down from the plane, at one moment I thought I was lost in the beautiful Ha Long Bay of Vietnam. No, this is only a small part of Ha Long because the total number of islands of Langkawi is only one third of the number of islands of Ha Long Bay.

Langkawi International Airport, located close to the sea, is quite modern with a runway of 3,810 meters long, capable of receiving large aircraft. The airport is busy everyday with dozens of flights from many countries bringing global tourists to Langkawi. Many 6-seater and 10-seater planes of Middle Eastern billionaires parked at a corner of the airport, indicating that Langkawi stays true to its name of a paradise.

Thai Quang Trung took us to Datai tourist area located on a high mountain, the car had to go back and forth for 40 minutes from the east slope to the west slope to Datai, many monkeys running on the street as if welcoming visitors. Lots of birds, storks and squirrels were flying between branches. The car stopped at the reception hall, where we were welcomed by the echo of the green forest, the birdsong, the cicadas chirping, the whispering wind, and the rustling of the trees leaning in the wind. From the reception to the beach of Datai Bay of the Andaman Sea, you have to ride a tram running under the winding forest for 2-3 km. The villas nestled in the old forest on the mountainside or by the stream, the roads were narrow with only one lane. We visited the spa, located next to a small murmuring stream; herbal's soothing and attractive aroma relaxed our souls. From the spa house, no nearby villa can be seen. Two days of advanced booking was required to get spa services. As for the summer, villas must be booked six months in advance. One night at the monotonous two-room stilt house we just visited cost as much as US$350 ++, or nearly US$400 in total. As for villas with swimming pools, one or two thousand dollars per night is the normal price. Breakfast can be served in room and guests can travel by tram, bicycle or hiking, sometimes at junctions, a polite guide will gently give tourist instruction and help.

What a unique idea! Choosing an old forest, a steep slope to build a 5-star resort was a breakthrough decision to bring people to the ecological nature, which Thai Quang Trung called green tourism. That was why he brought us to Datai first.

For lunch, we sat at a bar on the shores of Datai Bay of the Andaman Sea. Datai Bay is like two great arms embracing the whole sea; far on the horizon are the mountains and islands of the Indian Ocean; to the right is a small island, the nest of sea birds. The seawater of Malaysia and Thailand are mixed. The ships are still running back and forth without entry procedures, the sea has no boundaries, only humans define the boundaries. I said that to Thai Quang Trung, he laughed: "The most difficult demarcation is at sea". Keep silent for a moment, he said: "If only the world didn't have greedy invaders, the humankind's blue sea would be borderless". I added, "And let people open their hearts to love each other even more."

Thai Quang Trung then ordered some Langkawi dishes. I love skewered meat like the one in my hometown but marinated with spices and crushed peanuts and then grilled on a fragrant charcoal stove, known in Malaysia as Satay; grilled fish and shrimp are all seasoned with curry flavor. Finally, he ordered a bowl of Laksa for each person, which is a type of vermicelli with bean sprouts, eggs, fried tofu, shrimp, and meat or fish balls. They are served with a thick spicy sauce that is a typical

Malay dish. Laksa vermicelli is very rich in Malay flavor with the hotness of chili and sate. Every small wave pats the golden sand as if to reduce the spicy that is making each of us sweat by the Laksa dish. The seagulls flew close to the shore and looked at us as if wondering where we came from. They glided lightly and then flew off into the distance. On this beach, we were introduced to this beautiful archipelago by engineer Tay Min Seng, my dear Malaysian friend. Concluding the introduction, Tay said: "Natural beauty is eternal, its beauty does not bring wealth to people. Fortunately, Prime Minister Mahathir is interested in the island, perhaps because Langkawi is his homeland." He retained the pristine beauty of the island when planning, the beauty of heaven and earth. Mahathir built a mechanism on tax exemption, investment incentives, and employment policy to bring jobs and wealth to the people so that the island's GDP per capita is much higher than the GDP per capita of Malaysia.

Langkawi has a very good mobile market system; each shop owner carries their business on a mobile car and truck full of goods. Each day the market is opened at a different place, mainly in the morning to sell food, vegetables, meat, and fish. It only takes a week to move from North to South and then back. In contrast, the night markets is organized and also rotated. Cenang night market is organized on Thursday night, Kuah Town night market is on Saturday night, and some night markets in other locations are on Sunday... The market opens until 10pm; buyers and sellers are busy with all kinds of goods. Visitors to the island will surely visit the night markets once.

The island has very rich source of fresh water, but according to Tay, Prime Minister Mahathir only allowed moderate usage of the water supply because he wanted to keep the water source for the island to protect the ecology and keep the flora and fauna growing. He built an undersea pipeline to bring fresh water from the mainland to the island. The same goes for electricity, the island's power plant is only for backup. The main power line is an undersea cable that crosses the sea to provide electricity and water for today and for the growth of population and tourists many times in the future.

In the afternoon, we went to the primeval forest to visit Tasik Dayang Bunting freshwater lake. In the middle of the sea with salt water, on the mountain, there is a lake up to 14 meters deep, large, and full of fresh water. The birds and animals that come to live along the lake are very ecologically friendly.

Legend has it that once upon a time, a fairy, when passing by this island, had been attracted by the voice of a fisherman. She fell in love and decided to stay on earth. They lived together in a great limestone cave.

The Jade Emperor knew and summoned her, but she disobeyed his order. The Jade Emperor sent the God of Thunder to knock down the huge cave on this island. The cave that collapsed is now the 14-meter-deep freshwater lake on Machinchang mountain in the middle of this island.

It is said that, when hit by thunder, she was pregnant. Therefore she has become a powerful spirit. Many women come here for lake water and pray for pregnancy. Those who came here to pray became pregnant when returning, so the lake was named Tasik Dayang Bunting, which means pregnant maiden lake. Today Tasik Dayang Bunting has become a destination for couples on their honeymoon.

We travelled to the north of the island by a high-speed boat. This is the homeland of eagles, they live in flocks in the forest and hover in the sea during day time to catch fish. One of the tours in the island is Eagle Feeding tour. Seeing our canoe stop, knowing that the guests were coming, a few eagles spread their wings as if to welcome us. Each of us threw some fish into the sea to feed the eagles. Some called out for their companions, then hundreds of one-meter-long eagles suddenly appeared; one by one, each of them orderly swooped down and poked their legs like two small anchors to catch the fish very accurately. Many cruises docked on eagle bay and each ship was welcomed by the eagle. What a spectacular unique tourist corner.

After seeing the eagle, the ship continued its journey to the Northeastern port, the center of Langkawi. The Dataran Lang Square (Eagle) was built majestically, especially the gate which was made of two giant stone blocks, the statue of a pink-brown eagle spreading its wings flying into the sea. The eagle's feet hold a Manganese ore, which is abundant in the island. It was explained that in the past, the islanders saw eagle picking up Manganese ore flying away. Malaysians call Manganese Kawi. There is theory that by combining the word Lang of Helang (eagle) with Kawi, it is called Langkawi, which means eagle grabbing Mangan. The island government takes the eagle as the symbol of the island. On the day Tay took us to visit the administration building, the Chairman of Langkawi respectfully presented us with a bronze statue of a winged eagle and said: "We are striving to build our homeland so that Langkawi can take off like the image of this Lang bird".

We also headed to the south to take the cable car to the top of Gunung Mat Cincang at the altitude of 705 meters and from here we walked on the 125-meter-long iron bridge connecting the peak of two mountains. It was a fairy scene, standing here, clouds flying below, the wind blowing from every side, below our feet are the sea and the islands of Langkawi reflecting on the blue sea.

On Langkawi Island, there are so many tours such as boating through mangroves, visiting hot springs, caves, rice parks, eco-parks, water parks, and beaches, each with its own charm. In Malay, Pantai means the beach, Langkawi is lots of Pantai: Pantai Kok, Pantai Tengah, Pantai Cenang, Pantai Tanjung Rhu... Langkawi has dozens of beautiful Pantai. If Pantai Cenang is vibrant with many exciting games and bustling dining, Pantai Cenang is quiet, nestled under the mountain. But perhaps the most beautiful beach is still Pantai Tanjung Rhu with pure white sand, crystal clear water and gentle sea with quiet waves. Tanjung Rhu is ranked in the top of the most beautiful beaches in the world.

The next morning, we boarded a canoe in the Southeast of the island to travel twenty kilometers to the Southeast to visit Pulau Payar Ocean Park. The water is not very deep, a coral reef stretching thirty kilometers with many small islands of different shapes, it is truly paradise of the sea. We stopped at the Pulau Payar, the largest island in this park. This park is in the top of the best diving area in the world. Old coral reef and colorful young coral reef, with many colorful fish glittering under the rays of sunlight shining through the water. Many tourists dived or snorkeled to see the life of marine creatures: corals, colorful fish, shrimp, crabs, jellyfish, clams, oyster. We did not dive, but at the bottom of the canoe there was a bright glass door with lights shining into the sea. The slow-moving canoe gave us the scene as if we were diving. I suddenly thought of the sea in my hometown Phu Yen, also a lot of coral, many colorful fish; when I was a child I dived to catch snails, seeing countless sea creatures, but today it is no more. Humans have destroyed the environment; this loss cannot be compensated by money.

In the last afternoon we visited the Museum of Prime Minister Mahathir. It is actually a souvenir house, storing many gifts from different countries to the Prime Minister, who handed them over to Langkawi, including a brand new car and many pictures. Looking at the picture of Mahathir visiting Langkawi, I thought: "Without timely decisions, without an opening mechanism from the Prime Minister, Langkawi would not be what it is today."

The next day, returning to Putra Jaya, the new administrative center of Malaysia (also the world's first national administrative center), we visited and worked with the Prime Minister's advisory group, Professor Aman Awang, former President of the University of Technology of Malaysia, member of the Prime Minister's advisory group. When listening to our question about the role of Langkawi's planning, Professor Aman affirmed: "Yes, the Prime Minister has assigned us to work with the Ministry of Tourism to develop a breakthrough plan to turn Langkawi into a tourist pearl and adopt ecology as its essence". The Prime Minister warned: "We must protect the environment, people are only allowed to make the environment more beautiful". Professor Aman added, "The first thing when accelerating the industrialization of the country, Prime Minister Mahathir asked us to complete the master plans. We began with the plans to build Malaysia, Kuala Lumpur and Langkawi as they are today". I shook Aman Awang's hand: "Thank you, it was the planning and decisiveness of the Prime Minister that made Langkawi a legend".

22nd March 2017

Phuket – Jade Island

*P*rofessor Thai Quang Trung and Dr. Surin Pitsuwan were two friends of mine. Mr. Surin was the former Minister of Foreign Affairs of Thailand. I met him when he was acting as the 12th General Secretary of ASEAN. Thai Quang Trung was a Vietnamese - French intellectual. A man with great erudition, he had an ambition to create a "Green Economy" in Vietnam. Trung has traveled with me to many ASEAN countries. Both of them passed away suddenly. Surin was on a speech at a major conference in Bangkok when he suffered a stroke and passed away. Thai Quang Trung also was attending a conference on environmental protection in Quang Ngai when he had a heart attack and passed away the next day. I have many memories with Professor Thai Quang Trung, and with Surin. This article is to remember my two friends who suddenly left for heaven.

The night we were in Bangkok, Mr. Surin Pitsuwan took me and Thai Quang Trung to a dinner banquet at the private house of Mayor of Bangkok. The mayor is a member of the Royal family; his villa is unique, resembling a small palace inside the Royal Palace complex. The mayor in his elegant royal robes welcomed us in a corner of a beautiful garden. We had dinner, drinking wine, and having joyful conversation about the cooperation between ASEAN countries. At the end of the dinner, Thai Quang Trung told everyone that he would take us to Phuket the next morning and wanted Surin to provide us with some information about Phuket. Surin spread his arms: "Oh, this is interesting". Surin's hometown is in Southern Thailand. We had recently attended a three-day cultural festival held in Dr. Surin's hometown with the participation of six Asean countries including Indonesia, Singapore, Malaysia, Philippines, Thailand, and Vietnam, and with the Sao Bien arts company from Phu Yen province, my hometown, who gave performances as representatives of Vietnam and who were awarded the first prize and given flowers by the former Prime Minister of Thailand. Surin said that the abovementioned arts festival was also an opportunity for him to repay his gratitude to his relatives at home. He felt very happy that Thai Quang Trung and I had attended the event and now wanted to learn more about Phuket. Surin took a map and spread it on the corner of the table and began:

- Phuket is located in the Gulf of Thailand of the Andaman Sea, in the great Atlantic Ocean, over 850 kilometers from Bangkok and one hour flight. Phuket is the largest island located among thirty-six islands in Phuket province. The capital city of Phuket province is also named Phuket. The southernmost area of Phuket is in the middle of Kra, the narrowest part of Thailand connecting to Malaysia, but we are still discussing whether to invest in building the Kra canal to connect the East Sea with the Atlantic Ocean. At that southernmost point is the tip of Brahma, which we call Laem Phromthep in Thai. It's only a thirty minutes flight from there to the Malaysian island of Langkawi that you have just visited. To the north of Phuket there is a wildlife museum for animals and plants (Khao Phra Thaeo area), a typical wild forest of the tropics, about twenty square kilometers wide and a total territory of nearly one hundred square kilometers including the sea of Nai Yang, the birthplace of sea turtles (tortoises, turtles, etc.). This area is recognized as a National Park, named Sirinat (Sirinat National Park). Surin looked at us and insisted: I wish there were more sanctuaries like this so people everywhere can know how to love the forests, maintain them, and protect them together with the wild animals living in them, in order to protect our earth. He affirmed: Only if and when each person on earth understands this and it becomes the sentiment and consciousness of each person, the earth will be green and sustainable. Phuket today is still a pearl island, a main tourist paradise because it is still wild and able to maintain its ecological nature; people improve it and not destroy it. In Phuket there are many extremely beautiful beaches. Thai Quang Trung interjected: "The beauty of our sea, especially the central part of our hometown, is not far from the beauty of the beaches here." Surin said: "I hope Vietnam knows not only how to exploit the forest and the sea but also how to improve and preserve their ecology."

Surin suggested us to have a canoe trip to visit the islets at the southernmost and northeast of the island while in Phuket. "There are just a few beaches there, but the scenery is beautiful, it's like Ha Long Bay, the wonder of your country; these beaches are small and attached to the island through the connecting fishing villages, so it is easier to attract tourists." Surin did not forget to introduce us to Phuket. Phuket has a monument worth being visited, a sacred place to commemorate the two heroines who stood up to lead the insurgent army against foreign invaders and gain independence for Phuket island in 1785. Phuket people always remember and worship the heroines, whose names are Thao Thep Krasattri and Thao Sisunthon. Today, the reliefs, emblems, flags and seals of Phuket still represent these two heroines.

***

The next day, leaving Bangkok, we went to Phuket. It was the last days of the year, the weather was cool, the temperature about 27-28 degrees Celsius, ideally for tourists. Thai Quang Trung booked a room at Laguna Resort. This area, a few hundred years ago, was a tin mine exploited by the Chinese. Later, due to the dropping in price of tin, however, they stopped mining, thus many pits were left opened until this day. Tourist investors take advantage of this terrain to build resorts and turn open tunnels into lakes, building a system of over three hundred meters ditches connecting the lakes and running around hotels and villas. As you enter the resort, the first impression you get is the freshness and the azure color of the water that relaxes both our body and soul. Laguna Resort is located on the shores of quiet and peaceful BangTao Bay. The sea is so silent, the seawater a jade green. The first day of stay in Laguna Resort left many impressions.

More than two hundred years ago, under the leadership of two heroic female generals named Thao Thep Krasattri and Thao Sisunthon, the people of Phuket rose up to liberate Phuket from the Myanmar invaders. From that day, people had freedom, and the village was developed form a smaller one, previously named Jung Ceylon. The Portuguese and Chinese settled in to exploit the tin ore available in the region and also to grow rubber. Gradually, the village developed into a town and quickly became the provincial capital of Phuket. In 1929, the first hotel was built. Thanks to the famous movies shot here and the beautiful road connecting the Northeast to Phang Nga, Phuket is known to the world. Phuket is located in the center of the island and has a mountain road connecting it to the beautiful famous Patong beach on the west coast. After 2000, Phuket was recognized as a city with over sixty thousand inhabitants; Phuket City, especially Phuket FantaSea, is a monumental art center with a lighting and fountain system and famous with Thai traditional performances. There are also old villages, entertainment areas, and a shopping center for handicrafts. Especially, the buffet restaurant in Phuket FantaSea is the largest one in the world with four thousand seats, performing modern art mixed with mysterious Thai dances, attracting tourists from all over the world. Along with Phuket city, Patong is also developed one. If Phuket city is a modern industrial city, Patong is known for being a modern, eco-tourism city and soon became Phuket's best tourist attraction with Patong beach, which is several kilometers long in the shape of a bow with white sand, clear water and silent waves. The streets of Patong are crowded with all tourists from Russia, China, Vietnam, Europe, Australia, and America. Every year, Patong welcomes millions of tourists.

We dined on the Patong beachfront. The grilled fresh seafood emitted a mesmerizing aroma. Lobsters in Phuket was average 3-4 kilos each. In particular, the mantis shrimp here, perhaps thanks to their menu consisting of solely zooplankton of the Gulf of Thailand, is very big, sweet, and full of eggs. The last dish was chicken rice cooked with pandan leaves, with a strange and attractive taste. Thai people call this rice Kaomangai, a popular dish of the islanders and quite a delicacy for guests like us.

Patong at night was bustling with colorful lights. There is no such thing called night here because all activities are non-stop all night. I'm trying to figure out why they call it Sex City. Yes, in Phuket, there is Bangla Street where all kinds of entertainments with lady boy clubs performing all night, with bars and people in sexy dress dancing around the corner of the streets. Bangla Street is also known as the red-light district (the name referring to the place where prostitution businesses operate). The whole business in the red-light district, including that in townhouses with red lanterns, are strictly controlled by local authorities.

In the past, Patong city was an area where bananas were grown for export. Patong in Thai means banana. Banana leaves are used for wrapping sticky rice, rice, and grilled fish. There is very delicious and attractive grilled banana sticky rice dish here. Today, banana leaves and bananas can be only seen in tourism. Banana city (Patong) is really attractive, famous for its clean and beautiful beaches with both bustling activities and a quiet bathing area and also an area for water sports such as parasailing and windsurfing. Patong has fishing services and 4-5 star restaurants on board; there are ships for hunting and diving in the southern sea of the island. There is the largest supermarket in Thailand here named Jung Ceylon hypermarket (the previous name of Phuket), also known as "paradise", the heart of shopping. Jung Ceylon shopping center is located on the Ratuthit road, the main road of the city of Patong. The center is two hundred thousand square meters wide and has a parking lot that can accommodate up to two thousand cars. The hypermarket is newly built with many famous supermarkets, full of international brands. There is also entertainment, relaxing areas, and a food court... In front of the door is a lake with sailboats spreading their sails, creating a sense of the vastness of the sea and islands. The hypermarket has several basements called Siam selling jewelry and handicrafts, reflecting the traditional culture of Thailand with over two hundred busy shops.

On the streets of Patong, there are small streets that serve local food with many local cakes, pies wrapped in banana leaf, sticky rice cooked with durian and mango, and grilled rice with banana wrapped inside. The small shops sell street dishes such as spicy delicious Hokkien noodles. Satay means lean meat marinated in spices and grilled on skewers similar to a traditional meat dish in Central Vietnam, or like the Russian shashlyk, satay dipped with salty, both spicy, sweet and sour sauce and, interestingly, served with Thai beer. Many local dishes are sold here such as Kao Man Gai rice, Khanom Jeen curry noodles, stir-fry wild vegetable dishes, tapioca root and sprout soup, stir-fried sprouts with a different Thai flavor. Fresh fish wrapped in banana leaves grilled on charcoal, steamed shrimp and squid, spicy and sour fried dishes with crabs, all are so attractive to customers. There are shops with only a few dozen seats, so customers have to book in advance or wait patiently.

Once you are in Thailand and visit Phuket and Patong, you can see clearly that Thailand has a new mindset to bring its tourism industry from a static state to a dynamic state. Thailand is a country of temples and monarchy, and yet its tourism industry is very vibrant. There are, in particular, very dynamic types of entertainment that are similar to those in European and American cities. With that mindset, they woke up nature. With that mindset, the same mountains, the same jade green water, the same golden, sunny, white sand beaches, and the same local dishes, like chicken rice cooked with pandan leaves, or popular grilled or steamed seafood, suddenly became top specialties ranked high in any list of Phuket cuisine. Even those quiet hundred-year-old temples suddenly became crowded, busy and attractive to tourists.

Every year, in addition to tourist fairs, Phuket has dozens of other festivals such as Mid-Autumn Festival featuring boat racing tournaments

(Chaole), seafood festival, sports festival, Phuket King's Cup Regatta... And, in November, the annual tourist festival in Patong, hence the name Patong festival was held, and, in particular, the vegetarian festival. Thailand is the land of temples, and following Buddhism and vegetarianism is a common practice, but in Phuket there is a vegetarian festival taking place in the first 9 days of the 9th lunar month. During the festival, you can enjoy not only vegetarian feasts but also parades with colorful costumes and incense offerings at the temple, and a memorial ceremony for the two national heroines. Once the tourism industry is developed, they come up with many ideas to attract tourists. Ecotourism has made the roads and infrastructure more beautiful, the beaches clean, the trees and flowers green and colorful, the national culture well introduced. Local products, from seafood to fruits, vegetables, and the smallest things such as banana leaves, lotus leaves, potato tubers, flower branches, have all become tourism products. Nature is still preserved and embellished.

We embarked on a very new and modern touring canoe with twelve seats. The canoe ran at high speed, drawing impressive curves on the calm sea surface. It took us around the East, suddenly we were lost in the island of Kol Phi Phi. If Patong is the place for watching the sunset, Phi Phi is for the sunrise. The canoe took us up to Phang Nga Bay. The whole northeast of Phuket Island extends to Phang Nga Bay with many islands, some of which are exactly like Dr. Surin introduced to us while in Bangkok, which are extremely similar to Ha Long Bay, a small Ha Long with many strangely shaped limestone islands. There is an island that is just a block of limestone with the lower part carved in by sea waves, while the upper part is covered with trees, grass and flowers, looking like a sail from afar. In this region each island is a tourist destination. Kosire Island has a Gypsy fishing village, the largest one in Phuket. Far away, there are small islands such as Racha, Raya, Coral, Koh Bon islands, along with many other islets resembling tiny on the background of the sea. Panwa Peninsula with a long coral reef. From a boat or while diving, you can contemplate hundreds of species of marine life, colorful fish splashing around young bright pink coral reef.

In the late afternoon, the canoe took us back to Leam Promthep Cape, a cape located at the southernmost tip of the island like Cape Saint Jacques in Vung Tau. Leam Promthep in Thai means stone of God. The steep cliff is sixty meters above sea level, reaching out to the western sea, Koh Kaew Island for Buddhist meditation and remote small islands. In the afternoon sun, palm trees create vertical lines like the notes of Thai folk songs, increasing the gentleness and grace of the remote islands and Promthep cape. The sun is going down on the west coast of the Indian Ocean. The clouds curled up like dancers accompanying the sun in its descending down the mountain. The gentle red and yellow sunset light shone on a giant sea mirror with small gliding sails like birds flying in the sky in full harmony with distant clouds, all of which creating a wonderful picture of sunset in Phuket. On the tourist map, Leam Promthep is the place for watching sunset, and it has become the number one place for the sunset in Phuket.

From the north to this southernmost tip, Phuket Island has many beautiful beaches such as Nai Yang, Bang Tao, Surin, Kamala, Patong, Karon, Kata, and Nai Harn. All the beaches with fine white sand are located in the west of the island. From Mai Khao beach near the Phuket airport to the tip of Panwa in the Southeast of the island, there are twenty-six beaches with full high-class services. The eastern part also has some beautiful beaches, but the sand is mixed with mud so it can not attract tourists like the west coast of the island, but there are many beautiful islands and many coral reefs that are very interesting for those who like diving. The unique landscape in this island has been featured in many famous movies… And cinema has also contributed to bringing Phuket to the international and attracting tourists to Phuket, the pearl island of Thailand, contributing to making tourism become the key economic sector in this Golden Temple country.

In the late afternoon, we dined at the Promthep Cape restaurant of the "sunset" service area at this beautiful southernmost part of the island. The service area has a large parking lot that can accommodate thousands of cars. There are many eateries, souvenir shops and grocery stores. Standing on the high floor of the lighthouse looking down, you can see the peaceful and sacred silence of Promthep Cape during the moment of the sun going down the mountain while, in contrast, the whole area here is bustling. A group of four to five musicians with musical instruments are singing Thai love songs for guests. Seeing Thai Quang Trung who was wearing his hair and beard too long, they thought he was old, so they took off their hats and wanted to give him a song. Thai Quang Trung is four years younger than me and yet, while he shaves clean every summer, in winter he wears his beard and hair like an old man. We still call him "Elder Thai". The troubadour group asked "Elder Thai" what song he would like to hear. He discussed with us, I asked them to sing "Song Karan". The Thai lady in charge of Phuket's tourism in our group agreed. The group of amateur artists sang very passionately, the lyrics in the 2/4 rhythm kept rushing and rushing and concluding each paragraph with a long line, the more they rushed towards the end, the more vibrant it became. Her Thai friend explained the Song Karan ceremony to us: every year from April 13 to April 15, the whole country of Thailand organizes the Song Karan water festival, which is a festival to welcome the New Year just like the Lunar New Year in Vietnam. She said that if you think about the old way, this is the moment when the sun moves from the Pisces Zodiac to the Sun, it has a sacred meaning to Thai people, so it becomes the most attractive festival in ASEAN countries. CNN Travel considers Thailand's water festival the largest and most unique one in the world. Buddha statues are bathed in fragrant water, everything in the house is washed by water. People dress nice, but very gently they go out to the streets and splash water on each other. Bangkok, Chiang Mai and Phuket are the places where the Song Karan festival is most vibrant, crowded and spectacular. In the provincial capital city of Phuket and in Patong, the festival goes on all night, including a service to provide clean water for visitors to drink. Local people splash water using beautifully inlaid silver bowls, while Western guests bring plastic guns with very large containers to participate in the cheerful mutual water splashing. Thai people believe that water will wash away bad things and bring happiness for a new year. Opening the festival is an impressive parade including from cars to vans, and ships in the Patong Sea, all with brilliant flowers moving along the streets, on the sea and sounding horns. The streets of Bangla were packed with people who dance, sing the Songkran folk songs and then splash water. Whoever gets wet the most is the luckiest, happiest person. The girls are usually the ones who get wet the most, people get down to the streets to splash each other with water, and the elephants are also brought out to splash water with their trunks. After the water splashing ceremony is an all-night food festival for New Year Eve. The next day, there are fun and cultural events, including Miss Song Karan contest in Phuket, and a happy and joyful contest "Little Song Karan" for children; flowers are in every house, and streets are gorgeously beautiful.

"Elder Thai" ordered Thai seafood hotpot, lots of shrimp, squid, and octopus with spicy lemongrass, curry and chili, spicy to the point of making our body heated up. Thai Quang Trung did not forget to order a plate of Thai rice, a type of rice that is long and chewy like sticky rice to be eaten with hot grilled salted scad fish marinated with spices. A Thai friend told us the legendary story of Songkran. It is a long story, but, in short, the intelligent man has defeated the supreme god. It can be summed up like this: Once upon a time there was a handsome and intelligent boy. The God, also the owner of the Vedas (Brahma) came to the earth to meet and challenge this boy: if the boy could give the correct answer to the god's riddle within seven days, the god would be beheaded, otherwise the boy would die. The puzzle given by God is: where is the pride of man in the morning, afternoon, and evening?

The young man went to consult the birds in the forest, then one day he answered Brahma: "In the morning, human pride is on the face, so when people wake up, they have to wash their face. In the afternoon, the pride is on the body, so people often take a bath at the end of the afternoon. In the evening, the pride is on the feet, after going all day, going everywhere, and at night the feet must be washed before going to bed." The answer is correct, Brahma gave up and today his head is paraded respectfully during the Songkran water festival. Songkran means change for the better, getting rid of the bad, the old, and welcoming the new year with good things and happiness.

I told Thai Quang Trung: In Vietnam, we also have a place to greet the sunrise in Phu Yen, the easternmost point of the mainland; a place to greet the sunset in Phu Quoc, in Ha Tien, which is also on the shores of this Gulf of Thailand, but we're unable to organize events and festivals to develop tourism. Thai Quang Trung sniffed and praised the delicious grilled fish, then he looked up at me and said: That's it, Vietnam has been only focusing on the quantity, number of tourists per year, but we have not taken into account how to make each customer spend more. It is calculated that one tourist in Vietnam spends an amount equal to 25 per cent of what he would spend in Phuket. He affirmed: "We must develop many amusement parks in parallel with the development of hotels and resorts, more attractions and festivals to be held with attractive services." The Thai friend said as if to remind us: "Travel is to know how to "pickpocket" reasonably. Where to travel, where to visit, what to eat, what to buy, what to play."

That's right. Just look at Phuket Island, an island that used to only have bananas, rubber, and tin, now a tourist island, a pearl island. If we have new thinking, good planning, and synchronous development, Vietnam's tourism will quickly become a key economic sector. The Songkran song of the amateur group from the corner of the shop still echoes as a reminder to everyone to innovate and be creative. In the distance, the sunset light is still on the horizon...

The coast of the Gulf of Thailand,

Early December 2018.

Cambodia – The Land Of Smiles

My friend, journalist Ta Bao was assigned to be Head of the Youth Expert delegation sent to Cambodia to help in the country in the early days of its revival. After a few years in the land of pagodas, he returned and wrote a book about Cambodia. He gave me the manuscript, taking into account the fact that, during his years in Cambodia, I went to this country several times and accompanied him to many places in Phnom Penh, Oudong and Siem Reap, even during the Khmer Rouge time. He wanted me to help him choose a title for his work. In those days, he had a girlfriend in Cambodia, a member of the youth union, also a victim of the genocide regime, who was always smiling. Her smile and Bayon's smile at Angkor are deeply imprinted on us, so I suggested that he call his book "The land of Smile". Today, nearly four decades after, with Ta Bao having passed away, I sit down to write about Cambodia and still want to name my memoir with that eternal smile.

***

1. Ms. Penh and Phnom Pênh

I came to Phnom Penh for the first time in early June, 1969. I was urgently assigned to the South to serve the Southern National Congress of Deputies with an aim to establish the Provisional Revolutionary Government of the Republic of South Vietnam. We had to go to Guangzhou where we are to take a plane to Phnom Penh under the name of journalists. After two days of visiting and taking photos of Phnom Penh, we were back to the royal palace on the occasion of the 50th anniversary of King Sivowat's order on the construction of the main palace. On the third day, we secretly said goodbye to Phnom Penh and left for the Cambodia-Vietnam border at Tay Ninh province, where we took back seats on the motorcycles of the liberation army and rode them all the way to the Southern battlefields...

I went to Cambodia many times after that, including a trip to the royal palace to visit King Norodom Sihanouk, Prince Norodom Ranariddh, to work with President Heng Somrin, and the Prime Minister Hun Sen. My notebook is filled with information about Cambodia. What was recorded and seen during two days in Phnom Penh since 1969, however, are the crucial things imprinted in me about the capital of this pagoda country.

Legends has it that, about 650 years ago, the area of the capital of Cambodia today was a fishing village in the swamp area located on the banks of the Tonle Sap River. After a flood, a rich woman named Penh, while she was sailing, discovered a large log floating around the mound, pulled over to her boat and then drifted out, then pulled over again. This went on many times, which struck Mrs. Penh as very strange. She then came to pick it up and found four Buddha statues inside a Bodhi tree trunk. As a devotee of Buddhism, she understood immediately that this was a rare spiritual phenomenon, the manifestation of none other than Buddha in this land. She set up an altar and built a temple for worship. After that, she called on people to raise the mound into a hill to avoid flooding and build a temple on it for the worship of Buddha. The Cambodian word for "hill" is *Phnom*, whereas *wat* is the word for pagoda, that was why people called it Wat Phnom ("Temple on the Hill"). The temple was very sacred; people from everywhere came to pray. The fishing village was increasingly crowded and gradually expanding; people built houses and roads, which were to become the first streets of the capital city of Cambodia today. When Mrs. Penh passed away, people built a statue and shrine to worship her behind the Buddhist temple on the very hill that she herself had built in her lifetime. From then on the hill was named after her, Phnom Penh ("Penh Hill"), and the pagoda also came to be called Wat Phnom Penh. Later, the fishing village was renamed as Phnom Penh village and it was the precursor of the city of Phnom Penh as it is today.

I asked Prince Ranariddh, the son of King Norodom Sihanouk, who is a doctor from France. He was once Co-Prime Minister and President of the National Assembly of the Kingdom of Cambodia. He confirmed: This legend is well known to all Phnom Penh people, as recorded in history. Even King Sihanouk also recounted the same story.

Phnom Penh temple worships the Snake god Naga, that's why there are statues of God Naga, including God Nagas with three heads, five heads, seven heads and nine heads, respectively, all the way leading from the entrance gate to the temple. They explained: The three heads represent heaven, earth, and human. The five heads, the five elements (metal-water-wood-fire-earth). The seven heads, the seven colors of the rainbow, the practice of attaining enlightenment. The nine heads are the way to heaven. Today, Penh Hill Pagoda is visited by many visitors, truly a sacred tourist destination of the capital of the Kingdom of Cambodia.

***

2. The Royal Palace and Silver Temple

The heart of the capital city Phnom Penh and the most dazzling attraction of Phnom Penh is the Royal Palace.

The first capital of Cambodia that still remains today is Angkor Thom, the famous Angkor Wat built in the 800s. Due to the geographical barrier which was the Tonlé Sap River, however, it was difficult for the capital to keep contact with people from the South. On the other hand, the proximity of the capital to the Cambodia-Thailand border and the continuous wars between the two countries meant that it was increasingly necessary for the capital to be moved the south - first to Ba San, then to Lo Vek, then to Ou Dong, which still has a royal tomb on a hill. It was not until 1800 that King Norodom moved the capital from Ou-Dong to Phnom Penh and built the Royal Palace there. The first royal palace was built just by wood. At the beginning of the 20th century, the new Royal Palace was built magnificently with the participation of Cambodian and French architects. Many palaces were built, with Damnakchan Palace being the workplace of the King. I had once the honor to meet King Norodom Sihanouk at this palace.

The Bronze Palace (Hok Samran Phirum) is the royal palace for vacation. Especially, Phochani Palace, the place for welcoming guests as well as holding conferences and art performances, is built by artisans in Hung Ha, Thai Binh province of Vietnam. The Napoléon Palace is for Queen Eugénie of France, Napoleon's wife. The palace was built by Napoleon, that's why so many N letters can be seen in the palace. Particularly, Assembly Hall was rebuilt in 1919 by order of King Sisowath with an area of 1,800 m², and a 59-meter-high tower with three spires. In the middle of the palace is the throne for the king in the occasion of coronation or court ceremonies. The ceiling is brightly textured by paintings in indelible ink depicting scenes from the epic of the legendary Reamker, which was the Khmer version of the Indian epic "Ramayana", creating a dignified and also very attractive atmosphere. I was curious to learn about this epic "Reamker" because, here and in

Angkor, in the great temples, there are drawings of this story with consecutive pictures with bright colors. The story of Reamker can be summarized as follows:

The beautiful wife of Prince Reamker was kidnapped by an ogre and forced to marry him. With the help of the Monkey God called God Hanuman and his brother, Prince Reamker bravely attacked the land of King of Ogre, a war that shook the world. The King of Ogre used all his tricks but eventually was defeated, and, in the end, he cast a spell with the effect that all of his soldiers became Reamker's relatives. The prince, shocked, did not dare to attack, thus the King of Ogre regained the victory. In this dangerous moment, the prince suddenly heard these words of Thevada from heaven: "Do not hesitate, you must attack to win". Obeying the command, he took the move and win. The story was briefly told but drawn beautifully in continuous pictures, with a view to pass it through future generations, so that everyone becomes well aware of their task to protect their own happiness and that of the nation.

In the Assembly Hall, there is a real-size bronze statue of King Sivo Wath (who built this hall). Also, there are statues of the four kings of the four dynasties reigning here.

Next to the palace, as you pass the door of the Southern wall, you see the Silver Pagoda where the royal family worshipped Buddha, and also the place where the tombs of the kings and royal treasures were kept. The Silver Pagoda is known in Cambodian as Wat Preah Morakat. It is called Silver Pagoda because the floor is paved with 5,329 pieces of silver (each piece weighing 1,125 g). The temple is also the storage of 1,650 valuable treasures of the royal dynasties. In the middle of the pagoda is a sitting Buddha statue placed on a tower made of emerald. In front of the Emerald statue is a statue of Maitreya Buddha made of 90 kilograms of pure gold. And, mounted on Buddha's body is 2,086 pieces of diamond, the most remarkable of which is a 25-carat diamond on the crown and a 20-carat one on Buddha's chest. The inside path around the temple was also very beautifully decorated with paintings based on the epic "Reamker". In front of the temple yard was the statue of King Norodom riding a horse made by a French artist in 1875. When King Sihanouk ascended the throne, he added a roof, symbolizing the light of King Norodom and representing the independence of the Kingdom of Cambodia. To the right of the temple was the man-made hill of Mondop, representing the mountain Kai-lusa in Buddhism. In the tower built on the top of the hill, there is a footprint of Buddha and a display of 108 images of Buddha. In the courtyard of the temple near Mondop hill, there are tower tombs of the three kings and the daughter of King Sihanouk. The recently deceased King Sihanouk was also placed in a tower next to the Mondop hill. In front of the temple, on the left, is a tower that houses the relics of King Norodom, who built the Silver Pagoda. The tower and the statue of him riding a horse create a majestic scene symbolizing the dynasties.

I do not understand why it is that all cultural heritages and knowledge were destroyed under the genocidal hands but the royal palace and this temple, the Penh hill pagoda are still there, the precious Buddha statue is still there. On one of my visits to this place I asked King Sihanouk about this and he said: "Perhaps because Buddha is here, the souls of the ancestors are here. It might also be because of a mistake of mine."

I asked the king in surprise:

- High Majesty, why would You call it a mistake?

- It's a long story, but here's the summary, - he said. - In 1970, I was thrown off my throne by Lon Non, Vietnam helped me go abroad. In China, Pol Pot and Ieng Sari invited me to join them in the establishment of a unified front against Lon Non. I mistook them for communists, friends of China and Vietnam, so I agreed. They appointed me as "President", as "Führer". And I went to the United Nations to recommend them as future members of the organization. They invited me back to our country to be the "Führer", but in reality we were kept under arrest in this palace. It was terrible days. It was because they wanted to please the "President", to continue to deceive me and the international public, that they did not destroy this palace.

Hundreds of birds hovered overhead and perched on the spires of the constructions and on the equestrian statue of King Norodom. I stood and looked at the peaceful birds flying around in the blue sky with white clouds and suddenly shuddered, thinking about the terrible past of Cambodia, of Phnom Penh under the Pol Pot genocidal regime. How can a peaceful country like this bear such a tragedy?

***

3. The deadly field

Whenever Cambodia is mentioned, it is still impossible not to mention the terrible disaster of genocide regime, perhaps not in a few hundred years from now, even though almost forty years have passed since then. The above said Mr. Ta Bao, - a friend of mine that I have known closely since 1959-1960 when he was working at Tien Phong newspaper and, while he was Director of Thanh Nien Publishing House, was assigned by the Government to help revive Cambodia - has long been keeping a notebook filled with painful stories of the victims' families. Reading his documents made me sad and shocked. The Khmer Rouge, represented by the angkas (leaders) and the dothians (soldiers), committed unimaginably barbaric acts to humanity. As soon as they captured Phnom Penh, they quickly drove all the people of Phnom Penh out of the city. The streets turned into rivers of people quietly following the angkas and doths. Two million people, within a few days, were all driven out. Twenty thousand war victims, injured by American bombs and bullets and being treated at the hospitals, were also driven to the streets, people with broken legs who could not walk were killed on the spot, women who had just given birth a few hours had to leave... Embassies of all countries, except for the Chinese embassy, had to close and leave Cambodia immediately. The airport being closed, the ambassadors, embassy staffs, and diplomats had to take trucks to travel to the Thai border.

After only a few days, Phnom Penh was quiet, without a single person. The Khmer Rouge closed its doors to the outside world, the country had no marketplace, the currency was abolished, temples and churches were destroyed, and monks also left. All were trapped in the "communes", concentration camps and the purge began: Those who were intellectuals, educated and skilled people would have their heads smashed and dumped first. Phnom Penh became a dead city, a ruined ghost city. From that moment, Cambodians were not allowed to speak, to laugh, and even not to cry. They had only one thing to do, bowing to the orders of the doths and angkas, and waiting for death coming from behind their back. In Mr. Ta Bao's notebook, there were numbers that were terrifying to read:

"The ledger of Stung Leng prison (codenamed camp S21) recorded:

August 6, 1976 killed 100 people

August 21, 1976 killed 191 people

November 11, 1978 killed 1,000 people

Total in 8 months killed: 4,291 people."

He also recorded the way Pol Pots took human blood. They tied people to beds and took their blood, taking all the blood out of the body and the "donor" of the blood had to die. Three hundred Cambodian intellectuals having returned from France. the Khmer Rouge welcomed them joyfully at the airport, and then, a day later, killed them. They also did an experiment that was recorded in S21 prison log, "the bodies are soaked in water, if the corpses are tied both hands to the back, they will lie on their backs. A corpse that is not bound will lie on its stomach when floating" (?)

I got goose bumps reading the part where each angka took thousands of human bile. Before reading "Ca Mau's letter" by writer Anh Duc describing the act of dissecting people's livers to drink alcohol by the executioner Nguyen Lac Hoa in Ca Mau, I felt extremely terrified. Now, in this country of pagodas and towers, they took human livers and biles in a much creepier and more professional manner. Each of them had a very thin blade. If they wanted to get the bile, they tied the victims' hands in front of their stomach and then made them stoop down. If they wanted to take the liver, the victim's hands were tie behind their back and they were forced to stand with their chest up, then the Pol Pots lightly stabbed from the side with that very thin blade to take out the liver. They cut the woman breasts and smoked them as snack for drinks. I wonder whether there are on the earth any executioners, cannibals, and genocidal killers more savage than those?

***

We followed our Cambodian friends to visit the Choeung Ek field, fourteen kilometers from Phnom Penh in the mid-1980s.

A terrifying scene appeared before our eyes, the burial pits were dug up. That day, only a few dozen holes were dug, and skulls and bones were everywhere. Later, it was estimated that up to 20,000 people were beaten to death and buried here in this field of fruit trees. When these are excavated, the authorities estimated there was a pit of 100 infant corpses, the largest pit was of 450 people, and there was a pit of 166 headless bodies (?). Later, the government put up large boards providing this information, making visitors feel uncomfortable. The day we arrived at Choeung Ek, bones and skulls piled up on the crater. A group of people continued to excavate. The smell of rotten, cold air covered an area that was once a field of fruits. I met here a man who was a survivor of the genocide, he was sitting and picking each skull to see if he could find his children. He had an older son and a daughter who were killed here. I asked if he had any traits or marks that would help him recognize his children. He shook his head: "Just by feeling." And he said: I think that when I choose the right head, my children will say "here I am". He said in tears. At one pit, I saw children's slippers and small skulls, about 10 years old or younger. In another corner was a skull with a long braid of hair, and nearby, a plastic comb. I stared at the black hair and suddenly before my eyes appeared the Apsara dance that I had seen before. Female artists with lovely bodies, gentle feet gliding across the stage with charming smiles. Oh, this hair might well belong to an Apsara artist back then. Most likely, because the dancers, if they could not escape, they will be the first to be raped and killed. "Culture is a luxury", Pon Pol said (?). Here at S21 prison there was a sign: "No Smile". It was hurtful to come to the land of smiles and read this line. But perhaps there was no need for it, because who could laugh at such painful scenes.

During 1,355 days (from April 17, 1975 to January 7, 1979), by the hands of "Khmer Rouge" cannibals, three million innocent people were killed, nearly half of Cambodia's population. And almost all the intellectuals were completely annihilated. They made Cambodia the hell of the 20th century. I took a picture of skulls being juxtaposed. None of the skulls closed their mouths, all opened wide as if to scream, to shout, to send message: "Humans, people, beware of genocide".

***

4. Revival

The genocidal regime has pushed tens thousands and millions of Cambodians to flee to Thailand, Laos and Vietnam. Because the country was betrayed by the Khmer Rouge; the entire village of Ba Chuc along the southwestern border were attacked and destroyed. But the Vietnamese people still helped tens of thousands of Cambodians who had just escaped from the hands of murderers. It was these Cambodians who came back from the death along with the Cambodian citizens who were being helped by Vietnam to study and get together. They were the "princes" Reamker today. On December 2, 1978, the Cambodian National Salvation Front was established in Long Khanh (Dong Nai province) with 49 members. They gathered to form battalions of the liberation army with the unconditional support of Vietnam in terms of weapons to food and training. The National Salvation Front called for Vietnamese and international help. The team of Reamker era had gradually crowded. Ten thousand troops with 28 battalions. They began the historic battle to save the nation. The Vietnamese army stood side by side with them to enter Phnom Penh. And on January 7, 1979, Phnom Penh was liberated. Concentration camps, and "communes" were demolished. The people returned, even though they were hungry and in need, but they now were able to talk, to smile gently, the smile of the people of the pagoda country.

As writing these lines I still wonder, why, why? Many countries, even big ones, defend murderers. Why did Vietnam invade Cambodia, according to them? Tens of thousands of Vietnamese soldiers have sacrificed their lives and shed their blood for the revival of Cambodia, and still some people deliberately understand it in a different way and say untrue things. It was not until the genocides were brought to the international court that they understood (!). In this information era, why does it take them that long to realize it? Was it intentional? The day I visited President Heng Samrin (he was the Chairman of the Party, the Chairman of the National Assembly of Cambodia), I asked him about this. He was silent for a moment, then put his hand on his left chest and said with emotion: "My fatherland, we Cambodian people have engraved it in our hearts. Cambodia's history will forever remember Vietnam's great gratitude for saving our people". King Norodom Sihanouk, at the end of the reception, exclaimed "Thank you Vietnam for saving my people." Prime Minister Hun Sen, in his turn, has repeatedly asked the question: If we had only 10,000 fighters of the Cambodian Liberation Army, how long would it take us to expel 180,000 Pol Pot soldiers?" He once said: "Were it not for Vietnam, it would take five years to liberate the country, and then all Cambodians would die." He asserted: "Without yesterday, there is no today, there is no tomorrow. Without Vietnam's help, Cambodia could not be saved, that is objective history. This is the historical truth that no force can falsify and deny." Cambodia went from revival to rapidly developing its economy, becoming a developing and integrated country.

"Four Faces" is a unique feature of Cambodia. That was what I was feeling as I sat in the four-sided hall, admiring the Bayon statues with a gentle smile on each one of their four faces, the like of which cannot be found in any other country. Four-Faced Buddha, Four-Faced Hall. Where does it come from? Thinking about the mystery of the four faces, I realized that, in front of the Royal Palace, in front of this Four-Faced Hall is the four-sided river. The Mekong River from Laos flows here to meet the Tonle Sap River that takes its origin from the Great Lake, and soon after it divides into two branches, the Bat Sac River and the Mekong River which flows into Vietnam under the names of Tien Giang and Hau Giang. The Four Faces River has existed for millions of years, so "Four Faces" comes from the place of confluence and separation of the Mekong River as a mirror of the city of Phnom Penh. A few Thnot trees (Vietnam calls Thot Not trees) with their rounded foliage grow straight on the peninsula of the Four Faces River, reminding everyone that this is Cambodia. The Thnot tree has a small but sturdy trunk, rising high toward the blue sky and white clouds. It produces about 400 liters of milk every year. Cambodians take this milk and cook it into Thnot sugar, which has a different flavor from other kinds of sugar. The Thnot tree symbolizes the rise of the Cambodian nation.

***

5. The smile Bayon

The last night in Phnom Penh, we were able to sit in the Four Faces Hall to watch Apsara dance, listen to Cambodian folk songs:

"Here, Cambodia, the beloved country of thousands of times.

Anyone who comes to my hometown, please visit this place, the beautiful garden

It's Svay Chanty, sweet and bold flavor

It's the wonderful Svay Chanty, don't forget this place."

The lyrics of the folk songs are as sweet as the taste of Thnot, and the gentleness of the voice seems to stretch out over the fields. Cambodia has revived and is growing. That revival is imbued with the sentiments of the two countries of Vietnam and Cambodia, transcending the threshold of close friendship because it is imbued with the blood and bones of the two nations. Those who have once come to visit the Vietnam-Cambodia friendship monument will always feel this priceless sacredness. The gentle song suddenly brought us back to Angkor, the ancient capital of the country of pagodas.

The plane of Cambodia Airlines, a joint venture with Vietnam Airlines, painted purple, took off from Pochenton airport and then tilted its wings to the left to return to the north. The Four Faces River and the city of Phnom Penh are clearly visible under the wings. Only a few ten minutes later, the plane lowered its altitude, glided smoothly over the giant mirror of the Tonlé Sap to land in Siem Reap. Angkor Wat appears as a model. The five towers shimmer in the water and with white clouds and blue sky. Angkor in Cambodian means the capital. This is the first capital of the Kingdom of Cambodia built more than 1,000 years ago, it is Angkor Wat and Angkor Thom that the Vietnamese people still call De Thien, De Thich, is the world's largest temple complex with 600 constructions that were built in 802 (nearly 1,300 years ago) entirely of stone. Today they still retain the original features of an ancient capital. It is recognized, therefore, as a world cultural heritage. From the fences to the temple themselves, the whole complex, including the domes, is made of stone - millions of stone blocks, some of which weighing up to 2-3 tons. Of particular value are the stone carvings. First of all, stone blocks were arranged and put in their proper places. Only after this would the carvers begin their work. There are statues up to five meters high and, together with this, meticulous attention was paid to minute details such as those on bare breasts and fingers, or the wrinkles on the belly of Apsara dancers, some of whom had had a child as explained by our tour guide. How sophisticated and talented! Along the way is an epic story, still the story about Prince Reamker, but shown by the sublime stone carving skill that is very sharp, detailed, and holy, but also very natural and down-to-earth.

It was in this capital, in 802 that King Jayavarman II, after defeating the invaders and gaining independence for the country, declared the independence of the Khmer kingdom, opening a brilliant era for posterity... He mobilized tens of thousands of workers to create this project. In Angkor Wat, there is a unique architecture, creating a strange mystery. Visitors standing near the wall, clasping their hands and patting their chest gently will hear the echo like they are beating a drum. Around the wall are many sculptures of fairies playing together.

In the reign of King Jayavarman 7, with the policy of taking Mahayana Buddhism as the root, he built Angkor Thom (meaning the "Great Capital"). Angkor is a glorious architectural achievement in terms of using stone as its material. Up to 1,000 years later, modern scientists look at it in amazement and admiration.

I wandered in Angkor Thom, in the Bayon temple, the national temple of the 12th century dynasty. The temple has 37 towers and on the high and low towers there are four-faced Bayons. Bayon's faces, whether the eyes closed or opened, looking straight or looking down, were smiling, very gentle smiles, sometimes just a slightest smile. The Bayon statues represent the Buddha, most of all Bodhisattva Avalokitesvara, who is embodied in King Jayavarman 7 himself. A stone recording the words of King Jayavarman 7: "It is because of the desire to liberate mankind from the suffering that I have an oath to become Buddha." The Buddha looks at all four directions so as to observe life, protect the humankind, and keep the nation's independence.

Angkor has been neglected in the forest for 5-6 centuries, but even after 600 years, Angkor still stands there, the smiling Bayon still moves people's hearts. Hopefully Cambodia will always be the land of smiles, as desired by its ancestors.

29th April 2017.

Feeling The Land Of Cherry Blossom

THE MODERN LEGENDARY

In 1970, I came to Japan for the first time as a member of the delegation of the National Front for the Liberation of the South. Japan at that time was a developed country which, nevertheless, was not that impressive. Thirty years later, I returned to Japan for the second time. This time, I came to the country with a world-leading industry. Japan in the last years of the 20th century has been an economic power in Asia and the second developed economy in the world after the United States. Japan is famous for its electronics and non-ferrous metals industry, the country with a top high-tech industry, and a car-making sector which is among the leading ones in the world. Japan's Shinkansen bullet train is the fastest and most complete train in the world. But the most remarkable about Japan is the story of land reclamation and the creation of an island especially for the construction of the Kansai airport in Osaka, the world's most modern airport. People call it the "myth of modern times". Sitting on the plane at 9,000 m altitude, I tried to imagine that myth... And there, under the floating clouds, Kansai airport appeared like two giant floating battleships side by side parked in the middle of the blue sea of Kinki in Southern Japan. The plane circled around to land. Kansai airport is sparkling, light and elegant, like a giant bird spreading its wings in the middle of the ocean. The Airbus of Vietnam Airlines landed lightly at Kansai Osaka Airport at dawn.

I set foot on the legendary land of modern times. The more I learn about it, the more magical it is.

This place used to be the ocean, the sea of Osaka Bay. There was no land at that time. The Japanese decided to fill the sea to create an artificial island. First, they drove stakes up to 60 meters into the seabed to build 11 km of dikes covering an area of 511 ha. Then they poured sand into the sea, 180 million cubic meters of sand were poured into this giant mold, and an island of sand which was 33 m above the sea level was raised by the great strength of man. It took them 2,200 days, which was equivalent to 6 years, to build an island in front of Osaka's gateway. The bridge across the sea was built. At a length of nearly 4 km and an altitude of 108 meters, with 12 car lanes and a railway below, it crosses the strait to connect the artificial island with the mainland of Osaka. An airport was built on the basis design of the Italian architect Renzo Piano. It is not difficult for Japanese companies to build an airport, but the real challenge here was to build it on an island where the ground is not stable, the piles must be nearly 100 m deep into the seabed. They patiently drove each pile into the seabed with high compression techniques, and it took 1/5 of a century, 20 years and 1,500 billion yen to build a modern airport in the middle of the ocean.

The airport is 4-storey high and 2 km long with an area of 300,000 m², but there are absolutely no concrete pillars, all are stainless steel bars for installing stained glass. The airport has a runway of 3,500 m long to accommodate large aircrafts. It is the most modern and expensive airport in the world. Due to the high expenses for its construction, the cost of landing at Osaka Kansai airport is also the highest in the world. One landing for a Boeing 747 costs one million yen (equivalent to US$ 10,000). It's a very expensive airport, but also a great one, with its vast open spaces from all directions. By 2005, when we landed in Osaka, there were nearly 100,000 international flights of 50 countries landing at this airport, including those by Vietnam Airlines.

Today, the Japanese government is advocating the investment of an additional sum of 2,500 billion yen (about 25 billion USD) to expand the airport to be twice as wide, and to construct a new runway. In particular, it is being planned that there will be a special runway dedicated solely to flights that take place amid winds up to level 13, taking to account the fact that the airport lies in the middle of an empty ocean and Japan is the land of storms and tsunamis. This is a myth of the 20th and 21st centuries.

Kansai Airport is the manifestation of Japan's miraculous transformation. A country with the 10th largest population in the world (128 million people), poor in resources and minerals and always prone to natural disasters, earthquakes, floods, tsunamis and volcanoes, Japan is also the country with the most natural disasters in the world. On average, there are 7,500 small and large earthquakes each year. However, after the event of atomic bomb on Hiroshima, twenty years later, Japanese are holding their heads high in the pride of being able to overcome poverty and hardships so as to strongly develop their country. Today, Japan is the world's leading country in the fields of science and technology, one of the economic powers, and the country with the longest life expectancy.

***

In 2013, after many tribulations, natural disasters and the global storm of the economic crisis, we returned to Japan. Japan is still beautiful, clean, and standing as proudly as the victorious Tokyo Tower.

I have walked around the capital of Tokyo in sunny days on the occasion of celebrating 40 years of friendship between Vietnam and Japan. Tokyo is magnificent. The Japanese people have a respectful, principled and polite way of life. They treasure affection and promises. Many elderly politicians I have met express their sincere feelings for the Vietnamese people.

***

FUJI MOUNTAIN

Talking about Japan, people often refer to Mount Fuji, a scenic spot recognized by UNESCO as world heritage site. Mount Fuji is the highlight, the center of the world famous Fuji Takona Iza National Park.

Mount Fuji can be called "Fu Ji Shan" in kanji, "Shan" means mountain. There is also another way of calling it: "Fuyoho", which means the "top of the ephemeral flower". Mount Fuji is the result of a volcano eruption that took place as the result of certain tectonic movements over 100,000 years ago. New sediments began to cover the older ones of an ancient mountain to create Mount Fuji. Fuji is the intersection of the Eurasian continental plate, the Philippine mainland, and the Okhotsk continental plate. The latest eruption of Mount Fuji was in 1707, which means it has been dormant for 306 years so far. Geologists have measured that the volcano is still smoldering. Looking at Mount Fuji from the airplane, the summit and the crater can be clearly seen. It is measured to be nearly a kilometer in diameter and 200 meters deep. Let's pray for Mount Fuji to continue its sleep so that Fuji will forever be a world heritage site! Mount Fuji is 3,776 meters high, the highest mountain in Japan located 100 km southwest of Tokyo. With the vantage point from the tall buildings in the western part of Tokyo, you have an entire panorama of the snowy-white Mount Fuji against the blue sky. From an altitude of 2,000 m and above, Mount Fuji is covered with snow almost all year round, so there are no trees. The whole scene is only in one color, usually the white color of snow, but sometimes pink or red at dawn or sunset. In summer, looking at Fuji from other side of the lake, the snow-covered peak of Fuji is like giant hat on the green background of vegetation.

Around Mount Fuji, there are five freshwater lakes: Kawaguchi, Yamanaki, Motosuu, Shoji, and Sai. The Japanese call Fuji one of the three holy mountains (Sanreizan), the other two being Tate and Haku. Cherry blossoms flourish in the mountains of Fuji. It is said that Fuji is the embodiment of the goddess of beauty. Whenever spring comes, she's dressed in beautiful cherry pink chiffon. In autumn, when the trees change leaves, she puts on a brilliant red shirt. The blue water around the foot of the mountain is the huge mirrors with which she reflects herself. Such a charming painting!

At the foot of Mount Fuji, there is a forest called Aokigahara with many beautiful and mysterious caves, stalactites and waterfalls. This area has plenty of iron and metal deposits, so the compass and navigation devices do not properly operate here. The forest is thick with big trees so many people get lost in it forever. Thus the Aokigahara forest becomes a sacred place where the spirits are still wandering...

Japan in general, and the area around Mount Fuji in particular, is abundant in mineral springs. In the winter, at Mount Fuji, numerous snow houses and mineral springs offer winter-related services much popular to a lot of people. Mount Fuji is a famous tourist destination which serves up to 300,000 climbers every year. The best weather for climbing is July and August.

Dating back to the year 663, a monk discovered and conquered the Mount Fuji. He climbed the mountain at night with an oil lamp, and took a break every time the tube of oil turned empty. After 10 breaks, he reached the top of the mountain. This story is still recorded in the board on the top of Mount Fuji. The places where the monk stopped to refill oil are later set up as the stops. Today, cars can drive to the fifth stops and visitors only have to climb the remaining five stops. Each stop has simple motels and canteens, not hotels. Each stop provides visitors with futon which is free for customers of the restaurant, or it will come with a cost in case visitors do not want to eat at the restaurant. Hundreds of people lied in line to sleep overnight. Therefore, climbers must carry their own backpacks, blankets and warm clothes. In autumn, the weather is moderately cold, however in winter, the weather is freezing at the altitude of 3,000 meters, and sometimes the temperature drops to minus 40 degrees.

Visitors often try to reach the top of the mountain or the altitude of 3,000 m while it is still dark with a view to catch the dawn. Looking down from there, the clouds are as dense as a vast sea of snow; people passionately take pictures when the sun rises. Sometimes they choose their birthday or wedding anniversary to watch the sunrise here because Japan is the country who welcomes the earliest sunrise on earth and here, Mount Fuji is the place welcoming the earliest sunrise in Japan. They drink a cup of hot sake with dried fish or a cup of hot coffee in water bottles, and then take a walk around the crater and walk down the mountain with the joy of a person who welcomes the earliest sun of the land of the rising sun. Looking at the map, the Japanese archipelago looks like an arc located at the easternmost point of the globe. The Japanese flag has the symbol of the sun as it is said this country is the home of the sun goddess. Standing on Mount Fuji and watching the sunrise is a unique experience. Mount Fuji has its majestic figure. The white snow on the top enhances the brightness of the mountain. Looking up the Mount Fuji from its foot during spring season, visitors are able to admire the beauty of white clouds floating in the middle of the mountain, the sun, and the brilliant purple cherry blossoms. It is such a fairy scene.

Mount Fuji has been the pride of the Japanese for many generations.

***

CHERRY BLOSSOMS

Japan has another beautiful name that I want to mention, that is the "land of cherry blossoms". Cherry blossom has become the national flower of Japan. When spring comes, from January to mid-year, cherry blossoms bloom. Due to the weather, in the South region as Okinawa and Osaka where the weather is sunny, the cherry blossoms bloom first. Accordingly, from Okinawa in the south, flowers gradually bloom, to the north region and then to Hokkaido Island, according to the warmth of each latitude.

The Japanese cherry blossoms are called Sakura, belonging to the plum and apricot varieties, but originally from the rose family with white, pink and red colors. Some white varieties turn pink when blooming, others turn to pale pink. Some blooms after the leaves fall, while some have blooming flowers and growing buds at the same time. There are 6 types of cherry blossoms, of which the most popular one is the Someiyoshino cherry blossom, which is grown popularly in the capital, villas, and parks. This type of cherry blossoms has only flowers and no leaves, so the whole tree is full of flowers. On the tree, the flowers bloom, while the falling petals cover the ground like a carpet of pale pink snow. The whole country is in festival when the spring comes. The Emperors and the Prime Ministers of Japan often entertain foreign delegations in the garden of cherry blossoms. One day, we had opportunity to visit the office of the Prime Minister Shinzo Abe inside the National Assembly building. Looking down from the window at the Prime Minister's residence, the garden of cherry blossoms was blooming brilliantly. In the blooming season, young men and women have picnic under the cherry trees while the elderly invite their mates to drink sake. A falling cherry petal in the cup of wine symbolizes good omen. Groups of people are jubilant and happy with the lucky charm, and that usually happens to everyone whenever a light breeze comes, the petals fall into every cup of wine…. According to the legendary "Kojiki" ("Chronicle of Ancient Stories") of Japan, Sakura is the name derived from Sakuya, the name of the goddess Konohara Kakuya Hime who has a legendary beauty and also the first person to plant the seeds of cherry blossoms tree on Mount Fuji. When the first petal bloomed, she incarnated into the roots of the tree, so people named the immortal flower "Sakura" in her memories.

From mid-March to the first ten days of April, it is the opening of flower festival which is called "mankai" by the Japanese. In the capital city of Tokyo, cherry blossoms bloom in villas, temples, and on the streets. Branches of cherry blossoms intersect; its falling petals create carpets of flowers. The cars run on the flower petals and under the natural flower arches. It can be said that only few places in the world can be such vibrant that move the people's heart as in Japan. Cherry blossoms reflect themselves on river and lakes. Taking a tourist helicopter and looking down the Tokyo from above, you can contemplate how the whole city is covered in the color of pink. The fragrance of this flower is gentle and soothing that lifts the soul of anyone who enjoys mankai and makes them feel serenity and delightfulness. In the famous parks of Tokyo such as Ueno, Kitanomaru, Sumida, or Maruyama near the Yasaka Shrine, the large cherry trees, with their big, solid trunks and large foliage, are typical for the apricot family. Girls in bright traditional *kimono* walk under the cherry blossom, adding even more to the unique ambiance of Japan. I once had the opportunity to stand under the cherry blossoms tree and listened to the girls sing a Japanese folk song called "Cherry Blossom" - the folk song dating back to ancient times and has become the opening song of festivals. The folk song has the passage:

"...

On the grassy hills and mountains

Where there are fragrance and clouds

The fragrance shines in the morning sun,

Cherry blossom season, cherry blossoms bloom

The petals are showing brilliant colors

...

The music rarely goes up and down; rather, it is a moderate, subdued song that gently expands the human soul. Later, it was developed by musician Alfred Reed into the 5th symphony Cherry Blossom.

The colors, fragrance and rhyme of the folk song have left their deep impression in tourists' heart. We once asked for a cherry tree to bring back to my hometown, Vietstar resort in Phu Yen. We have multiplied it; it was able to grow easily just from a single branch cut off from the tree. Today, cherry blossoms have covered some of the roads in the resort and in front of the villas; there is also a villa covered with cherry blossoms named Cherry Villa. The road in front of the entrance to the villas and the entrance to the spa area is shaded by the branches of cherry blossoms tree. When spring come, the cherry blossoms bloom in light purple color in the morning dew; on the ground, it is a whole carpet of fallen cherry petals, the feeling is just like being lost in the world of cherry blossoms. One of my friends said, "There must be cherry festival in Vietstar resort!" The cherry tree from the land of the rising sun has such pervasive and inspiring power. It is the flower of friendship.

In Japan, apart from cherry blossom season, there are other two interesting things. It is autumn when certain trees, like maple, oak, etc. change their leaves from green to red. Those kinds of trees are referred to collectively in Japanese as "momiji", and so, autumn is also called *momiji* season. The leaves of trees in the mountains, the hills and on the streets, all change to the red color, putting a brilliant autumn dress the entire country of Japan. The Japanese watch the red leaves and start their autumn festival. In contrast to the cherry blossoms that bloom from south to north, momiji season starts from north to south.

Japan has hundreds of craters, so there are also many mineral springs. There are 3,000 hot springs in Japan. It is said that this is the magic medicine from heaven, available there to be exploited to satisfy the needs of humans. The public mineral baths and hot mineral springs are highly popular. In contrast to their daily strict adherence to traditional rules and customs, the Japanese seem to become different people once in the hot spring, they open up and behave friendly, take off all their clothes and, totally naked, casually immerse themselves into the hot mineral water until their skin becomes pink or red, then they dry their body and take a sip of Japanese wine, as if in order to absorb the entire resonances of heaven and earth.

The Japanese love nature, they enjoy what nature has to offer. Their main dishes, sashimi and sushi, are full of natural taste. In order to have delicious chicken sashimi, chickens must be raised according to strict formulae to preserve its nutrition and ensure its hygiene safety. Japan is also famous of beef, especially Kobe beef. It is said that cows are fed with clean food, they let them listen to music and drink beer in order to create the most delicious and expensive meat in the world. Once you are in Japan, grilled beef and sushi are definitely must-try.

Our friend, Mr. Shimamura, the Minister of Agriculture, Forestry and Fisheries under three Prime Ministers, invited my wife and me to have sushi at a traditional restaurant. That was a small restaurant with just over a dozen seats close to the chief. The restaurant is simple in design, but it is the oldest sushi restaurant in Japan and requires booking in advance. They served us with a lot of different delicacies, from various types of fish to squid, shrimp, and snails, all perfectly fresh and absolutely without the fishy smell and the feeling of eating raw food. All are delicious and crunchy. What a delightful experience!

The high life expectancy of Japan might be because they know how to enjoy what nature offers. Nature is pure, whereas humans turn evil when their minds run after money. Only humans make nature worse and turn delicious and nutritious food to deadly poison. A message from Japan that I have learned: Dear humans, let's keep the purity of nature and put it to the service of humans.

THE SACREDNESS

During all of my three trips to Japan, I have been taken by Japanese friends to visit ancient temples and pagodas that is said to be very sacred. In Japan, no matter how modern they dress and live, their facial expressions and mannerisms still express how strongly they believe in God. In any temple I have visited, whether in a remote area or in a city, I feel dignified. Children in uniform and girls in beautiful kimono line up to visit temples. Casual clothes and unbecoming behaviors, if any, can only be seen in a few tourists.

In Tokyo, the most spacious, splendid and dignified temple is the Meiji Temple, which worships Emperor Mutsuhito who made great contribution to the Meiji Restoration Revolution in 1868, bringing Japan from a feudal country to a modern civilized country and creating conditions for the development of Japan today. Meiji Temple is located in a vast piece of land in the heart of Tokyo with an area of more than 70 hectares. The temple has 365 kinds of precious trees and nearly 200,000 green trees. The most beautiful and impressive one is probably still the green pine forest right in the heart of Tokyo.

During our trip to Japan this time, our Japanese friends took us to the oldest temple in Tokyo, named Asakura Temple, also known as Sensoji Temple. Asakura Temple is located in Taito City next to the gentle and poetic Sumida River. This area is usually called Taito "City". In fact, however, it's just the Taito district. Asakura is the name of the northeast area of Tokyo. This is the oldest temple in Tokyo which was built in 628. Legend has it that there were two brothers of the Hinokuma family who worked as fishermen on the Sumida River. One day they pulled the net and saw a wooden statue. They quietly returned the statue back to the river, and still they pulled it up for the second and the third time. They then brought the statue back to the village's chief. Aware that this was a sacred omen, the chief decided to repair part of his house to build an altar. Then several monks came to visit the statue. Upon realization that Buddha had appeared, they built a temple which gradually grew up to become the largest and oldest one in Tokyo with a history of more than 1,300 years.

Today, Asakura Temple is like a miniature city surrounded by shopping streets and dozens of hotels from 2 to 5 stars.

The temple has a gate called Kaminarimon which means "origin of thunder". On both sides of the gate stand the two statues of the God of Thunder (Rai Jin) and the God of Wind (Fu Jin), respectively. A red lantern weighing up to 670 kg hangs up from the middle of the gate, on which is an inscription that reads, "Thunder Gate". From the Thunder Gate, there is a straight path leading to the temple gate named Hozomon (which means "Gate of Treasure"). Next to the temple, there is a 5-storey tower called Dempoin. There is the statue of Guanyin in the main hall, which is only opened for worshippers on December 13. Visitors only pay their worship in the lobby by placing incenses in a large copper burner outside, and then pray after throwing coins. In utmost seriousness, the Japanese stand in front of the God statue and ask for sacred water with which to wash their hands before entering the temple to perform their rites. There are 5-6 festivals organized in this temple every year. In the Buddha Day on April 8th, people are well dressed, and one hundred children from four to five years old, in uniforms and with purple cherry blossoms on both sides of their heads and a big flower in the middle of their foreheads, stand in line along the road. Seen from above, it is quite a magnificent scene of cherry blossom purple. The Buddha statue, placed in a golden palanquin mounted atop a real-size artificial white elephant, is brought to the middle of the yard and is respectfully washed with clean water in shiny copper ladles by hundreds or thousands of people. After bathing the Buddha and taking Him into the temple, people wash their faces with the water just used for Buddha's bathing and then happily enjoy cakes, tea and leave contentedly.

This sacredness, in my thought, has raised the awareness of the Japanese to a new level. They are not superstitious, not made ignorant by their traditional religion. The faith that comes from their hearts, and the sense of their origin, their ancestry and tradition, with which the blood of every Japanese, young as well as old is imbued, are perhaps what creates their confidence and beautiful style of living. The sacredness has been reminding the Japanese to live honestly, crave for knowledge, and nurture a desire to strive for a prosperous Japan.

I would like to mention the way Japan exploits the aspect of spirituality to do tourism. The distance from the Thunder Gate to the main temple gate is about 300 m long. On both sides of the path, red painted columns and two rows of kiosks with 90 shops are built to sell souvenirs and consumer goods. A real market street, and still dignified, orderly and clean. Around this market street are intersected streets selling all kinds of things. The streets are old but clean. A group of rickshaws just like in the old days with young men as "drivers", good at English, cheerfully welcoming the guests (in Japan, people do not normally speak much English). The smile is always on their faces. They pull the rickshaw to take guests go around the temple for 30 minutes. The driver's legs are covered with red cloths. They take guests for a visit around the temple while introducing beautiful places with a perfectly professional manner, which makes you feel quite comfortable. The lesson of spiritual tourism and religious tourism can be seen here. The Japanese have properly taken the advantages of temples for tourism business, they have created a great tourism product. They deliver the information about national history to the people from all over the world while making effective commercial business at the same time.

Just a few minutes of walk from the temple is Hanayshiki Park with full of flowers and entertainment. Nearby is Sumida Park next to the gentle river which is full of cherry blossoms in spring season. We took a walk in the middle of the park to breathe in the fresh air and to feel Japan in our hearts.

Japanese people love flowers, love red leaves, and love nature, it might be true that nature has made Japanese people love their country and believe in their ancestors. Ancestors and their sacredness give people confidence and strength. I feel that the source of creativity and breakthroughs that makes Japan truly great is derived from this trust and strength.

November 2013

From Seoul To Busan

The flight of Vietnam Airlines that took us to Korea departed at midnight and landed in Korea at dawn. Incheon International Airport is located on a cluster of islands more than 50 kilometers from Seoul. We arrived at Incheon at dawn; the car took us back to Seoul crossing the world's 5th longest bridge - Incheon Grand Bridge. At a length of more than 21 kilometers and a width of thirty-three meters, it crosses the sea, connecting the small island and Yeongjong Island where the airport is located with the mainland. The modern cable-stayed concrete bridge can withstand storms with winds of 72 m/s, that is, above level 17, the most destructive level, and also earthquakes up to seven on the Richter scale. The car kept rushing through the blue sea in the brilliant dawn. If it were not for the rows of trees and cherry blossoms, we would not have known we have reached the mainland. In the middle of late spring, it was chilly, cherry blossoms bloomed all along the way like Korean girls in traditional clothes gently welcoming guests. I recalled how I used to see, in Japan, abundant cherry blossoms, big trees with foliage overtopping on the road. Here in Korea cherries have only been planted for about 3-5 years now, they are just young trees, and yet the flowers they yield were simply brilliant, white cherry blossoms, pure pink and dark pink cherries jostling all the way back to the capital. The morning dew glittering in the early morning sun made the cherry blossoms even more gorgeous. The cherry blossoms woke us up after a dreamy night on our plane.

Seoul appeared in front of us with Han River, the aorta of Seoul stretching out in front of the car. Many Vietnamese people mistakenly call this river "Hàn", this may be due to fact that the name Korea, in Vietnamese, is "Đại Hàn". In Chinese Korean, the name of this river is "Hán". Looking at the winding Han River, I suddenly remembered the historical period of Korea. After the war, Korea was founded on ruins, poverty and hunger. As it was written in Korean history, Korea back then had to live on American aid. To get this aid, however, Korean men had to joint the Vietnam war. It was during this period that Korean soldiers entered Vietnam and the brigades and divisions named Tiger and White Tiger committed their heinous crimes in Phu Yen and the provinces of Zone 5, my hometown. More than 5,000 Korean soldiers had died in battle in Vietnam; another 35,000 soldiers were wounded. In the 1960s, Korean people's life was very difficult, their income per capita was only 100 USD. However, by self-reliance, using its people as the driving force, the Korean government has found ways to stimulate workers to achieve high productivity, sometimes as high as 2-2.5 times over that in the United States, although the salary was only 10% compared to that of American workers. They developed from technical industry and, 40 years later, Korea had a gross domestic product of one trillion US dollars, becoming the Asian Tiger. Seoul, its capital, became a global city, home to global corporations such as Samsung, Hyundai, Daewoo, Lotte, to name a few. At that time, the world called this city the "miracle of the Han River" or the "legend of the Han River". It has once been hailed as the "miracle of the Han River" by Vietnam's press.

The Han River has the shape of giant dragon gliding at the foot of the mountain to embrace ancient Seoul including the Sam Mountain and the N'Seoul TV tower. Forty bridges with different designs span the river to connect the North and South banks, some of them having being ranged among the most beautiful bridges on the planet, including Paurpo Bridge at dawn with water sprayed on both its sides in magical colors. The Han River, connecting the old city with the Gangnam area on the south bank, is newly built, highly modern, with the towering sixty-three-storey Danlsup Sam building.

We stayed at the much famous Lotte hotel in Korea. The hotel is nearly forty floors high and is connected to a busy ten-floor supermarket. This style of linking the hotel with a supermarket is perhaps unique in the world. In Seoul, hotels are always fully occupied and the supermarkets crowded with buyers even on weekdays. This is an indicator of the health of the economy.

Today Korea is the country with the largest direct investment in Vietnam. By 2018 there were over 4,000 Korean projects investing in Vietnam with registered capital of USD 36.7 billion. Samsung Group has contributed significantly to the growth of Vietnam's GDP. Today, Korean industrial and financial corporations are actively investing in Vietnam, both directly and indirectly. That is a good sign, Deputy Prime Minister in charge of finance and strategy of Korea Kim Dong-Yeon affirmed in the office of the Prime Minister on the next day. "Korea is always interested in investing in Vietnam, because this is a stable market with good growth rate." The Korean government has policy of 'The new south'," he said.

I have been in Seoul many times. The country has both modern hustles and traditional nuances of a bold Asian country. Locate near the Vietnamese Embassy is Bukchon Hanok Village, this village was built 600 years ago. I do not know whether it was the first village of Seoul, but today it is the oldest village; hundreds of houses with cursive roofs, antique bricks and tiles clustering together. Many couples can be seen wearing traditional clothes called Hanbok, many international and domestic tourists have rented Hanbok while visiting the ancient village and walking around the Royal Palace where they can take pictures and footages. Bukchon Hanok Ancient Village has become a tourist destination and a natural cultural reserve.

Two hours away from Seoul by car is the Minsok ethnic village, which also preserves hundreds of ancient houses of ethnic minorities. Today it is an attractive film studio where the famous "Dae Jang Geum" was filmed.

From the old village we travelled back to Sejong Avenue; this avenue is called Daero in Korean and Sejong is name of the king who, five hundred years ago, created the national alphabet for the Korean language. Situated on this Sejong Avenue is a statue of King Sejong sitting leisurely, looking down at people going up and down. In front from him is a standing statue of General Yi Sun-shin, who bravely fought against foreign invaders. Sejong Avenue leads to Gyeong Bokgung Palace, which is "Cảnh Phúc Cung" in Chinese-Vietnamese, built more than 700 years ago. This was the palace of the dynasties between 1300 to 1910. It can be said to be the largest, most modern, most magnificent, and most ancient Royal Palace in Korea with a great number of magnificent palaces including the royal court, the king's main workplace, the king's residential quarters, and that of the queen, with its lovely small garden full of blooming flowers...

There is also the National Palace Museum in this Royal Palace, which preserves the cultural royal artifacts by the Joseon Dynasty. Visiting the Palace Museum can help better understand the life of the royal family, royal religious activities, and the architecture of the Royal Palace.

Notably, you can find in the grounds of the Royal Palace the National Folk Museum where the daily items of the Korean people in the ancient times and the folklore features of the Koreans from ancient to present are displayed. The Folk Museum is the upper tower of an ancient white building, a 5-storey tower house with ancient arched roofs creating a vantage point as if to lift people's souls, today as well in the years to come. Looking at the image of museum tower on the background of the mountains in the distance, with the green building of the Korean Presidential House floating in the blue sky amid white clouds, I understand more deeply the fact that whatever valuable each country possesses today represents the accumulated results obtained from its cultural and traditional legacy.

Gyeongbokgung Palace still retains main features of the oriental culture. Visitors must respect the solemnity, behave properly, dress politely, walk silently, and speak softly. The changing of the royal guards is performed from morning till 3 pm and taken place every hour. The group of soldiers is about dozens of people including drummers, trumpeters, and sentinels wearing brightly colored clothes with belts, wide-brimmed hats with straps like a large pearl chain, holding flags and flying dragon banners. The red-shirted generals would go first, then the blue-shirted generals, all of them with short mustaches. On their hats you can read the three words "Gatekeeping Generals", which roughly means "commanders of the group of guards protecting the city". Next is the carrying team with twelve people, then the flags of all kinds and finally the trumpets and drums, with two soldiers blowing conches majestically.

The whole palace, from the main entrance with three main arches, to Gyeonghoeru Pavilion, to the palaces and the museums, are elaborately carved with sophisticated motifs, which remind me of Vietnamese craftsmen, a similarity and closeness which results from a shared religious culture and royal culture between the two countries.

*

* *

On the morning of the last day of the trip, a Sunday, the Samsung corporation invited the Vietnamese delegation to play golf. They said Samsung has a very large golf club and their An Yang golf course is the number one in Korea. In Korea, golf is an economic, cultural and sports industry, a driving force for tourism development, and a part of life for many Koreans. The Korean golf industry has developed phenomenally, the country has nearly 600 golf courses, and Seoul, with a population of 10 million, has 100 golf courses. The country has thousands of golf courses and tens of thousands of screen room, a type of playing and practicing golf through electronic screens, still actually use clubs and play through 3-D screens. The Korean golf industry is among the top 10 countries in the world. Every year, tens of millions of people play golf courses, and the Korean golf industry contributes to the country's economy up to five billion US dollars each year. In Seoul there is a Golf Research Institute. As I know, Korea is cooperating with Ton Duc Thang University, a Vietnam-based international 4-star university, to open a golf course in Vietnam.

We got up at five o'clock to go to the East Valley golf course located in the eastern valley of the city, on a high hill area, the car climbing uphill. The early morning sun shone through the foliage of the big cherry trees which stretched their branches over the road, the cherry petals shimmered in the morning sun, the remaining dews made the petals sparkle like diamond, and the faint pink color of cherry blossoms in the early sun seemed darker. The flowers were beautiful, so as the branches. Cherry branches are not as elegant as apricot blossoms, but they also have soft foliage that moves people's hearts. I stopped the car to take some pictures of cherry blossom branches in the mountains and forests outside Korea. It was very cold; I rubbed with my right hand the hot pack to prevent frostbite, and leaned over to record these rare images. In Korea, in the cold season, there is Hot Pack, Koreans call it "hat peck", which is a small bag with tiny seed; by tearing the plastic bag and rubbing both hands on the seeds inside, the bag will gradually heat up to 38°C - 40°C and staying hot for 10-15 hours. You have just to rub it with your hands, put it on your neck and warm up your chest, then put it in your pocket for it to warm up when it turns cold. The golf course is located between the valleys of two mountain ranges. Winter here is full of snow; snowmobiles are available to keep the golf course running. In Korea, there is red leaf season, winter months when the trees lose their leaves, waiting for new buds in the spring.

***

On our arrival in Seoul, the TV tower can be seen from any direction. Koreans call it N'Seoul tower (N' stands for Namsan mountain). Namsan means the South Mountain which is at an altitude of 243 meters above sea level and is also an ecological park. Walking around, you can hear the birds chirping in harmony with gentle winds swaying the foliage, freeing visitors from the fatigue of the long journey. Looking down the calm Han River from Namsan, the swallows swoop down as if the spring is still there. A small boat was carrying a group of young men and women wearing traditional clothes and happily singing the Korean folk song "Arirang". The lyrics keep humming as if stretching on the mountains, on the fields and on the Han River. The choruses "Harida" "Harida" keep echoing, reminding me of the day when the Vietnam U23 football team won the Asia's runner-up prize, the Korean singer Jin Ju singing this folk song in dedication to the Vietnamese team and their coach, the Korean Park Hang-seo.

Right at the foot of N'Seoul tower, there is an area full of love locks where young couples would come with a lock of their own, engrave their names on it, then leave it here and throw the key down the mountain. I have seen this love lock tradition in Russia, Germany, Italy, France... but this is the first time I ever see it here, in Asia. Unlike in European countries, young couples are very serious, they hold their hands to pray and promise in front of heaven, earth, and rivers and to wish for eternal love. N'Seoul Tower is 240 meters high, which equals to the height of the mountain, making the tower in total 483 meters higher than sea level, and 500 meters high including the lightning rod. At night, the tower appears with multiple colors which represent the purity of the air in this capital city. If the tower shows up in red, the air is very polluted; yellow means polluted, green, average good air, and blue, good air. When we went down the tower and walked in the big forest, the tower appeared blue above us. Our Korean friend accompanying us said: It is late spring with clear sky, light wind, and fresh air.

***

On leaving N'Seoul Tower, we visited an ecological stream that some called the wonder of Seoul, Cheonggyecheon stream. The name is too long to read. Cheon means stream, I call Cheong-gye for short "Chong-gy", which our Korean friends still can understand. A very beautiful stream, it starts near Sejong Avenue and runs through the city center, up to 6 kilometers long. The stream is not very deep, the water is so clear that fish swimming upstream can be easily seen. There are two wide walking paths on both sides, stone benches along the way where you can sit and admire the scenery. Many tourists come here to take photos and videos. Korean men and women wearing traditional Hanbok crossed small bridges leading to the middle of the stream to have a closer look at the beauty landscape. The stream is nearly two meters below the street level, with two thick concrete walls built along its banks. Along the walls were paintings depicting how the king walked on the road, accompanied by a long entourage riding splendid horses. The gentle afternoon sun shone on the surface of the stream, drawing bright lines like water paintings with magical colors. Twenty bridges, high and low, and even bridges over the water like "underground" one during the war in Vietnam, each bridge has cultural design such as Naruto Bridge representing a butterfly spreading its wings, Gwanggyo Bridge representing the harmony of past, present and future.

The history of this stream is full of twists and turns. Originally, it was just a small stream with the function of draining waste water from the capital during the Joseon Dynasty. The kings made it a point of dredging, embanking streams and building bridges for people to pass through - "Cheng-gye" was called Gaecheon (meaning "open stream") at that time. After the devastation of the war, many poor people migrated to the capital in the 1950s to build makeshift houses on both sides of the stream, making the streets dirty and slum, the consequences of which, were garbage, sluice, and the stream becoming the worst place in terms of sanitation.

Twenty years after the rising era, a highway connecting the central boulevard with the President House, the Prime Minister's Office and the Royal Palace run through the center to connect with the eastern area. The road had replaced the filthy stream and cleared the slums. The stream was just an underground drain for drainage. The road made the traffic become convenient, but it also brought about noise, smoke, and dust from the traffic; smoke even on high-rise buildings...

In 2003, the Mayor of Seoul (later the President) decided to abandon this highway and elaborately re-opened the stream. The stream was opened and connected with traditional rich areas such as Bukchon, Jong Dong, Nam Cheong... which, collectively, are called the Cheonggyecheon cultural ring. After the re-opening, all six kilometers of the center of Seoul becomes a peaceful, ecological place thanks to the cool water, the average temperature being always 3-4°C lower than that in other neighborhoods. In order to turn an ecological stream to a center of tourism and culture, the city has to spend 281 million US dollars, equal to more than 6,500 billion Vietnamese dong.

***

Seoul in particular, Korea in general, has very typical dishes, such as chicken ginseng soup (Samgyetang), grilled beef... We visited the traditional Samgyetang restaurant near the Royal Palace to enjoy chicken ginseng soup. Korea in general and North Korea in particular are rich in ginseng. In our country, ginseng is rare treasure, the same also applies to Korea. For cuisine, however, ginseng is considered as a kind of vegetables here. Despite being located in an alley, Samgyetang restaurant is very crowded. We came on weekday but still had to wait for our turn. Each bowl of soup had a small chicken, ginseng roots and was stewed with rice; the broth was very sweet. The chicken ginseng soup was served together with kimchi and pickled radish, all of them perfectly rich and delicious. On another evening we went to a grilled beef restaurant in a small street in front of Lotte hotel. Enjoying grilled beef next to the hot kitchen and drinking Shochu felt extremely exhilarating in the cold weather. Korean beef meat is very tender and sweet, grilled beef being served with lots of fresh, attractive-looking vegetables and kimchi. In Vietnam we have kohlrabi pickles, salted onions and eggplants called traditional dishes. In Korea, kimchi is also a pickle dish, but comes with so many varieties, with over 100 types of kimchi from vegetables. Koreans people are gourmets, the famous grilled beef is not only attractive to domestic customers but also tourists, who are all to eager to enjoy it at least once. "Koreas eat everything from the ox," is a common Korean saying.

Koreans call grilled beef Bulgogi, which is marinated with sesame oil. They make soybean oil into a kind of sauce with which to marinate beef together with ginger, garlic, onions, sugar, and red wine, during up to four hours before grilling. Korean grilled beef is only used with fine ground salt without any other seasoning, which makes the meat more flavorful. Whether it is grilled beef, grilled pork or grilled seafood and chicken ginseng soup, the famous restaurants are always crowded. In one of the most heavily populated cities in the world, with income per capita over US$ 41,000, more than sixteen times higher than that of Vietnam, the purchasing power and number of extraordinary number of guests is all too obvious.

On the flight from Seoul back to Vietnam, I was introduced to the evening menu by a very charming Korean flight attendant in Vietnamese ao dai. She suggested that we try mixed rice dish that Koreans call Bibimbab. That night, above 9,000 meters altitude, I enjoyed delicious and rich dish of mixed rice. White soft rice with little boiled vegetables, carrots, radishes, mushrooms, bean sprouts, onions... all served together with shredded beef, sweet and sour dried shrimp mixed with sauce and chili sauce, and kimchi. Bibimbab is full of sweet, sour, salty and spicy flavors. Carrots and radishes are crispy in the mouth. The flight attendant said this is common and traditional dish of Korea. Although the plane had left Korea, I still found myself in the middle of Seoul, eating as I was a traditional Korean dish while warmly talking with a Korean girl.

***

Seoul has many scenic sites to visit, but we had to keep moving. Lee Jung Jun took our group to Young Pyong Mountain, which is 150 km from Seoul. This is the valley in the northeast of Seoul, a skiing city and weekend resort for wealthy people. Some Korean Presidents also have vacation villas here. They usually have a private villa, under the canopy of this pine forest. The Young Pyong Valley is located at an altitude of 600 meters, about 30 kilometers from the sea and only a few dozen kilometers from the Korean border, with fresh air, peaceful and ecological scenery.

In late spring it was still snowy here, there was a white ski slope filled with snow. As people from a tropical country, my group was so excited to rush into the snow to take pictures and hold a handful of snow to feel the cold running through our body. We stayed at Lee's No. 19 villa, sitting by the pine wood fire at night, making barbecue with warm Sansachung wine. I kept thinking about the divided Korean peninsula. Perhaps Vietnam is one of the rare nations in the world who deeply understand the division of the country. There was time when the country was divided into two regions, suffering from death and hunger for 21 years. The 38th parallel has divided the Korean peninsula into two regions and the two governments have been governing their respective territory for 68 years. Many families have been separated, parents remaining in the North while their children being in the South. The Korean people still want a reunited, peaceful and developed Korean peninsula, so that Koreans, Southern or Northern, could shake hands and sing together romantic folk songs in the language of their own nation, and cooperate to build a strong and prosperous Korean peninsula.

Next morning, we left the Young Pyong valley and headed east for 30 kilometers to the Jumunjin coast of Gang Won province. At noon Lee did not want us to eat seafood here because there would be abundant of them in Busan. Lee told the driver to turn the car into a mountain village with rice and vegetable fields like those in our midland provinces. A small and traditional restaurant is located at the foot of the mountain, with a pine tree dangling its branches in front of the alley. The rural restaurant is named Chaw Rum (meaning as you wish). This restaurant offers traditional Korean dishes made from cod fish braised with soft melons, braised chicken with spicy and sweet spices, marinated pork with spices grilled on skewers, and lots of boiled vegetables, pickles, etc. Especially, there is a dish of Gulbi fish which was dedicated solely to the king, so it is also called "King's fish". This fish looks nothing special, even too ordinary, much like croak fish and shellfish in Vietnam's sea, but it has less scales and you can't guess how it is dried out: the meat remains soft and fresh like freshly caught fish, and especially its intestines are very fatty. The gulbi fish eaten with crispy pickled radish is very rich in favor in Korean countryside cuisine.

After lunch we headed to the south, travelling 250 km on the highway along the east coast to the second largest city of Korea, the coastal city of Busan.

****

We arrived in Busan in the late afternoon; the bright sunshine pushed away the cold of the northern mountainous region. In Korean, Bu means good opportunity and wealthy, San means mountain, so Busan can be understood as a rich and prosperous mountain city. Three sides of Busan are surrounded by mountains, the city being located in a valley between the two rivers Nakdong and Suyeong. The hills and mountains keep overlapping, getting higher and higher. Geum Jeong San Mountain is so high as the peak of Busan. According to feng shui, Busan is the city "leaning against the mountain and facing the river". In fact, Busan leans against Geum Jeong San all day long, facing the big sea. From our car, our Korean friend used his mobile to open the radio channel that tells us the history of Busan. According to the channel, this area belonged to legendary Korean God leaders in the second century. By the 300s, these leaders had conquered the whole of Korea, the period itself being called the Three Kingdoms. This was the golden era of the ancient Korean dynasties. It was not until the 15th century that Busan was established and became the first seaport of Korea.

Aware as I am that we would go through a bridge named Gwan Gan, the longest one in Korea, as Lee has warned us as we were riding toward the city, I could not help but get surprised and amazed at the sight of the most impressive, 7,500 meter-bridge spanning the three small channels of the Busan Sea, at less than 200 km from Japan. The bridge, 25 meters at its widest and 18 meters at its narrowest, has eight lanes and two floors, all of them for one-way traffic. On the right of it are modern houses and seaport with many large ships coming in and out. The afternoon sunlight highlights the docked ships with many designs including 2-3 storey cruises looking like floating hotels and many sailboats resembling white birds gliding through the calm surface of the sea. High-speed yachts, one by one, drew white curves on the blue sea. In the distance were islands and ships like dotted lines made with high-tech watercolor strokes. The section of Gwan Gan Bridge connecting to the central of the city winds its way in an S-shape, much close to the busy marinas, creating an indescribable impression.

Busan is the largest port in South Korea, the first seaport of Korea to be opened for trade with Japan, nearly 25 years ago, Busan became the first international commercial port of South Korea. Today, Busan not only has the largest seaport but also features the most popular tourist city in South Korea. The famous beaches of Busan including Haeundae, Gwangalli, Songjeong, Dadaepo, etc. are always over-crowded in the summer, the less crowded one of them still having a hundred thousand visitors, while the largest one holding up to 150,000 people. Different festivals are frequently organized on these beaches; there are also seafood restaurants, yachts taking guests to go fishing, and all-day attractive games such as rope swing, wrestling, and darting. They even have a library on the beach, a music stage where people can sing at will...

We stayed at the five-star Paradise Hotel & Casino Busan for the night. From the high floor looking down, we saw an entire row of large and small swimming pools with Jacuzzi; there are pools with only a few couples; the pools are connected to the beach and always have warm water even in the cold season. As night fell, the weather was cold because it was still spring, and the sea was empty. The colored lights interspersed with LED lights shining several kilometers along the coast. The waves gently fell on the sand creating smooth movements; the white sand under the colored lights and the white waves looked like the laces of the giant chiffon dresses worn by ancient fairies, making the beach even more magical. The silent, curvaceous coast runs north, a small faraway island looks like a dot on the background of this fairy beach. Looking to the south, Gwangan Bridge becomes more shimmering and even more magical by the play of colored lights. This bridge at night is always changing lights - there are up to a hundred thousand different lighting effects that change every hour, every day, and are even more brilliant in festival days.

In Busan, it seems that everything can be turned into attractions to visitors. In the world, wherever there is a sea, almost there is fishing village and fish market. In Vietnam, the fish market stretches over three thousand kilometers along the S-shaped coast. But only in Busan the fish market is so special; Jagalchi fish market is located near the coast on a long street and operates almost all night. The lights are bright, and the fish shops are neat and clean. They sell fresh fish and seafood: shrimp, squid, snails and especially a lot of abalone, octopus still alive and squirming, and the fishmongers are very happy middle-aged women. At the two ends of the fish market street is a seafood food court with all kind of grilled, fried dishes, and hot pots being served with lots of vegetables and kimchi. There is great supply of abalone here, so the price is very reasonable, almost the same price as that for shrimp in Vietnam; it is not that strange to eat dozens of abalone at once here. Tourists love to drink wine while enjoying fresh seafood here. In October, crowded and noisy Jagalchi Festival is also held.

Busan has many places for tourists to to visit and spend their money, such as the 14-storey Shinsegae Center hypermarket, over 500,000 square meters, the largest hypermarket in the world, where you can shop, eat, practice sports, and play golf.

After walking around the supermarket, our Korean friends invited us to "visit the ocean". Indeed, after visiting the three underground floors of the aquarium (Busan aquatic park) with thirty-five thousand kinds of fish of the North Sea, it felt as if we had just returned from exploring the deep sea of Busan.

In Busan, there are many cruise ports which welcome the world's big ships to bring tourists to Busan and many small yachts of all kinds, six-seaters, ten-seaters and twenty-seaters, which bring visitors to this North Sea and also providing fishing services; each cruise port can at least welcome a hundred ships. We had the opportunity to visit the beautiful cruise port of Busan and also the "number one beauty" in Korea, which is the Marine City cruise port located on an estuary in the middle of the city with skyscrapers standing leisurely reflecting themselves on the water. On the estuary hundreds of large and small yachts were parking close to each other in perfectly neat order. The yachts gently left the port and went out of the estuary, undulating like flocks of birds gliding across the sea, painting a picture of wealth and prosperity.

Looking out at the South Busan Sea, you can see five small islands with different shapes, some of which look like a giant taken down to the sea, some resemble a sentry at duty, and some that reminds you of a pen that writes poetry on the sea. Busan people call this scenic spot Oryukdo relic, which represents the five elements Metal, Wood, Water, Fire, and Earth. Standing at the Busan gateway, it seems to welcome the ships coming to Busan and say goodbye to those leaving it.

On the last day of the trip, early in the morning we were able to visit Haedong Yonggungsa temple located close to the beach. It is somewhat strange that monks often choose high quiet mountains to build temples. The temple is located right next to the rocky cliffs. Haedong Yonggungsa Temple, built in 1376, has three floors with three connecting halls. Four lion statues lie there facing the sea with four faces which represent joy, anger, sadness and happiness, respectively. On a large stone, some features of the temple are introduced, the philosophy of temple being "to pray from the heart". Yonggungsa means "dragon's palace".

Legend has it that there was a bodhisattva riding a dragon over the seashore. The messenger of love and forgiving, this bodhisattva stopped at this cliff. People built a temple to worship him and called it the holy place of Boddhisattva.

The path to the temple with 108 steps is built among the blooming cherry trees swaying in the wind; the cherry blossom, the whispering waves, and the cool breezes make visitors more spiritual. Many people come here to pray for good luck.

At night, I followed young Koreans to visit the "Moonlight Dalmaji" road winding along the mountain, going up and down along the coast. On a bright moonlit night, the moonlight penetrates through the branches of the trees, along with the moon-shaped lamps on the ground giving off a soft light. On dark days, the artificial light is enough to make people think they are walking under the real moonlight. People seem to relax their souls in a romantic fantasy world. I walked on the Moonlight path, listening to the waves crashing into the shore.

Busan is like that: the nature is preserved, embellished, made more beautiful by people, becoming a cultural destination and a driving force, a key economic sector contributing to the "smokeless industry" of Korea. The tourism and service industry of Busan contributes 70 per cent to the Busan economy annually. I found myself still on the path of Moonlight with the thought as of what breakthrough is needed to reinforce the contribution of tourism and service industry to the development of the coastal cities of Vietnam, like it does in Busan? A question that followed me all my way along the path of Moonlight. Yes, only humans, the creative thinkers, can create a breakthrough. I plucked a cherry blossom branch of the "Moonlight" road as I returned to the hotel, with a dream about the future of the coast of my home country, of Vietnam's tourism and service industry.

Spring 2019.

Jeju Island, The Wonder Of The World

JEJU – THE ISLAND OF "TRIPLE ABUNDANCE"

Before coming to Korea, I read a lot about Jeju Island. The island is located at the southernmost tip of Korea. It can be said that Jeju has a deep and strong attraction to us. It is not only because of its beautiful names such as "love island", "tourist paradise", "world wonder..." but also because of the fact that Jeju itself has gone a long way from being one of the poorest regions in Korea to becoming an international tourist destination. While Vietnam welcomes 5 million foreign tourists annually, Jeju Island, with its 500,000 residents, welcomes 5 million tourists from all continents. It is said that, 20 years ago, Jeju was a poor island of prisons, and nowadays, the income from tourism per capita has reached 5,000 USD per year. What makes Jeju so developed? That miraculous growth is a strong attraction for me.

From Seoul we went to Gimpo domestic airport in order to get to Jeju. I thought there would be about 10 flights to the island every day like in European countries. But it is not the case. Jeju Airport is an international airport. There are direct flights from Hong Kong, Japan, Beijing, Shanghai, Taiwan, and Singapore to Jeju, apart from the many domestic flights. On average, there is a plane landing on the island every 5 minutes, most of which are large aircrafts. There are many airlines with fixed routes to the island, including Korea Air, Asiana Air... Especially, there are many low-cost airlines such as Eastar Jet, Jin Air, Jeju Air...

It only takes 45 minutes by flight from Seoul to the island. It's absolutely amazing to watch the whole island through the plane window before landing. The whole island appears in the middle of the ocean: blue water, waves crashing on the rocks and creating white foam. The coast is mainly rocky, black rocks mixed with golden sands. The whole island is a gentle green land, peaceful and quiet.

Jeju Island is also known as Samdado. Our Korean friend explained that Samdado is the island of "triple abundance". It means that the island has "three things in abundance", namely, abundance of wind, of rocks, and of women.

Yes, Jeju is a windy island. The wind from the ocean blows in all directions and seems to help us wash away all the dust from the trip and give us the pristinely fresh air as if we are right in the middle of the sea.

Jeju is the island of rocks. The entire area of 1,846 square kilometers of the island is from volcanic eruptions millions of years ago, so the whole island is black rock covered by basalt and ancient alluvium. Jeju people distinguish between block stone, small stone, and honeycombs stone... They call them Basalt, Uldam, Olretdam, and batdam. "Dam" maybe is a Korean sound coming from the word "dol" meaning "rock". Rocks stand in rows at the coast, stones "grow" at the base of the mountains, stones form blocks at the top of the village, stones used to build houses, make fences, raise statues, pave roads... And far away are the rocky mountains, and volcanoes... Jeju is full of rocks and wind, the gift from nature that anyone who comes to Jeju can easily recognize. The third "abundance" thing is especially curious. Why "women" out of everything else? It turns out that Jeju people lived mainly on fishing in the past. Men had to go to the sea, where many of them fell victims to storms and wars, never to return. Korean women, in accordance with Confucian culture, are very humble, taking upon themselves the task of looking after the household and caring for their husbands and kids, while earning money for the survival of the family falls within the man's responsibility. However, in the case of Jeju, with 70 percent of its regular population being women, they become leaders of the family. I met groups of women in tight diving suits, wearing glasses and snorkels, dive and catch seafood with a big net bag. I see women working in hotels and restaurants, fields and gardens, as fruit and vegetable vendors, as taxi drivers. All of them are women.

****

JEJU – THE ISLAND OF LOVE

A quarter of a century ago, Jeju was still a poor island, living mainly by farming, raising cows, horses, and fishing. Agriculture is based mainly on growing oranges, tangerines, radishes, rice and corn for animal feeding, just enough for self consumption. In feudal times, Jeju was an island where prisoners were exiled. It can be said that Jeju was an island of prison and poverty, where people had to raise pigs using both garbage and human waste (called black pigs).

But Jeju also has beautiful scenery, virgin, poetic, lyrical and rustic beauty, and still retains many traditional cultural features. I asked Lee, my Korean friend: what makes Jeju change?

- It can be affirmed that the first breakthrough is the TV series.

- Can a drama change the face of the island?

- Around the early 2000s, the 20-episode drama "Winter Sonata" with many beautiful and romantic scenes filmed on Jeju Island and featuring famous actors such as Choi Ji Woo, Park Yong Ha, was premiered. It tells the story of a man and a woman who love each other compassionately. The director brought the original Jeju landscape, its sea, its cliffs, its forests, its flowers, its waterfalls... into the film. People were amazed. "Jeju is so beautiful", so they all want to visit Jeju.

Movies, the landscape on the screen, and the appearance of famous actors, are the main attraction to people. "Winter Sonata" has also been screened by HTV Ho Chi Minh City in recent years. Hundreds of other dramas have been filmed in Jeju including "Lady Dee Jang Geum", "Slave Hunting", "Spring Day"... with famous actors the like of Jang Dong Gun, Ko So Young, Bae Young Joon, Kim Young Jin, Lee Byung Hun Cinema has drawn visitors to Jeju and made Jeju become the top of its kind. Today, numerous human-size figures and photos of famous actors and artists are displayed on the island, where visitors can take pictures with their favourite characters and artists. The films made on Jeju Island are all love stories and this is also one of the reasons behind the name "The island of love". I once stood on a peaceful corner of the hill full of yellow canola flowers to witness the whole view of Jeju. How truly poetical! The small village roads crossed the flower fields leading into the forest with rows after rows of maple trees turning red under the change of seasons and, far away, the waves whispering the love song together with rocks and rapids. The waves "kiss the rapids forever", "shall I stop crashing / only as my kisses make the whole world melt", as Xuan Dieu wrote. It is worth calling Jeju the island of love if only because of its wild and modern beauty, its charming mountains and sea. My hometown, Phu Yen province, also has a beautiful sea like this. Da Dia Reef, the national heritage, is more beautiful than the cliff of Dragon Head on Jeju Island. Phu Yen is also the place to welcome the earliest dawn in the country like Jeju. Phu Yen tourism, however, is only at its starting point. Why? How? Is Jeju the lesson for the breakthrough of tourism in Phu Yen and the central coastal provinces?

As far as Jeju is called the island of love, you cannot fail to mention the park of love. The park name "Love Land Park" and the prohibition of children under 16 years of age has attracted even greater curiosity in visitors. The park is not that large, just a few hectares, where 140 statues, from white and colored stones with meticulous, detailed, sharp and bold outlines, are placed. The statues are all in human-real size. Nude males and females. Kissing couples. Couples making love in all different positions, which makes event adults blush and, at the same time, keeps everyone excited. The director told me: "This is an indispensable aspect of life, also the tonic. Just one more smile from the heart makes you more youthful." He said this is also one way of sex education. I thank him for the bold idea to create a unique tourism product that seems to be profane, yet elegant, and civilized... Visitors to Jeju, especially young people, can hardly fail to visit the park of love at least once.

JEJU – THE LAND OF TRADITIONAL CULTURE

In the Jeju tourist map, you can see the Seongeup ethnic village with 3,000 traditional cliff cottages. The walls are made of Jeju black stone, and the roof is made of 7-8 layers of thatch. Only few kilometers from the center of Jeju city, the ethnic village still retains its ancient nuances. Originally, Seongeup village was the capital of the Cheong-eui Hyeon tribe (since the early 15th century). The road to the village is abundant in trees and colorful flowers. In summer, mustard flowers bloom brightly and purple peonies extent to the horizon. This is also the place where the famous movie "Dae Jang Geum", directed by Lee Byung Hoon, was filmed. The big boat at the entrance of the village serves as a monument, the medicine millstone of the past. It was Dae Jang Geum who had used this legendary millstone as she learnt the profession of medicine. People here are very proud of their own culture. They know how to live in modernity and at the same time retain their traditional culture. The ethnic village is a living museum on Jeju Island. The local people are very hospitable, they invite guests to try their handmade dough cake dipped with honey. The costumes, the farming, worshipping, and community activities are kept unchanged, without being mixed. Just a little improvement has been made so as to provide it with something "modern". Visitors can see a unique tradition of the island, reflected in that each house has a stone gate with 4 rows of holes. If one bamboo tree is hanged, it signals that the owner will be away for a while and will be back soon. If the second bamboo is hanged, it is a signal that the owner will come back at night. Hanging all three bamboo trees is the signal that the owner has been away for a long time, and guests should not be waiting. When four bamboo trees are all hanged up, it means this family has only women. I am confused about the 4th signal, whether they try to tell other men not to disturb them or it means they need more attention and help. Anyway, this is transparent. In Jeju, opposite to "triple abundance" is "triple absence": absence of house gates, of beggars, and of hospitals. The first two "absences" speak of a wealthy society without crimes where people live honestly. The third "absence", on the other hand, left me a bit confused. It's obvious that healthy people do not need hospitals, but what about the old and the sick? A Jeju official said: "There is an airplane to transport the sick to Busan", and then he shook his head: "The people on the island are very healthy". He said the state has preferential policies for islanders in medical treatment and education, in addition to tax exemption and visa-free entry for tourists, and, especially, special policies for preservation of the island culture. Besides the ethnic village, Jeju also has a museum: the Folk Village with 117 houses, a recreation of the old villages on Jeju Island of the last century. More than 40 hectares of land were used to build "the mountain villages", "the steppe hill villages", "the fishing villages", "the religious villages"... The items for daily use and production in the island have traditionally been brought here for preservation before the tall glass buildings and the central city of Jeju are developed. In 2006, they built an amusement park at Folk Village which is very attractive to tourists.

JEJU – THE WORLD WONDER

Few years ago, 400 scenic destinations in many countries were introduced to the world with a view to be selected as the "wonders of the world". 28 destinations were shortlisted for the final round, from which the "Seven wonders of the world" were voted, including Ha Long Bay of Vietnam. Of those, Jeju Island is selected with a high number of votes.

Previously, in 2007, Jeju Island with the volcano and its craters was recognized by UNESCO as a world heritage. Three main attractions of

Jeju have been selected by UNESCO: the sun mountain, the Halla peak, and the Geomunoreum cave.

Koreans call Seongsan Mountain the place to welcome the earliest dawn in Korea because it is located at the easternmost point and reaches out to the sea of Jeju. It is the pearl of the port city of Seongsan-po.

This crater slept millions of years ago, forming the 200-meter high Seongsan Mountain whose crater is the round Seongsan peak just like a stadium, called the Sunrise Peak, which is surrounded by the black cliffs of 99 side-by-side rocky outcrops like lotus petals. The Sunrise Peak has diameter of 600 meters. Viewed from above, the Seongsan Peak looks like a giant crown. To the west there is a small pedestrian path, a small steppe, and Seongsan ethnic village. During the radish season, its flowers bloom highlighting the great crown of Jeju. In the morning when the sun rises at a corner of the sky, Seongsan Peak is the place to welcome the first dawn. At the foot of the mountain, the sunrise time is clearly informed to the visitors to catch the sunrise. A lot of people from all over the world come here to watch the dawn. The road to Seongsan is very beautiful and visitors only stay at the top for no more than 50 minutes. On bad weather days, Seongsan Peak does not welcome visitors. Many Korean movies have been filmed in Seongsan, the most beautiful island in Jeju.

Geomunoreum cave is the longest and widest cave in the world, with nine caves connecting with each other into a complex covering over 22 square kilometers. According to the UNESCO delegation who came to evaluate the caves, they must meet both criteria "vii" and "viii" regarding the lava system. The cave in Jeju has outstanding and unusual beauty because of the colorful arches and the cave floor created by limestone (carbonate), standing out against the black background of the lava walls. The arches and cave floor have a lot of stalagmites "growing" from the ground and stalactites hanging from the top, creating a unique and attractive landscape. Compared to other caves in the world, no cave is as beautiful, wide and long. The cave structure is very well protected - a separate path is designed solely for visitors so as to avoid infringement on the existing structure. This entire cave system is located in the ecological forest of Jeju National Park at the altitude of 500 meters above sea level_ it has cool temperatures even in the summer, which is ideal for hikers. The wind and the coolness of the air create a magical feeling. Legend has it that three gods named Go, Yang and Bu appeared from Jeju cave and married three girls from the mainland, then they gave birth to Jeju indigenous people. Those are the ancestors of the people on the island. They lived through the Stone Age, hunting, gathering for a living, fighting the cold with animal skins. In those days they ate raw seafood and raw meat. The ancestors planted 70 species of precious trees that stood upright and blocked the sun from shining on the entrance of the cave, creating mysterious and sacred atmosphere. They were the founders of the T'amla Kuk country, which changed to Jeju in ancient times and later belonged to Korea.

The sacred mountain: this is the roof of Jeju, located in the center of the island called Hallasan (In Korean, san means mountain, Halla means volcano). But it is closer to the word Hala, meaning God in religious language. For Jeju people, Hallasan is the sacred mountain. The Halla peak is 1,950 meters high and contains the legend about the sacred life of God and the spirits that Koreans call Yeong. The last eruption turned the crater into a lake. From there, the water flows down creating lyrical waterfalls. The top of Halla is usually covered by clouds. In clear day, Halla is like a tower reaching to the sky. This is the highest mountain in Korea. It is the center of rich and diverse semi-tropical ecological forests. Around the mountainside is a national park with many rare species of flora and fauna. On the slopes of Halla Mountain, there are many caves and waterfalls, the most famous one of which is the "Heaven and Earth" waterfall, which Jeju people call Cheonjeyeon, meaning "the place where the sky touches the ground". The waterfall falls like white silk. The Jeju people built a large lake to keep "the water from heaven". Nearby are three ancient rocks, where people come to pray for peace and prosperity. Legend has it that this is the place where seven fairies came to earth, so it is also known as the Fairy Waterfall. The waterfall is ringing, the birds are singing, the wind is gently pushing the clouds, all creating fairy scene of Halla mountain.

The Yeongsil trail is one of the main routes leading to the top of Hallasan. The nearly four-kilometer road crosses through the forest of the national park; in leaves changing season in autumn, the forest is like carpeting to welcome guests, the road passes through rocky mountains and lava with many magnificent shapes. The visitors will pass through a valley full of fragrant flowers and butterflies before reaching the top of Hallasan.

UNESCO has selected the sacred mountain (Hallasan) of Geomunoreum cave, and the peak of the sun mountain (Seongsan) in the east to be recognized as the world heritage of mankind, collectively known as: "Jeju Volcanic Island and Lava Tubes". Juju's lava also includes the cliffs on the west coast, especially the **Dragon Head Rock**, which is called Young Dam Rock by Jeju people, located to the west of Yong Yeon Bay; looking far away, the reed looks like the dragon head reaching out to the sea. Along the western seashore, there are also rock formations that make up the **Jusang Jeollidae** landscape as arranged by human hands. Here, the rocks are also created by nature like Da Dia Reef in Phu Yen. It is fair to say that Da Dia Reef in Phu Yen is more beautiful than the Dragon Head Reef and Jeju Jusang Reef. However, these places have become popular and busy destination because of human embellishment. The vertical rows of pine trees, souvenir shops, flower gardens, restaurants, galleries, theaters, rocky coastal roads... have raised the cliffs to the international level. At this beach, there are two things that make strange impression on me: pebbles and small rocks are everywhere but no one can take them. Even if you take, you cannot take it out of Korea as it is national property. Visitors can only buy it at the souvenir shop and a stone with the inscription of Jeju island is taken out of the country, meaning the stone is "exported" only when it has been crafted. The second thing is that there are many stalls serving fresh seafood without cooking, called traditional dishes. The stalls have only few rows of simple tables and chairs, few large barrels of sea water, abalone, octopus, and sea cucumber. The shop owner picked it up, washed it with clean sea water, then cut it thinly and neatly before arranging it on a plate which is deliciously served with kimchi. The diners have it with Soju which is said to be superb. This country has a lot of abalone, in the past being served only to the king, today it is everyone's favorite dish. They say: eating this way, the seafood is fresh, clean and sweet. Koreans love to enjoy seafood while still alive. The saleswomen are also the ones willing to wear diving suits to plunge into the sea to catch abalone, sea cucumber or octopus to sell to diners. I noticed that it seems there are no empty tables in the stalls, young men and women even have to sit on sidewalk to enjoy the seafood when it is full of seats. Seafood has long been the favorite source of food for people living in the bays as in Vietnam. Jeju also has impressive specialty which is Jeju red tangerine. On the island, in the season of ripe tangerines, red ripe tangerines are everywhere, in the garden, around the house, and along the way. Jeju tangerines have red, shiny skin and sweet taste.

Jeju, just over a decade since the Winter Sonata aired, has grown with full range of high-end travel services. Jeju has casino, racecourse, and stadium for international football tournaments... Jeju has 30-meter-deep diving boat for tourists to watch the coral sea and natural colored fish. An island with only 500,000 people but has 20 golf courses and has a 36-hole and 27-hole international golf course, lots of 5-6 stars hotels, the main road has six lanes each way. In Jeju, on average, every two people have one car. This rate is even higher than the capital city of Seoul. A Jeju that has reached the standard of the world's tourist paradise. Modern civilization has developed on the background of ecology and traditional culture which has made Jeju wonder of the world.

***

I stand on the windy Jeju Port looking at Seongsan Mountain at dawn and realize that in order to become a tourist country, marketing, tourist product, the embellishment and exploitation what nature offers and preservation of indigenous culture and promoting people's awareness of traditional culture are all the must. I realize that one of the spectacular ways to promote tourism is through cinema which is extremely important and effective. It has stimulated the breakthrough of Jeju tourism, turning the prison island into tourist paradise of mankind.

September 2nd, 2014.

Taiwan – The Pearl Island

I came to Taiwan for the first time in the early years of the 21st century, that day Taiwan together with Korea, Hong Kong and Singapore were the 4 dragons of Asia. The development of Taiwan is seen as a miracle. In the 1960s, Taiwan had income per capita of only $170, on par with Central African countries. Yet in the first decade of the 2000s, income per capita (GNP) has reached $33,000, the Human Development Index (HDI) is ranked 18th in the world by the United Nations and its foreign exchange reserves is ranked 5th in the world. In the same year, Taiwan has celebrated the completion of the "Taipei 101", a 101-storey supermarket, apartment and office building which is one of the tallest buildings in the world and as the symbol of the economy of Taiwan. Taiwan is one of the biggest investors in Vietnam.

In the country of Taiwan from North to South, the mountainous region occupies two thirds of the territory, with the peak of Mount Yushan reaching 3,952 meters high. The big island is nearly four hundred kilometers long. Taiwan has 64 islands in the Penghu archipelago and 21 other small islands. Taiwan covers an area of 38,000 square kilometers. Looking at the map, Taiwan has the shape of a giant leaf floating in the sea. If Taiwan is called the pearl island, this is the jade leaf that people in the mainland always desire for. In the past, when Spanish sailors discovered the island of Taiwan, they were amazed by the sacred wild beauty of the island, so they named it Formosa, and called it Ilha Formosa, which means beautiful island. Today, Taiwan is also known as the Green Island because of Taiwan's rare ecological nature.

When I was still in school, I thought that in 1949, when the Kuomintang was cornered by the Liberation Army of Chinese People, they abandoned the mainland and fled to the island and founded Taiwan. Some say that it was only then that Taiwan was born. That is the misconception that is far from the truth. So what is the truth?

According to archeological research, humans appeared on this island 30,000 years ago and the ancestors of Taiwanese aborigines settled on the island 4,000 years ago. The Taiwanese aborigines have many genetic characteristics which are closed to the Indonesians and the peoples of the East of Australia which is called the Austronesian group in ethnography. Taipei was home to the Ketagalan tribes in the 18th century, who had an independent language system. The Han people did not know about Taiwan until the Three Kingdoms period.

Taiwan was a colony of Portuguese in many years (1594), Spanish (1626), and Dutch colonists. Europeans came for the purpose of resource exploitation, including "seducing" the Aboriginal people to take the antler velvets and then bring the alters back to the West. They set up agricultural production facilities and brought Han workers from Fujian (China) to here.

In 1662, the Ming Dynasty collapsed, and the Qing Dynasty ascended the throne. A group of loyal protestors to the Ming Dynasty gathered to drive away the European colonialists in Taiwan and establish their own territory to escape the control of the Qing Dynasty. But not long after that, Taiwan was back into Japanese hands. Japan has ruled Taiwan for over 50 years. Being resisted by the aboriginal people, Japan launched hundreds of fights to destroy the aboriginal people, sent Japanese workers and attracted Han people on the mainland to the island as labor forces. Japan constructed the North-South railway, built roads, hospitals and schools. The agriculture was developed with abundant crops, in 1939, Taiwan was the 7th largest sugar producer in the world. The civilization of Japan has changed part of the cultural identity of the island, and this was also the beginning of industrial and civilized development on this island with many infrastructures construction, including some temples built by the Japanese. Today, the Presidential Residence is the former Governor-General of Japan. After Japan surrendered to the Allies in 1945, three hundred thousand Japanese immigrants in Taiwan had returned home.

All those to say that although Taiwan has the Chinese as its national language, the foundation of the economic and cultural development of Taiwan cannot be without the influence of Japan and Europe. Taiwanese people are polite and always say thank you just like the Japanese, but they do not have bowing gesture. Taiwan also has red leaf season; the whole street and the mountain turns red when the autumn comes and when the spring comes, the brilliant blooming cherry blossoms touches the heart of people. Taiwan does not have cherry blossom festival like in Japan, but many groups of people still hold tea parties under the cherry blossoms. They laugh and wait for the gentle breeze to blow the flower petals on the girls' hair and in the cup of tea, thinking it as blessing and good news just like the Japanese. It is that mix of culture that makes Taiwanese culture unique.

***

Taiwanese people call the capital city Taipei. Taipei is the land located along the valley created by rivers. Taipei is bordered to New Taipei and Keelung, the urban connection forms massive and bustling Taipei with the population of over seven million people which is the political, economic and cultural center of Taiwan and is recognized as the global city for manufacturing high-tech products. Taipei has two international airports, North-South express train, and high-speed subway and is the leader in economic development in Taiwan. Taipei alone has 30 billionaires ranked 16th in the world, even before Los Angeles (United State) and Sydney (Australia). In 2017, the IESE Cities organisation ranked Taipei as the number one smart technology city globally and number one in Asia and sixth in the world for entrepreneurship development. Taiwan has many prestigious universities. The whole island has 121 universities. Taipei alone has 24 national universities and academies, many of which have long history such as the Soochow University, which was founded 100 years ago, the Taipei National University of Technology (1912), the University of National Defense (1906), the National Pedagogical University (1922). Particularly, the Taipei National Pedagogical University was established in 1895 and is now 126 years old.

National Taiwan University Hospital is a leading international medical research center.

Professor Hwang, who teaches at National Sun Yat-sen University, has introduced me to the education system of Taiwan. He said: Unlike Vietnam, graduating from high school is not always followed by university degree. In Taiwan, up to 60% of high school students do not apply for university degree, instead of that, they take vocational classes when being in high school and receive the vocational diplomas. Education in Taiwan, especially in university and vocational programs, the creativity is always promoted by the school. Taiwan is a country that recognizes the great importance of open universities. Many adults and hundreds of thousands of people have been trained through this open system. The educated rate of children is 99.91%. The education system of Taiwan is recognized to satisfy the international standards by the world organizations.

Thanks to the focus on education and training, Taiwan has human resource with high technology and intelligence and also teams of expert doctors. The development in medical industry in Taiwan is not inferior to other countries. Many hospitals welcome millions of international patients annually for medical examination and treatment. Taiwan hospitals has expert doctors and modern facilities that are trusted by the world.

Coming to Taipei, one must visit museums, night markets, and beautiful scenic areas of Taiwan. Perhaps the most signature symbol is the Taipei 101 building (also known as the World Financial Center) which consists of 101 floors being divided into 8 segments. The Chinese considers number 8 as the symbol of prosperity and wealth and in each segment, there are 8 floors just like 8 knots of a bamboo tree. In 2004, Taipei 101 was the tallest building in the world at the time of its opening at the high of 508 meters. In 2010, it ranked second after the Burj Khalifa of Dubai which is 829.8 meters high. Taipei 101 is the building of modern construction that withstands the seismic of the largest earthquakes ever occurred in 2,500 years and the storms with speeds of up to 216km/h. The building is installed with UV-resistant double-glazed glass which reduces the heat caused by the sun by 50%, and these glasses are resistant to the impact of up to nearly 8 tons. In sunlight, the glasses turn green just like the color of bamboo. Taipei 101 is recognized as the tallest green building in the world. At night, the color at the top of the tower is changed every night, red on Monday, orange on Tuesday, yellow on Wednesday, green on Thursday, blue on Friday, purple on Saturday and violet on Sunday. Just by looking at the top of Taipei 101, one can know what day it is.

Mr. Chen, one Taiwanese friend of mine, took us to visit the Taipei 101 building. The first five floors are busy shopping center, the 85th – 86th floor, 88th – 89th floor and the 91st floors are the observatory deck where people can see the city of Taipei with 360-degree view. Through the magnified lens, you can clearly see the mountains surrounding Taipei and the Tamsui River formed by the Keelung River and the Xinjian River in the middle of valley. Three rivers winding like dragons embrace the mountainside and enhance the beauty of city. Far away, the Keelung seaport lies at the end of the river, blazing in the afternoon sun with ships looking like the birds on the calm sea. Leaving the 91st floor, we went down to the 5th floor to look for place to rest. Mr. Chen was previously a businessman in Vietnam and married a Vietnamese wife, now he returns to Taiwan to open numbers of high-end tea shops. I have watched him making tea, his hands were as fast as the hands of magician, putting water in, then rinsing the kettle and the cup, pouring out the first tea water which is called tea washing, after those process, the tea is poured into cup to invite guests.

On the 5th floor, Mr. Chen took me to a tea shop with milk tea that Chen said was "very good". In Vietnam, milk tea is also the favorite drink of my grandchildren, only to know that the milk tea is origin from Taipei. Young people of this island also love milk tea. The milk tea in the tea shop on the 5th floor is very delicious because it is made from Oolong tea with fresh milk and rich black sugar, mixed with pearls to bring about delicious taste. Sitting at the tea shop, Chen talked about Taiwanese tea, an island with many hills and mountains which is covered by green tea gardens, the higher tea tree is planted, the more valuable it is. Taiwan has variety of teas which are made from tea buds and leaves; there are over 100 types of tea, but Chen only mentioned his three favorite types: green tea, oolong tea and black tea. Each category comes with dozens of famous brands. Green tea is the type of tea with low level of oxidization, famous as Longjing tea, Biluochin tea (this type of tea will have a spiral shape when being dried), ... Oolong tea, which is slightly oxidized is considered high-class tea in the world with variety of famous types such as Baozhong Tea which is naturally curly leaf tea that is wrapped in half a pound and one pound bag and has yellow green water and sweet taste. Guan Yin Tea and Si ji Chun Tea also have golden water, Alishan Tea is grown on high mountains, after being processed, the leaves curled like seeds, the taste is no longer bitter but very fragrant. All of those are the top names of tea which are well-known by tea lover. The black tea is highly oxidized and fermented which also has many famous varieties such as Sun Moon Lake being grown around Sun Moon Lake, large lake located at 7,800-meter-high mountain, and Alishan (Ali mountain) black tea which is grown at 1,000 meters high or more, this type of tea is processed and brewed very carefully, packed into expensive package and being sold for thousands of dollars, this tea has healing effects and good for intestinal, digestive and heart support. I do not understand where it comes from, but people call it tea tree, tea hill, tea garden, and when the tea leaves are processed, it is just called tea. I do not know when Chen bought it, but in front of me was a box of Royal Palace Oolong Tea, also known as the King of Tea. Two tea bags were neatly wrapped in a wooden box covered with gold with the lid engraved with two elegant and sophisticated dragons curling up. The packaging must account for 60% of the cost of the tea box.

Although being culturally influenced by the Han ethnic group, when it comes to tea, it shows significant influence from Japanese tea culture. Taiwanese teas have long been exported to the world.

Once after the party, I was invited to taste the dumplings that are only available in Taipei or in Din Tai Fung in Singapore, which is Xiao long bao, small dumpling with very thin and smooth cover, the meat is very delicious and especially it has very rich sauce which is easily leaked out when eating. After tasting the dumplings, we were invited to drink a cup of high mountain Oolong tea, then a cup of black tea to make our stomach "lighten".

The tea tree is an example of the transformation of agricultural industry in Taiwan. The proportion of agriculture in the national economy is not significant, but it is the basis of the Taiwan's economy. The Taiwanese government has strategy of "Developing industry through agriculture and developing agriculture base on development of industry". The industry comes to the field, the processing industry comes to the product area. In the agricultural processing factories such as processing asparagus, tomatoes, vegetables, tea, meat, milk... farms are transformed into business models. Universities and research institutes are also associated with agricultural enterprises, so science and technology are practically applied in agricultural enterprises. People do not have to move to the city. In rural areas, there are still demand for engineers and high-quality human resource such as PhDs and Masters.

The policy of private land ownership has promoted the ownership and production of households, in addition, the government investment in transport infrastructure for rural areas and irrigation along with price subsidies, tax reduction and protection policy has brought agricultural development of Taiwan miraculous leap. And it has become the foundation for the development of Taiwan's economy. More than ever, we see the close association among the state, the scientist, the banker, and the farmer in rural areas in Taiwan.

We took the express train from Kaohsiung at the southern to Taipei at the northern of the island. The express train passed through the fields, the hills, and the cities. Only by travelling by train to see the rural areas of Taiwan, one can clearly see the foundations of Taiwanese agriculture: all the mountains and hills are covered with green, the higher the mountain, the bigger the tree. The fields are straight and massive with irrigation system bringing water to the field. It is hard to see "The buffalo goes first, then the plow following" here, the field has been mechanized. In the corner of large fields, there are clusters of green trees which are residential neighborhoods, the cars run leisurely in the fields. People are not in a hurry as if they want to relax and enjoy the fresh air of the countryside. I just suddenly remember the night before when we went to night market in Kaohsiung, perhaps the most impressive thing is the fruit, watermelon weighing up to 7-8 kg, each mango and mangosteen weighing up to 0.5 - 1 kg. Guava is very big and juicy, types of Taiwanese fruit is plentiful, 36 farms have grown all kinds of fruits from oranges, tangerines, grapefruits to quarries, gourds, squash... All kind of fruit is big in size and has sweet taste without any chemical fertilizers like in my own country thanks to the success of biotechnology and the research result of universities and agricultural-associated institutes. On the occasion of visiting the research Institute in Taichung, we came across varieties of rice which was purple, brown and orange. An engineer joked: "We want our eyes to enjoy the meals too, it means that there must be color in the bowl of rice".

It is impossible not to mention orchids when mentioning Taiwanese agriculture. Taiwan has lots of orchid production farms. This island country exports nearly 90 million branches of Phalaenopsis orchid to 86 countries annually, earning nearly 200 million USD. Taiwan has the largest orchid park in the world, up to 150 hectares with the participation of 80 orchid growing companies. Orchids are transplanted in a cold room and incubated with the appropriate light from the LED system, all are grown in the greenhouse with scientific automatic watering system.

In 2019, Taiwan held the international orchid exhibition and the Kaohsiung agricultural renovation center won 4 awards for the "dancing" orchids which is created from thick round Phalaenopsis orchids with red spots on yellow petals and sweet fragrance, each branch has more than 10 flowers (meeting the commercial standards) so it won the first prize and also the silver award.

The two plants of Phalaenopsis orchid the "Girl" and the "Ballet" have very strong yellow-red petals, but also gentle and graceful shape and long-lasting fragrance, so they both won the third prize.

Taiwanese orchids are biologically elaborated, and the orchid technology has been recognized and respected by the world.

Trees, flowers, vegetables, fruits, rice, sugar cane, corn, tea... and meat, fish, dairy products... have made Taiwan's agriculture an advanced model which has been studied my many countries, including Vietnam. Taiwan has successfully developed agriculture associated with tourism. Farms, agribusinesses and villages all develop tourism. In many places, the hotels, amusement parks, parks are next to the farm like rural tourist area. However, there are also many villages that only develop the model of homestays, and rooms in the villagers' houses... There, they sell the local dishes that are hard to find in restaurants. There are still ethnic minority villages in the mountains and valleys. Their colorful traditional costumes and unique dance festivals have attracted tourists.

Tea gardens and tea farms today are agricultural tourism destinations to many tourists. The Sun Moon Lake is located on 800-meters-high mountain and surrounded by tea hills. Visitors come here and stay in the middle of the forest while enjoying the traditional dishes of the indigenous people such as grilled rice in bamboo tubes dipped in salt and chili mixed with garlic. Or San Bei Ji chicken (fried chicken with sesame oil, soy sauce and rice wine) served with rice ... And drinking fermented wines poured into "glasses" skillfully made of small piece of bamboo.

Agricultural tourism has changed the face of rural life. The clean and fresh countryside with friendly people has made rural Taiwan the "Green countryside". Tourism has improved society, making rural Taiwan more civilized and modern, and the living of people have been rapidly improved. Tourism has helped people earn high income. The products from village from poultry meat to fresh fruits and vegetables are "exported" on the spot.

***

In early 2020, before the Covid pandemic, we went to Taiwan by Vietnam Airline, landing in Kaohsiung and also departure from Kaohsiung. I have time to discover Kaohsiung. This is the second largest city of Taiwan and has the largest port in this island country. Kaohsiung Port is in the top of the major ports and ranked fourth in the world. Kaohsiung is not as busy as Taipei and is the industrial city and the gateway to the great ocean of Taiwan.

Professors of National Sun Yat-sen University arranged us to stay at the 5-star hotel "The Grand Kaohsiung". The hotel is built in royal style, at first glance, it looks like an ancient palace with painted gilded exterior, but very modern inside. Behind The Grand Kaohsiung, it is quiet lake. The air in Kaohsiung City is not as pure as in Taipei as this is the industrial city. So, it is rare to have such huge quiet lake behind 5-star hotel right in the heart of the city. That is Cheng Qing Lake Park. Cheng Qing Lake is large natural lake. The road surrounding the lake is up to 4-5 km. The trees are dense as old forest with plenty of kinds of flowers being grown here. The cherry blossoms are reflecting on the blue lake surface and swaying in the wind. The jogging track next to the lake with flowers and green trees is as supporting the steps of those who exercise, walk and jog here.

Kaohsiung also has many tourism attractions such as the landscapes, busy and crowded night markets all day and night. I was taken by Professor Hwang to visit Cijin Island which is the ancestral fishing village of Kaohsiung. Farewell to Sun Yat-sen University, a prestigious university with magnificent campus located on the shores of Sizihwan Bay where Mount Shoushan charmingly reflecting on the West Kaohsiung Sea. We stopped at the Ai He River (the river of love) to get off the ferry to Cijin. Cijin Island is a narrow and long island like giant dam lying in front of the city as if to protect the peace of Kaohsiung from the waves. Cijin Island has been inhabited since the 30th year of the Kangxi Dynasty (1691). On the island, there is Cijin Tianhou castle which is the oldest palace in Kaohsiung. There are many monuments and attractions in the island such as light tunnels, wind power parks, two giant seashell monuments with the statue of fisherman's hands, the wooden walkways along the coast... also streets and cars but perhaps the distinctive characteristic of Cijin is the "smell" of the sea. From the ferry terminal to the food market, which is the barbecue street. Fish, squid, shrimp, oysters, and snails are fragrantly grilled on charcoal stove. The smoke rose up and filled with the scent of the sea. All the visitors are welcome by this rich smell of the sea when setting foot on Cijin. The seafood here has been freshly caught from the sea, so its taste is very rich and fresh. Therefore, Cijin has become must-visit destination for Kaohsiung people and international tourists. They come to Cijin not only for sightseeing and swimming, but also to enjoy the taste of seafood. Cijin has many seafood restaurants cooked in Taiwanese style.

***

In our last evening in Kaohsiung, we asked Professor Hwang to introduce us simple and normal Taiwanese meal. He happily accepted our request and took us to a small restaurant located on the outskirts of the city. The owner of the restaurant is an ethnic person with strong physique, dark skin and open smile like the Bana and Ede people in the mountains of my hometown. He is the owner of the restaurant, and also the chef. He cooks local Taiwanese dishes. Still the fried chicken, but he fried it and made it as flat as a pizza; the crispy, sweet and fragrant fried chicken was dipped in spicy sauce. The braised pork rolls were served with grilled bamboo and crushed salt with wild leaves, creating very strange salty, sweet and sour taste. I remember the dish "Seo chu" which is deep fried small fish soaked in thick local maji, mixed with lemon, crushed garlic and lots of green chili. It was so spicy that we were sweating, but everyone loved it and made compliments on it. The owner of the restaurant sincerely invited us to taste his homemade sticky rice wine. The wine is made by the traditional method of fermenting and brewing, with slightly sweet, sour and bitter taste that made his dishes even more flavorful. What a simple yet unique meal. This meal is an unforgettable memory.

What impressed to me while staying in this city was the word Kao of the name Kaohsiung. The city has the flag with the symbol of Kao written in one-stroke calligraphy style. Kaohsiung has built the symbolic building of the city in the shape of letter Kao. The tower, including columns and spire, is up to 378 meters high and was built in 1997 with 85 floors. Before "Taipei 101", it was one of the tallest buildings in the world. The tower is named Tuntex Sky Tower, but I still used to call it the Kao tower. Professor Hwang took me to the 74th floor by the express elevator system in only 43 seconds. The 74th floor is also where the visitors can take the panoramic view of Kaohsiung. We had tea break and watched the sunset on the west side. 180 kilometers from

Cijin Island is the Fujian of China. The sun like a red ball slowly descended to the western coastline, the sun shined the clouds in all kinds of colors, red, purple, violet and blue in many spectacular shapes of dragon. The sun painted the surface of the sea in brilliant pink. The boats left the port like the birds leaving their nest, rushing out and heading to the south to the fishing grounds in the East Sea. Next to the cup of premium Taiwanese oolong tea, we talked about the word Kao. Kaohsiung represents the supreme, heroic will and aspiration to development. Professor Hwang said to us: Our generation is the successor, but I know that our ancestor also shared the same passion to raise the knowledge and aspirations of the people. He said: "Taiwan has its position as today because people know how to raise the word Kao in their hearts. That is to have high intelligence and high determination." Knowing I agreed, he excitedly told me the story of Taiwan manufacturing IC (Integrated Circuit) also known as "Chip", type of electronic integrated circuit for industry. It is well known that the global industry is growing smarter thanks to electronic devices. From industrial control, control systems of aircraft, cars, missiles, satellites to modern weapons ... all must use "electronic chips". He pointed to the phone and asserted: This small phone is smart because of those chips. The electronic chip is the heart of all industrial systems in the world. Professor Hwang said: From being the outsourcing producer for the United States, Japan and Germany, Taiwan has become the home of the microelectronics industry. He said that it took Taiwan twenty-five years from 1970 to become the world's fourth largest manufacturer (along with the United States, Japan and South Korea) and by 2003, the integrated circuit industry of Taiwan has accounted for 80% of the world market share, becoming the world's leading country and earning billions of dollars for the country. Professor Hwang said: "The Institute of Technology Research (ITRI) is where the scientists are gathered, they have overcome the failures with high intelligence and high will. The small chip which is the heart of the world technology, is the testament to the crucial role of people, intellectuals, and scientists.

It is true that in order to become the Pearl Island, having beautiful nature is not enough, one must have high aspirations, will, and intelligence. More than ever, I deeply understand the importance of knowledge, science and advanced technology to Vietnam./.

April 2021.

Visiting Algeria

The Airbus of Air France took off from Paris bringing our group across the Mediterranean Sea, from the North to the South, to Algeria. Our group included some members of the Vietnam Peace and Development Fund accompanying Ms. Nguyen Thi Binh, the Fund's President. Ms. Nguyen Thi Binh, before her appointment as Vice President of the Socialist Republic of Vietnam, was the Minister of Foreign Affairs, Overseas Ambassador of the National Liberation Front and then Head of the Delegation of the Revolutionary Government of the South at the Paris conference. At that time, I was fortunate to be a foreign affairs officer from the South, a subordinate of Minister Nguyen Thi Binh - a gentle and erudite minister, whom we still often call 'sister'. Sister Nguyen Thi Binh had visited Africa and Algeria many times during those years. I also, wearing broad-brimmed hat and in liberation army uniform, has visited this country that was enthusiastically supporting Vietnam. The plane is at an altitude of 5,000 m in the clear blue Mediterranean sky. Through the window frame, looking at the clouds floating under the wings, I reminisce about those exciting days...

I

The Algerian revolution shared many similarities with Vietnam. As Algerian friends usually said, Vietnam has 'planted the seeds of revolution' for Algeria, the victory of Vietnam over the French colonialists was to pave the way for Algeria to liberate the nation. Uncle Ho at that time told Saden, the Algerian revolutionary: "Let Vietnam fight the French first. As Algeria has fewer friends, you need to learn from experience". Shortly after the Dien Bien Phu victory in May 1954, six Algerian soldiers opened fire attacking the French post in Hamidou, Rais District, starting the revolution on November 1, 1954. The revolutionary organization - the National Front for the Liberation of Algeria - was officially born, declaring to the world their revolutionary struggle for national independence. The revolution against the French colonialists lasted eight years, like that in Vietnam, and, in 1962, achieved complete victory, liberating the country after nearly a century of domination. Later, the three-kilometer road in the capital ran along the sea, with Hamidou, the place where the first shot of the Algerian national liberation was fired, being named Ho Chi Minh Boulevard. We were taken by friends to visit and walk the whole avenue named after our dear Uncle Ho, our hearts filled with emotions...

The days when Vietnam fought against the America, Algerians wholeheartedly supported Vietnam. It can be said that anywhere, whether in the city or in the countryside, on faces of many colors, black, brunette, white, we would always meet with friendly smiles and bright eyes full of enthusiasm for Vietnam. The young Algerians used to organize white nights in the desert to welcome us... On that day, when they welcomed us, they used to chant a chorus of "Vietnam -Vietnam - FINAL". (FNL is the acronym for Front National de Liberation) as their greeting to us.

The plane had lowered its altitude, tilted its wings to greet Algeria, the blue Mediterranean Sea appeared in front of us and then the Algerian winding coast with its many rapids. Just like the southern coast of France, the beaches in Nice, in Toulon and even in Monaco, here they are all rocks crushed by the waves from the Magma granite... Occasionally I see a few sandy beaches but not as white as in the center of Vietnam, the sand is opaque yellow, perhaps caused by volcanic eruptions millions of years ago with the sand being diligently filtered by the Mediterranean sea waves, so it has lost its red color, only being left with this ivory white. The Algerian coast running from Tunisia to Morocco is just less than a kilometer from 1,000 kilometers long.

Alger, the capital of the People Democratic Republic of Algeria, is clearly visible under the wings of the plane; the tall and low houses stretching from the mountains all the way to the coast are all pure white, the color of the national religion of Islam. The President of Algeria before 1975 was the Minister of Foreign Affairs, the counterpart and close friend of Ms. Nguyen Thi Binh. After signing the Paris Agreement, Sister Binh gave the President one of the pens she used to sign the Agreement as a special gift.

Ms. Nguyen Thi Binh, over 80 years old, returned to visit Algeria at the invitation of her old friend, who is the President. I thought she would be warmly and cordially welcomed, but only in the form of close friends...

The plane had just stopped, the stairs were open, and Ms. Nguyen Thi Binh and our group were invited to go out first. The head of the welcoming party came to the door to welcome us. A female Minister in the Government was sent by the President to the airport to welcome our delegation. Vietnamese flags and Algerian flags flew at the top of the tower. We were escorted to the guest house of the President House by two rows of motorbikes, in the same way a nation is welcoming the head of state from another country. Only four of us accompanied Sister Binh - only one car was enough for us but five or six cars were arranged. The streets of Alger had changed a lot, with eight lanes of traffic, many villas and high-rise buildings replacing the familiar flat-roofed box houses of Africans. The modern capital of Alger has reduced the number of date trees along the road, replaced by the greenhouses and industrial city.

Algeria covers over two million three hundred thousand square kilometers, the largest country in Africa, stretching over 2,000 km from the Mediterranean Sea to two countries Nigeria and Mali. The authority hierarchy under the government is at the provincial level and the commune level with 1,541 communes. A few places, due to ethnic characteristics, have district level, but without council. With the population of nearly 35 million people, the state subsidizes a lot of things, from education, health care, to electricity and water supply and other necessities. People do not pay for medical treatment. Large loaf of bread only cost ten dine (2,000 VND), a box of two liters of milk only twenty dine. All the tap water of the capital of five million people and the water systems of the cities are mainly filtered from sea water by expensive modern technology, but it is subsidized by the state. People's lives are stable. Children who go to university are also given air and train tickets by the government and are paid for education and living cost. The Algerian government pays great attention to education and training, thus it has established three Ministries dedicated to this cause: the Ministry of Education, the Ministry of Higher Education, and the Ministry of Vocational Training. Funding for education and vocational training accounts for 18 per cent of the total national budget, the second largest after national defense. In Algeria, refusing to send their children to school and refusing to allow family members to receive medical treatment is treated as violation of human rights. It can be clearly seen that studying is compulsory in Algeria. There are 48 provinces in the country, each province has a modern university that is training one million two hundred thousand students, fully funded by the state. The government also invests in vocational training. Algeria has 900 state-funded vocational schools and 500 private vocational training units with nearly half a million people attending each year.

The President of Algeria affirmed: In order for Algeria to develop into Africa's first industrialized country, the first thing to do is to train people. The Minister in charge of science and training, who was assigned by the President to accompany Sister Binh, told me: "We are interested in academic training, but we are also very interested in vocational training, because we must have a class of skilled technical workers in order to industrialize the country."

II

After a few days of working in the capital, visiting the ancient city of Tipasa from 2nd century BC, we were introduced to Sahara Desert by the President, who dedicated his private plane to our delegation. The 12-seat Boeing with the symbol FT-VPS is equipped with modern, shiny gold-plated doors. This type of aircraft is often called an Air Force One in other countries. The plane took off over the Oran delta of the Chelif valley and flied over the Tell Mountain range that separates the northern fields and the mountains, heading to the Sahara Desert. Looking down from the plane, it is clear that the capital of Alger and this country is literally an archipelago, just as in Arabic name, Algeria is called Al-Jazair "Island of life" because of the entire farming and population area are located in the North, with one side being the sea and the other side just mountains and desert. Perhaps it's why the Arabs call this country the island of life. The small Boeing flew at an altitude of several thousand meters, gliding over the desert. The straight road across the country was visible under the wings. It was in dry season, the rivers were dry, the sands of the golden desert are endless, and the wind gently blows the sands like the golden silks under the wings, few green oases and rocky mountains in the distance.

Yesterday, while visiting the Algerian Revolutionary Museum, I was introduced to the Sahara. The entire Sahara Desert is eight million six hundred thousand square kilometers with 5,600 kilometers wide from east to west, and 1,600 kilometers long from north to north, stretching over the territory of 11 countries and occupying one third of the entire area of Africa. Geographers call this the prime desert because it is the largest desert in the world. Unlike other deserts, the Sahara is not just wild sand but rather a desert because the characteristics of the Sahara are sand, rocky mountains, gravel, and exposed lava standing side by side on the sandy sea like a Ha Long Bay on land. Under the sand layer are mostly crushed lava and pebbles, so the desert has quite a solid foundation. It is said that on the border of Algeria and Libya, there is Forzgaha stone gate which is nearly 50 m high and has the largest 27 m archway in the Sahara, called the "heaven gate" by the aborigines. Under the gravel and sand are petroleum and other minerals. Africans say that under Sahara there are about 200,000 square kilometers of oases, underground streams and lakes. This groundwater is an invaluable resource that gives life to the people and animals of the Sahara.

In the Sahara it is said that: when walking in the middle of the hot weather above 50 degrees Celsius, people have to wrap 2-3 layers of cloth to insulate heat, people see the illusion of villages, grass and lakes in the distance... which disappear when coming closer. The Berber people say it is the gift from the God to help people go farther on the Sahara, to be happier and closer to life in order to reach the destination with less fatigue, but it is actually an illusion caused by refracted rays reflecting in this vast sea of sand creating an illusion.

Sahara also has a "legendary tree", also called horsetail, which grows root and green leaves just 10 minutes after the rain, and, ten hours, creates a magical field of grass spreading over the desert. It is also food for animals living in the cave such as antelopes, ostriches, lizards, and camels.

We landed at Tamanrasset airport at the southern tip of the Sahara which is 2,000 km from the capital Alger. The Sahara Desert covers three-quarters of the land area of Algeria. Looking at the map, it is clear that the major cities are located along the north coast, the rest are deserts. The towns and cities in the desert, like Hoggar - Tassili where we visited, are very small, just an oasis in the valley, but there are still lakes, dates and trees here. The whole desert is usually at an altitude of 1,000 m above the sea level, during the day it is very hot, sometimes during the day up to 50-57 degrees Celsius, but in the afternoon it is all cool breeze and followed by cold night. The villa we stayed was at the top of the hill and was the President's residence. Looking over the valley from this vantage point, all what you can see are a few blocks of streets with flat-roof box-shaped houses, which made me think it was a difficult deserted place. On the contrary, however, everything is available here, from bread, meat, fish to vegetables. I had accidentally broken the digital card of my Sony 3-D and thought it was impossible to buy a new one in this country. The guest house staff, however, bought a new one for me only 30 minutes later. Here the women are mostly pure black, with only ivory white teeth and black eyes as the color of longan seeds in our country. Women are not very tall, but men are the opposite. Our driver was a young man in his 20s from the Touareg ethnic group. I am 5 feet 8 and reach just over his shoulder. The young man wore a thick long coat with his head wrapped in a scarf, covering his mouth and leaving out only his eyes. Unlike the Northern ethnic people who wear white, they wear blue and purple shirts and take the mother's last name, following the matrilineal regime.

Calmness and sincerity are inherent traits of Algerians. The politics in Algeria has been stable for many years, but terrorists and radical Islamic groups with the instigation from outside forces still use mountains and forests and some deserted oases as their bases to attack and destroy the stability and development of Algeria. Therefore, in the capital, the number of police and military are significant, every three citizens are protected by two polices. When our plane landed in Sahara, we saw two military helicopters and the police arrived first to protect the safety of the delegation. Security forces, police and military are always closed together; they are soldiers keeping the peace for Algeria. I was told that the military helicopter team still regularly patrols to detect vandals and uses infrared glasses at night to find and dismiss them, especially in the area of Cabili near Libya and the western border with Morocco.

After a night in the Tassili valley at the end of the Sahara, the next afternoon we were able to visit the Sahara by car, a Toyota two-wheeler. Looking down from the plane, I thought the sandy desert has only one path. But it was not the case, there is rubble under the sand, the car kept going and then speeded up when the ground is flat. The aboriginal people are very familiar with the road, they run at 70-80 km/hour, moving smoothly on the sand, drawing on the Sahara sands spectacular curves not unlike the lightning drawn by boats on a lake.

The place we came to is the desert, in the middle of the sea of sand, rocks, granite, and unburned volcanic rocks that have created majestic shapes. The wind builds the sand up into different dunes in many artistic shapes as if made by artisans. I took out the camera to capture image of the sand under the shadow of the sun going down with a fiery red to the horizon of the desert; it reminded me of the sand dunes of Mui Ne in

Binh Thuan province. There are also traces of stone carvings from two million years ago as told by Algerian friends. These are picture of animals like fossils, crying cows, and many dancing figures. From a nearby village, a group of men and women with their heads covered, wearing colorful clothes and carrying drums and props walked towards us while singing and dancing. They sang in their own way. They danced to chase away evil spirits, welcomed the gods in the middle of the desert, and took pictures with us until the sun went down. Saying farewell to them, the car took us to the 40 ha Brahim Brimat farm located in an oasis at an altitude of 1,800 m. The farm is located by a stream that has water all summer, so they can grow oranges and big, sweet and fragrant dates. Here we heard ethnic men and women play the oùd, a musical instrument which has a round body and strings larger than those of a guitar. They played the instrument and sang lovingly; their voices were deep and humming as vast as the Sahara sands. In the Sahara Desert, there is a fragrant grass called Prémet which is food source for sheep, so the lamb here has very special flavor without the sting smell as the ones from Northern China. A thin, black man was sitting in a corner of a silver tent, boiling water to prepare tea for guests, no table, no chair, only a carpet over the sand, beautiful silver tea pot and silver cups made by local people. When the tea was brewed, they raised their hands to pour it directly into the cup, the water flows into a gurgling stream. I wonder whether this was the way to create the sound of flowing water to cool down this hot and windy desert. They let us drink tea with the honey of the Sahara, the patriarch told me in the Sahara there is a Jujubier bee that produces the best honey in the world, a honeycomb of 50 kg costs twice as much as the honey in the northern delta. I drank half a teaspoon of honey; it had sweet taste, not overly sweet and fragrant smell. Taking a sip of honey and drinking a cup of local tea in the middle of oasis was even more interesting. After the tea, we went to the main party which I had never seen even though I had traveled to many countries around the world. Our group, including the Ambassador and his wife, were only 7 people and about twenty local officials, but they set up five tables as tall as half a person's height, set up on carpets, each table had a cooked lamb perhaps weighing a few tens of kilos, still hot and fragrant. Placed around the cooked lamb were onions, carrots and cutlery without bread. Six or seven people gathered around the lamb and used knives and forks to cut each piece of cooked meat. No fish sauce, soy sauce, no alcohol, and no beer but very rich, fatty, sweet and fragrant in favor. We thought how six people could eat a whole lamb. We were full after just few bites, and returned to our seats to drink tea. The local friends continued to their dinner and. half an hour later, no meat was left. I must say that their cutting skill were excellent. And maybe it is because they eat so well that they are tall and strong enough to cope with this fierce nature. Tourists from all over the world love to visit the Sahara and enjoy grilled whole lamb. The weather here is usually good in May; so many tourists come to the Sahara during this time. In recent years, three thousand people from many countries come to visit the southernmost part of the Sahara in Algeria annually.

The Sahara has no water, the small area of farmland they have is used for breeding cattle, mainly goats, sheep, and camels, the latter having become friends of the aborigines. I met herds of camels without a shepherd, moving in line and following the leader in search of grass in the oases. People here said that camels from Mali, Nigeria sometimes cross the border looking for grass, which they ate for ten days and then came back. Aboriginal people love camels, they have camel-riding festivals. Young men and women, colorfully dressed, ride on their beloved camels with beautiful saddles and race across the desert. Hardly any animal has the patience and ability to bear the thirst like a camel, it walks leisurely with its head moved forward, without drinking water all day. Long before the time of cars, camels were the means of transportation of goods and people in this desert.

The Sahara hides oil, gas and many minerals under the sand, which feeds the country of Algeria. Every year Algeria produces five million tons of oil. The government has exploited oil and used it to take care of living of people and education. The Vietnam Petroleum Group is present here, in the Sahara. The day we arrived, the Vietnam and Algerian oil and gas joint venture had explored a new oil field and was preparing to exploit it. This was the first oil field being exploited and explored by Vietnamese officials in Africa. The Algerian government was as happy as we were when hearing the news.

Sitting in the middle of the Sahara at night, I remember how, when I was in Paris, I was told by a group of scientists about the Sahara optical energy project of Algerian and Japanese scientists working together to build the largest solar plant in the world. As I known, the scale of this project is considered as significant as the moon project by the Japanese scientists; they call it the "super polo" project. They will use sand to produce silicon used to make solar panels and build power plants in the Sahara desert with the plan of providing 50 per cent of the world's electricity demand by 2050. Science will exploit and conquer the nature. The Sahara will continue to provide human with this solar energy after oil and gas. Thank you, Sahara.

***

The special plane took us to leave Sahara and head to the second largest city of Algeria, Constantine, located on a high area of 600m above the sea level like Bao Loc district in our country. The city is only 280 km from the country of Libya. As a city located in the mountains, at the foot of which are dangerous rivers, many roads inside it have to go through mountains. We were sitting in the car, looking out at the deep cliffs. The city was founded over 100 years ago with one and a half million people, has the largest mosque in the world which took 27 years to complete. The city is also a center of training and scientific research, an interesting tourist city of Algeria.

Everywhere in Algeria, whether it is Alger, Tipasa, Sahara or Constantine, we always meet with the most sincere and loving affection of the Algerian people for Vietnam. I remember how, as I was once walking down the street taking pictures, I did not know whether it was because of some secret hidden in this street with many tall date trees that the police came to ask us for papers. They asked me if I was Chinese. When they found out that I was Vietnamese, they did not ask to see our documents anymore but showed their joy. They took me to take pictures with sincere trust. My friend who works at the embassy said: Once he went to the street to have breakfast and coffee at the shop of a veteran. When he knew that my friend were Vietnamese, he insisted not to take any money and earnestly invited my friend to have coffee every day.

III

Before leaving Algeria, we were invited to have dinner by the President. Welcoming us that day with the President were important authorities such as the President of the Senate and the Ministers. The President introduced us and said, "These are my friends from our beloved Vietnam."

At the end of the party, the President gave us dessert with the Algerian Néple. Néple fruit is like ambarella fruit in the South of

Vietnam but with smooth skin, beautiful red color, sweet and a bit sour taste. I suggested to the President that I'll bring some Algerian fruits back home and have them planted at the Sao Viet Resort in Phu Yen, my hometown. The President accepted this with great warmth. He called the waiter to bring us a basket of about thirty, forty fruits. The President said: You try to plant a few trees, then we will name them the Algeria-Vietnam friendship tree. Sister Binh smiled and suggested: "If Mr. Phu can grow it in Vietnam, let name it Bouteflika (the President's name)". He smiled happily: "I agree."

I have brought whole basket of Néple fruit to Vietnam, tried to plant it in many different ways, from dried seeds to whole dried fruit and fresh fruit... and planted it in many lands, from sandy soil to mixed soil and alluvial soil. After one month and then two months, the seeds did not sprout. By the third month, the whole dried fruits began to sprout and only fifteen trees grew healthily. Despite my excitement, I did not inform the President of the good news, instead I chose to wait for the trees to grow more. Surprisingly, the Algerian Ambassador informed me that the President asked about the Néple tree grown in Vietnam. On the occasion of the 400th anniversary of Phu Yen, Mr. Chief Chikhi, Ambassador Extraordinary and Plenipotentiary of Algeria in Vietnam returned to Phu Yen with Sister Binh and visited Sao Viet Resort to take pictures with the Algerian Néple tree that had grown up to one meter. Today, as I write these words, the Néple tree, the Algeria-Vietnam friendship tree, is taller than an average person's head and blooms for first time. We have taken a picture to send to the President of Algeria and hope that the trees will be full of beautiful ripe fruit to contribute more to the friendship of two nations on two continents but always close to each other.

Ho Chi Minh City, 2012-2014.

In Memory Of France

France has left me with many unforgettable memories. I once went to France from the North bordering Belgium, then crossing through France to Nice, the southern tip bordering the Mediterranean Sea. Another time, I traveled from the Atlantic coast in the west of France, crossing the fertile fields to ride the cable car to the top of the snow-covered Alps in the east. My friends in Phu Yen and I, my family, and my grandchildren had the opportunity to stay one day in the famous town of Chamonix in the middle of the Mont Blanc valley in the Alps, the roof of Europe. We sit in the four-star hotel Auberge du Bois Prin, surrounded by snow-covered mountains, to watch the snow peaks change color according to the color of the sun. Mont Blanc snow mountain has 82 peaks from 2,000-3,000 meters to 4,808 meters, the highest peak is Mont Blanc (meaning: the white peak), also known as the roof of Europe. The French have taken advantage of these snowy "deserts" to exploit mountaineering and skiing services. I call the snowy "desert" because it is as vast as the Sahara in Africa, but only with snow. Many crisscrossed cable car lines bring millions of people to the snowy mountains. The cable car line in the center of Chamonix town takes visitors to the top of Aiguille du Midi at 3,842m high, the highest cable car in the world. In the middle of the vast snowy mountains, there are shopping streets selling all kinds of things, including Mont Blanc pens but more expensive than ones in the cities. Chamonix town is at an altitude of 1,035m, full of hotels and restaurants. From Chamonix, visitors can take the climbing train to the top of Mer de Glace to see the Vallée Blanche glacier winding at the foot of the Midi range; this is also the second longest glacier in Europe. The Alps run along the east as the border between France, Switzerland, and Italy and to the southern coast of France to connect with the kingdom of Monaco.

France has the shape of a hexagon with 6 sides, each side does not exceed 1,000 km, and is also the largest country in Europe, bordering 9 countries, namely the United Kingdom, Belgium, Luxembourg, Germany in the North, Switzerland, Italy, Monaco in the East; Spain and Andorra which is at an altitude of 3,000m in the southwest. France is surrounded by the Mediterranean Sea, the Atlantic Ocean and the English Channel in 3 sides, which is convenient for waterway traffic and marine tourist areas. The sea of France, no matter how much human has tried to renovate it, its water quality is still far behind the sea of Vietnam, especially in Central Vietnam. I have been to the Atlantic coast of France and the English Channel, including the famous coastal city in the North, Le Touquet-Paris-Plage. Although the coast has been embellished a lot, the sea water is still cloudy, not blue and the sand is not white; it is also cold and lacks sunshine... Once I landed in Nice city on the southern coast. Looking through the airplane window, thousands of people were swimming in the sea, lying on the beach for a sunbathing. I thought this was a wonderful beach, but when getting there, I saw that the beach had no sand, only crushed rocks, and the sea was also cloudy. Standing on the southern coast of France and overlooking the Mediterranean Sea, the more I see the great value of the clear blue sea with smooth white sand, wind, and sunshine in the coast of Phu Yen, my hometown, that have been offered by nature.

From the South to the North of France, immense green fields can be seen everywhere. The more you travel to the North, to Arras, Lille... the more you see the immense steppes, the North has no mountains, only vast fields just like great golf courses. In the season of radish flowers, mustard flowers bloom brightly. The rivers of France: the Loire, the Rhone, the Garonne, and the Seine, all originate from the eastern mountains, running along and across France and accreting fertile alluvium for the vast fields which have created riverside cities with magnificent ancient castles. I cannot help but mention the valley of the Loire River, a 1,018km long river flowing entirely in France that has created many fields of the four provinces of Loiret, Loire-et-Cher, Indre-et-Loire and Maine-et-Loire. This is a beautiful golden valley of France, known as the "valley of the kings" because there are up to 100 ancient palaces located along two banks of the Loire River and was built in the 4th century with the leading materials of white granite and colored marble. It is considered the natural premises of Paris in many dynasties, the residence of the kings for holidays, entertainment, and hunting. The castles were built in the style of antiquity and renaissance, which are majestic, magnificent, and gentle romantic with gardens of flowers, charming nature, and especially the quiet Loire River running between the castles. Each castle is an architectural marvel, many of which were built 500 years ago. Chenonceau Castle is the "castle of beauty", which has recorded the memory of many famous females in the history of that time. We sit on a canoe on the Loire River to travel to the "castle of beauty" the river surface is quiet in the afternoon, and the castle reflects on the river like a princess looking in the mirror. The whole building is ivory white, with its tower immersing in the purple-red sky with light clouds in the afternoon sun. Such a fairy scene.

Also standing on the banks of the Loire River, opposite the "castle of beauty" is the great castle Chambord built under King Francois I (1515-1547) which is the largest castle in this region with 440 rooms in the premises of the forest covering an area of 4,440 hectares. Many kings of French dynasties have lived in this castle, where hold many important events. Over time, many courts have been destroyed by wars and natural disasters, but there are still 65 castles in the Loire valley. The castles keep and preserve their unique history. More attractive attractions are the gardens and parks of each castle. France has held international garden festivals in this valley of royal castles, and many people's favorite place is the forest of Chambord castle. The beauty of these ancient castles seems to be enhanced by vineyards and famous hundreds-year-old wineries. Because of that uniqueness, the Loire valley (from Sully- Sur-Loire to Maine-et-Loire) has been recognized by UNESCO as a world heritage because of its charming beauty, cultural features, and architectural and historical value of the Loire valley.

Speaking of France, it is necessary to mention the ancient features, historical culture, and famous castles from North to South and speciality the capital city of Paris.

The French people are diverse in origin. In the past, the people of France came from many tribes of the Mediterranean people, the people of the Alps, and people from Northern Europe, from the tribes of Gaulois, Romans, Germans, immigrants from Poland in the 19th century, Italy, Belgium in the North, then Algeria and African countries in the South. Therefore, the body features are also very diverse. The people in the North are tall, blonde, and have blue eyes. People in the South are short, tanned, and have dark eyes; they seem more laid-back and sincere than their northern neighbors. Despite their diversity, the French people speak a common language, French, and they are always proud of the civilization of France. For me, since decades of the previous mid-century, France has been a modern industrialized country with an advanced civilization, politeness, and the land of perfumes and fashion. France has left me with many beautiful impressions, especially the great support of French intellectuals and people for the national liberation of Vietnam.

1. The impression of Paris:

I have traveled to the capitals of many countries around the world. It can be said that Paris is one of the most beautiful cities with its own impression, a city of splendor, majesty, and silence with castles, palaces, ancient churches, squares, and parks with many bright flowers. The Seine River, nearly 800 kilometers long, gently flows through the North's fields and into Paris to give Paris charm, richness, and serenity. Thirty-five bridges of different designs across the Seine have enhanced the elegance of Paris. The River Seine connects Paris to the world by the Atlantic Ocean. Paris has its magical attraction, which is why there are 100 million visitors to Paris annually (accounting for 10% of tourists in the world). It is one of the top destinations in the world, partly because of the attractiveness of the Seine and its graceful banks.

I once walked on the Champs Élysées at sunset. The Arc de Triomphe appears majestically and contemplatively. The Champs Élysées is lit up with colorful lights. This is perhaps one of the most glorious moments in Paris. Champs means field. In ancient times, Elysees used to be a field. Queen Medicis gave the order to build a 2-k-0]\m road with trees along both sidewalks to connect the palace with Chaillot hill, the Champs Elysées today. Standing at the Arc de Triomphe, in the breeze from the Atlantic, looking all the way along the Champs Élysées, it is the Louvre Museum, the bell tower of the Sacré-Coeur cathedral, and Eiffel Tower at the end of the avenue. The other side is the modern towers of the new city of La Défense. The Arc de Triomphe is located between twelve intersecting avenues and streets, including Kléber Street, where the historic conference on Vietnam took place. The line of running cars is like groups of turtles in the middle of a big river where the Arc de Triomphe is a floating island. Many countries in the world have Arc de Triomphe, but the most famous and massive one is still the Arc de Triomphe in Paris.

The Arc de Triomphe was built by Napoleon in 1806 but had been postponed when Napoleon fell in 1814, and it was completed in

1836. Today, at the Arc de Triomphe, there is the tomb of unknown soldiers who sacrificed in World War I and II with undying flames burning day and night. The Arc de Triomphe is engraved with the names of famous French generals during the Napoleonic dynasty. Coming to the Arc de Triomphe, it is impossible to ignore the decorative reliefs such as the "Volunteer for battle," "The Triumph of Napoleon", especially on the façade, "Resistance in 1814", and "Peace in 1815"... by sculptors Francois Rude, and J.P. Cortot Antoine Etex. The Arc de Triomphe is the place of national mourning for French leaders. In 1840, Napoleon was brought here from the island of Saint Helena and was the first Head of state to be mourned at the Arc de Triomphe before being buried in the Invalides Palace. Architect Jean Francois Chalgrin designed the Arc de Triomphe in the style of the triumphal monument of Rome in the 18th century. Therefore, the Arc de Triomphe is both ancient and modern. It has a majestic and civilized character, worthy of being the Arc de Triomphe of France.

On the other side of Champs Elysées, opposite the Arc de Triomphe, is the Louvre Museum, which preserves the top human quintessence. The Louvre Museum is located on the banks of the Seine River, formerly a fortress under King Phillipe Auguste (1190), and was renovated into the royal palace at the end of the 15th century. When the Versailles castle was chosen as the royal palace, the Louvre palace was used as the place to keep the royal collections. In August 1793, during the French Revolution, the Louvre was officially turned into a museum. The 25-hectare Louvre Museum holds nearly 400,000 precious objects from ancient civilizations. However, only 35,000 objects are displayed. Visitors can admire famous one-of-a-kind works such as the statue of goddess Milo and the god of victory, Samothrace, and the paintings of famous artists.

Nowadays, when it comes to Paris, people often refer to the Eiffel Tower, the symbol of the soul of France. Millions of people worldwide have come to admire the Eiffel Tower, the most admired tower in the world.

On the 100th anniversary of the French Bourgeois Revolution (1789-1889), the state decided to build an iron tower symbolizing the industrialization of France in the 18th century. More than 700 designs were considered, and finally, the proposal of engineer Gustave Eiffel was accepted. The tower was completed after 25 months of construction with a height of 300m, and it was the tallest tower in the world in the 18th century, named Eiffel (name of the engineer who designed the project). The tower has three floors, and the top floor is the television and radio antenna and the laboratory for meteorology and aeronautics. This is also the place to set the international time standard in Europe. There are restaurants and observatory services on all three floors. Especially, in the restaurant on the 3rd floor, from the cups, and plates to the roses on the table, all are black - the restaurant is named after the French fiction writer Jules Verne as if to create the feeling of magic and illusion when sitting on the top floor of Paris.

In 1985, the tower was installed with a system of artistic lights to lighten up the Eiffel Tower at night, and the tower could be seen even from afar when coming to Paris. Sitting on the 2nd floor of the tower, drinking a cup of Parisian coffee, watching the Seine River winding at its feet, the Notre-Dame Cathedral far away at the right side, the historic Concorde square and Champs-Élysees boulevard straight to the Arc de Triomphe, Paris appears visibly in from of my eyes. A modern Paris still retains the ancient features and especially the greenery in large and small parks as the clean lungs of the city. Although the population density is so high with 21,800 people per square kilometer, each Parisian still has 10 square meters of greenery. And this green area has not been narrowed down for many years, despite the continuous development of the urban areas.

In Paris, there is a very sacred destination which is the Panthéon temple. In Greek, Panthéon means temple of the gods.

In 1746, King Louis XV laid the first stone of the construction of this temple, and it was not until 9 years later that it was completed. The Panthéon is built from monolithic stones, and its majesty is even emphasized by 16 huge stone columns in the entrance hall. The dome of the temple is roofed with glass, and it always changes color according to the color of the sun, making the colors of the paintings and reliefs in the temple also change continuously. In the summer, there is still light until 9 p.m., creating the majesty of the temple. The dome of the main hall is 75 meters high, so magnificent that taking the human soul to the fanciful and sacred space.

Initially, the Panthéon was the shrine to the gods. In 1791, the leader of the French Revolution, Mirabeau, died and was buried by the French government in the basement of the temple. Then, Léon M.

Gambetta, founder of the French Republic (1869) was also buried here (1882). Since then, the French parliament has decided to use the basement of the temple as the resting place of great people who have glorified France. The first great person who was buried here is the great writer Victor Hugo (1885) followed by scientists and talented artists. The French government has engraved a large inscription in front of the temple: "Aux Grand Hommes, La Patrie Reconnaissance" which means: "The fatherland is grateful to the great men."

We visited the Panthéon and visited each grave - all 73 great people resting here - except for the two founders of the country mentioned above. The other 71 great people are great writers, poets, talented artists, and scientists who have made outstanding contributions to humanity. We bowed before Victor Hugo, Emile Zola, Voltaire, and Dumas, the great writers of the world, and saw here others, especially the two great husband and wife scientists, Pietre Curie and Marie Curie; neither presidents nor politicians are buried here.

In the area of Panthéon Square, there is also the University of Law, the City Hall of District 5, and especially on the right-hand side is the Sainte Geneviève library, where the names of the great works are displayed on the front foyer with two words S.G. as the abbreviation of the Sainte Geneviève. This is one of the largest and oldest libraries in Paris. Uncle Ho, in the early 20th century, came here many times to read, study and write his works.

***

When it comes to Paris, people often think of castles, palaces, and churches, famous as the Palace of Versailles, the Palace of Fontainebleau (in the suburbs), the Louvre (now the largest museum in France), the Palais Royal, the Élysee Palace, now the presidential residence, and the ancient magnificence in Houses of Parliament, Senate, Paris City Hall. The glorious palaces, castles, and churches of the 18th century have made Paris more magnificent.

Ambassador Trinh Ngoc Thai, a former French-speaking teacher who understands Paris even better than many people in France, was the Ambassador Extraordinary and Plenipotentiary of Vietnam in France and also participated in the delegations of the Vietnamese Democratic Republic Government at the Paris conference on Vietnam. He has just been awarded the Order of the Legion of Honor by the

French Government for his contribution to the development of France-Vietnam friendship. He accompanied me on my visit to Paris and introduced me the French culture, especially the heritage of Paris. We visited the Notre Dame Cathedral together, which was portrayed by the great writer Victor Hugo in his novel of the same name. I looked at the ancient stone church located on the small island of Ile de la Cité in the middle of the Seine River. This ancient church was built of stone in a medieval Gothic style of architecture that can accommodate up to 6,500 people and took 187 years from 1163 to 1350to complete. King Henri VI was crowned at this church, and Napoleon was also crowned by Pope Pier VII in 1804 here, especially in 1455. The holy vestment for the French national heroine Jeanne d'Arc was also made in this church. This 850-year-old stone church has a bell tower with the bell named Emmanuel weighing 13 tons and a tree used to ring the bell weighing up to half a ton. Every time the Emmanuel bell rings, it echoes across the Parisian sky. Standing in the stone square of the church, I got lost in the world of the great writer Victor Hugo, to see the hunchback Quasimodo hiding in the bell tower? Was that place where Esme Vanda "twirling on the old Persian carpet" to dance and sing, was that where the cardinal took her into hiding that was described by Victor Hugo?

In the Notre Dame Cathedral, the most majestic structure is the giant columns and splendid dome with many ancient patterns. The lighting system is a work of art that makes the dome look higher, and the image of the statues embodying the Jewish Judas stands out, shimmering in the lights and candles during day and night. The church has the Orgue guitar made of 7,800 copper pipes with different sizes and shapes, of which the sound echoes throughout the church.

No matter from which direction the church is being looked at, the bell tower is still an impressive attraction of the church. Possibly this is the second tallest tower in Paris just after Eiffel Tower which is 97 meters high and covered with shiny copper, making it look like an arrow. This tower marked a historical event, which was during the first meeting of the four-party conference on Vietnam in Paris on January 18, 1969, the day both America and the government of Nguyen Van Thieu had to sit down for negotiation with the delegation of the National Front for the Liberation of South Vietnam. The next morning, the half-blue, half-red flag with the five-pointed yellow star was hung on the top of the tower of Notre Dame Cathedral. The whole of Europe and Paris were shaking; the flying flag was waving as if to show appreciation to the great support of the world and of the people of Paris. This is the greatest event of the international movement in supporting the National Front for the Liberation of South Vietnam. That flag was later taken down by the French government by helicopter.

***

I have had many years of working closely with Lawyer and President Nguyen Huu Tho, who was sent to France to study at the age of 13 and studied Law at the University of Aix-en-Provence, a peaceful city near the port of Marseille. He lived in France for decades in the second and third decades of the last century, but he was always Vietnamese, he did not marry a French wife and did not acquire French citizenship. Regarding France, Lawyer Nguyen Huu Tho commented: "France is a public country. Everyone follows the law, and everyone respects the law in a rigid way, thus making people constrained and less disruptive". I also feel the same way. The famous architectural works of Paris were mostly built from the 18th to 19th centuries, and after that, there are few impressive works. Perhaps the limitation has made the French people lose their self-control and creativity. The law has tied the mechanism, creating rigidity and formality. Charles de Gaulle airport of France, in the past ten years, has changed a lot, but it still creates an uncomfortable feeling due to the complexity of transport. Every time I land in Paris, the feeling of old France at this airport appears in me. I joke that it is just like the image of an old man leaning on the cane printed on Johnny Walker's wine bottle... I hope that France, with its traditional civilization, will break through, remove the old mechanisms, and become glorious as the Champs-Élysées of "Paris by night".

2. The historical trace of Ho Chi Minh in Paris:

When he learned that I was researching Uncle Ho, Lawyer Nguyen Huu Tho introduced me to one friend of his, Ms. Cong Thi Nghia, who was living in France. She took the name Thu Trang when going to France to study; she used to be Miss Saigon, worked as a spy in the headquarter of the enemy, was arrested, and was acquitted by Lawyer Nguyen Huu Tho in court. She was a Doctor of History in France and also studied Uncle Ho.

I met Ms. Thu Trang - Cong Thi Nghia when she was 75 years old but still kept the beauty, cheerfulness, and gentleness of a Vietnamese woman. She looked just about 60 years old. She gave me the works she wrote about Uncle Ho in Paris. Her suggestions and documents and the collections I have obtained have enriched my journey in researching the footsteps of Uncle Ho in Paris.

In 1911, as a sailor under the name Van Ba, Uncle arrived at the port of Marseille, this was the first place in France where Uncle Ho set foot when he came to France. The ship Amiral La Touche Tréville continued to bring Uncle to the North of France, Le Havre Port. He worked and studied French here. Then Uncle traveled around the world, from Africa, to America to England. During his years in England, Uncle was able to contact Lawyer Phan Van Truong, and Mr. Phan Chau Trinh, the founders of the Friendly Council of People, and Uncle decided to go to Paris to work for his people.

In 1917, Uncle went to Paris and stayed at the house of Lawyer Phan Van Truong in No. 6 Villa des Gobelins, District 13. This was a small and quiet house. Mr. Phan Chau Trinh was working there as a photographer for a living. Uncle lived in a narrow loft. At first, he studied and worked as a photo editor with Mr. Phan to make a living. However, this is where Uncle Ho finds his heart open. After 6 years of traveling around the world, he came to the capital of the country that was invading Vietnam. The country was theoretically liberty-equality-fraternity (?)Especially staying with the patriotic journalist Phan Chau Trinh and working in the Friendly Council of People, Uncle was like returning to the warm heart of Vietnamese compatriots. Many of his first activities were from the house at No. 6 Villa des Gobelins in District 13. It was from the small attic in Villa des Gobelins that Uncle wrote the 8 points of claiming freedom and independence for Indochina. At that time, Uncle was not very good at French; his main ideas were contributed by Mr. Phan and translated into French by Lawyer Truong. These 8 points were signed by Uncle Ho under the name of Nguyen Ai Quoc. Perhaps Uncle started taking the name Nguyen Ai Quoc after signing this famous claim.

In one document being preserved in France, the reply of Uncle to an American reporter in early September 1919 was recorded as follows:

Q: What is your purpose when coming to France?

A: To claim freedom for the people of An Nam

Q: How?

A: Work hard and keep moving forward

Q: Since coming to Paris, what have you done?

A: I have met congressmen who are willing to help us. The congressmen and socialists thought that the government of France would not accept my request, but they said they were willing to help. Changing perception is important. Here I activate in different classes.

Indeed, two years of these activities in France made a great impression not only in France but also in Vietnam and the world. Overcoming the danger and the control of French secret agents, Uncle worked very enthusiastically, as he said. The French secret agents followed him every day. Rereading the archives of the French secret agent, the image of a patriotic young man in Paris gradually appeared in my mind. Arnoux, the Head of the Indochinese affairs department of the French Secret Service in 1918, when commenting on Uncle Ho, predicted the end of the colonial regime in Indochina: "You should believe that this young, slender and energized man will be the one who put the final cross on French domination in Indochina" – commendable Arnoux for his right assessment. I quote below some diary entries of the French secret agents in December 1919 to see more clearly the revolutionary path of Uncle Ho in Paris.

December 14, 1919

Nguyen Ai Quoc received a letter from the editorial office of L'Humanité newspaper.

At 10:30, Quoc went to the tailor Charon at 8 Bis Gobelins Street. They went for a drink at pub No. 1 Gobelins Street. Then Nguyen Ai Quoc took the subway to the headquarters of La Dépêche Coloniale newspaper.

Returning home at 12:45. At 13:15, Nguyen Ai Quoc left the house again and disappeared towards Italy Square.

It was almost 5:30 p.m. when he returned home, and 15 minutes later, he went to Charon's house again.

At 20:30, Nguyen Ai Quoc went out to drop off letters at the Gobelins Street post office.

December 15, 1919

Nguyen Ai Quoc received a stamped letter from Paris du Nord station.

At 10:50, Quoc left the house and bought a copy of L'Humanité. Then go to the library Sainte Geneviève, stay there until 11:55, then take a walk in the Luxembourg flower garden.

At 13 o'clock, Nguyen Ai Quoc returned to the library, stayed there until 16 o'clock, then went for a 20-minute walk in the garden before returning home.

At 19:00, Nguyen Ai Quoc arrived at the house at 16 Fosse Saint Bernard Street. Later, with Verdegene, he went to a pub on the same street.

At 20:10, Nguyen Ai Quoc returned home.

December 16, 1919

At 14:35, Nguyen Ai Quoc and Ai Cam (a photographer who had been to Nguyen Ai Quoc's house for a few days) left home, went to the post office on Claude Bernard Street to look up the Paris Yearbook, and then went to the Torah bookstore to buy books. Then go to see a typewriter at 27 Claude Bernard Street to hire him to copy an article titled Politics of Indochina.

Nguyen Ai Quoc and Ai Cam also went to the following addresses:

- Mr. Louis Blanchard's house, selling pictures, at 40 Écoles Street - L'Incompara Shoe Shop

- Franco Chinois restaurant at 11 bis Carmes street

- The headquarters of the La Dépêche Coloniale newspaper

- Number 22 Châteaudun street.

At 17:10, Nguyen Ai Quoc and Ai Cam left the house at 22 Châteaudun Street to Le Peletier metro station.

December 17, 1919

Nguyen Ai Quoc left home at 9:45 a.m. to go to the Sainte Geneviève library.

At 14:15, out of the library, go to the House of Commons, write a request to meet Marcel Cachin.

At 15:45, left Bourbon Castle to buy Journal Official and then went home.

On the same day, Nguyen Ai Quoc also went to the offices of two newspapers, L'Humanité and Le Populaire, to ask for a job as a photographer for Phan Chau Trinh.

December 18, 1919

In the morning, Nguyen Ai Quoc left home at 10 o'clock, and went to the Sainte Geneviève library.

At 11:50, left the library, went to the Panthéon, then went to the Lachon et Renouf bookstore to buy a book, then returned to the library.

At 14:30, Nguyen Ai Quoc went to the House of Commons to ask for a meeting with Marcel Cachin; 25 minutes later, left the above address and went for a walk. At 16:30, Nguyen Ai Quoc disappeared into the crowd near the Louvre Palace.

At 17:35, Nguyen Ai Quoc returned home.

In the evening, Nguyen Ai Quoc debated with Mr. Phan Chau Trinh, Phan Van Truong, and Khanh Ky at 6 Villa des Gobelins Street.

December 20, 1919

Nguyen Ai Quoc went to the Sainte Geneviève library from 10:20 a.m. to 11:45 a.m. Bought a copy of L'Humanité.

At 17:30, went to Academie Saint Louis to play billiards with Phan Chau Trinh.

At 18:30, left Louis and returned to 6 Villa des Gobelins Street.

At 20:10, Nguyen Ai Quoc and a Vietnamese man got off the subway to Bastille and disappeared.

December 23, 1919

Nguyen Ai Quoc and Phan Chau Trinh left number 6 Villa des Gobelins at 14:10, went to Claude Bernard Street, Berthon dye shop to deliver laundry, went to Dr. Trinh, but he was not at home, met a student who stays on Montparnasse Street. Three Vietnamese came to see them.

At 17:30, Phan Chau Trinh, Nguyen Ai Quoc went out to drop the letter, Nguyen Ai Quoc went home first.

At 18:25, Khuong went to meet Nguyen Ai Quoc at number 6 Villa des Gobelins.

And even when Uncle got sick and stayed in the hospital, the French secret agents continued their records.

January 14, 1921

Nguyen Ai Quoc was admitted to Cochin Hospital to operate on an abscess in his shoulder.

The surgery was performed on January 19.

On January 20, many people visited, including Mr. Vigné d'Octon.

On January 25, Nguyen Ai Quoc asked a nurse to deliver a letter to Vo Van Toan directly.

On January 31, Phan Chau Trinh, Tran Tien Nam, Vo Van Toan, and Ba Soc visited Nguyen Ai Quoc.

On February 21, knowing that Phan Chau Dat - Phan Chau Trinh's son had died, Nguyen Ai Quoc, from Cochin hospital, asked a nurse to deliver his letter of condolences to Phan Chau Trinh.

The documents of the French Secret Service have become rare historical evidence that preserves his activities on the revolutionary path.

Arriving in Paris, following Uncle 's footsteps, we went to Compoint Lane. In 1920, a comrade in the French Communist Party helped Uncle Ho rent an apartment at No.9 Compoint Lane. Firstly, this place was near the photo shop where he worked for a living, then this quiet place did not attract the attention of people. I was fortunate to have a chance to visit his room at house No.9 and met the landlady. In 1983, the French Communist Party attached a bronze sign stating: The residence of Comrade Nguyen Ai Quoc-Ho Chi Minh...

During his stay at this house, Uncle Ho had attended the founding congress of the French Communist Party in 1920 and was active in the Union of Colonial Countries, the Association of Annamite patriots, and worked as a journalist and photo editor. In this house, Uncle Ho met many patriots, including Nguyen The Truyen and Nguyen An Ninh. These two young patriots, who were studying for a doctorate at the Sorbonne, had dropped out of school to work in the patriotic movement with Uncle and Mr. Phan Chu Trinh, lawyer Phan Van Truong. They were active and friendly and were called the Five

Dragons at that time. The Compoint Lane hold the memories of these five patriotic Dragon.

The room on the 3rd floor looks a bit square, 3m on each side, the bed is close to the wall, and the head of the bed has a wooden wardrobe to store clothes. Only one old wooden table, one antique table lamp, and one rustic chair in the room. Uncle was sitting at this table to edit photos, to read, and write. A small window overlooks the brick wall next door, the wind blows in, but you cannot see the blue sky through that window. The winter was cold; on snowy days, Uncle had to use a brick that was kept warm in the fireplace; he wrapped that brick in a newspaper and put it in the blanket to kept warm through the cold winter days. Also at this place, in this small room, Uncle Ho had read the Theses on the National and Colonial Questions of Lenin, and he shouted in joy, "my country, this is what we need." Mr. Xuan Thuy, as Head of the Government Delegation of the Democratic Republic of Vietnam at the Paris conference, visited this room and wrote the poem "Visiting Compoint". A few quotes as follows:

"I visited Compoint one afternoon in September

The early autumn sun shines over my path."

...

"The small bed must have been left by someone

Or is it still your bed back then?

How rustic is the cabinet

Will you have enough clothes?

The cold corner where you wash your face

Still shining in the mirror.

I heard about the snow winter days

A brick is enough to keep you warm

How many abysses out there?

The country is at war, dear Vietnam!

You sit here and think about the country

Open the window it's windy outside

It was here that you found your ideal."

...

This house is no longer there, the Compoint lane has been demolished to rebuild, Uncle Ho's room, including the wooden door, was brought back by the French Communist Party to place in the history museum in the town of Montreuil outside Paris. The town was led by the French Communist Party for decades. There is Montreal park, as large as a botanical garden. Right at the entrance is the History Museum of Living. The French friends have built a statue of Uncle Ho here, a bronze statue placed next to the purple peach tree with brilliant tulips at his feet. An inscription engraved on the base of the statue: President Ho Chi Minh 1890-1969. National Liberation Hero, Outstanding Cultural Personalities of Vietnam according to UNESCO 1987. (Président HoChiMinh 1890-1969. Héros de la Libération Nationale et Eminent homme de Culture du Vietnam). When the house at No. 9 Compoint Lane was demolished, the French friends has brought back and restore Uncle Ho's room to its original form in this museum. The main door, window, bed, standing cabinet, washing lab, small glass frame and small table used to be his work desk were brought into the small room on the 2nd floor of the museum. Thank you, French friends.

The French Communist Party respects Uncle Ho not only because he is not only the leader of Vietnam, great cultural personality of humanity, but also a founding member of the French Communist Party in 1920.

***

In Paris, there is a castle that holds the memories of Uncle Ho; it is the magnificent Palace of Versailles with a royal garden of 815 hectares, the largest and most beautiful castle in Europe, a world cultural heritage built in 1623. In addition to the magnificent palace, Versailles is famous for its 65 lakes, highlighting the attractive flowers of the palace of love and the royal garden. I stood between the bronze statue of King Louis XVI riding on horseback, and the statue of the goddess of love in this magnificent park, and imagined which was the route by which the 29-year-old Nguyen Ai Quoc had walked toward the international conference to submit the eight-point claims for Vietnam, Cambodia and Laos.

Back in Paris this time, I visited the Sainte Geneviève library (referred to as S.G.) located next to the Panthéon, where Uncle Ho used to come to read, research and write every day. Uncle Ho once said: "Library is the repository of human heritage". The S.G. library is the place where Uncle Ho frequently visited, where he had read, learnt, and written in the middle of this priceless treasure of human heritage.

French secret documents prove that Uncle has come here many times. On December 13, 1919, the French secret agents recorded: "From 8:55 to 12:13 and from 13:10 to 13:50, Nguyen Ai Quoc stayed at the Sainte-Geneviève library. Then left the library to the Luxembourg garden to take a walk for about half an hour as if waiting for someone." It was continuously repeated. Another quote asserts that:

"Usually, Mr. Nguyen only works half a day, working in the morning to earn money for living, and in the afternoon, he goes to the library or attends political talks. In the evening, he went to the meeting in Paris."

"Literally, Mr. Nguyen enjoys reading Shakespeare and Dickens in English, Lu Xun in Chinese and Victor Hugo, Zola in French, Anatole France, and Léon Tolstoi may be literary patrons of Mr. Nguyen"

We followed Uncle Ho's footsteps, from house No. 10 to the S.G. library located next to the Panthéon, from Sougglot road to Luxembourg park located on the banks of the Seine.

The park is full of flowers and smooth grass under the luxuriant ancient trees. The park is like the royal garden, which was up to 15 hectares, and built in 1612. The park is famous for its vastness and complex of tree species, especially an apple garden with 200 different types of apples and pears, many old trees over 100 years old and home of many bird species. The park has a garden of queens' statue and an artificial lake built 100 years ago. Especially, the castle of Queen Médicis in the garden today is the magnificent headquarter of French Senate (Sénat). We took a walk under the canopy of the forest to try to imagine the path of Uncle Ho. He breathed fresh air and meditated on the world on the streets full of fragrant flowers. It was the French secret agent who followed Uncle Ho, who thought that Uncle was walking around as if he was waiting for someone, and from the secret agent's documents, it can be seen that the library and the park are two of his favorite places. He might have come here to see people with the same ideal as him, or it might be truer that he was waiting to see people with great ideals. Perhaps the souls of the great men in the Pantheon also wandered in this royal garden and supported Uncle Ho's intellectual soul.

Parks, libraries, and the Panthéon are places where Uncle Ho had his ideal, information and knowledge about the way to save the country. He welcomed great ideas and met great people in the world. This library and park were his great university. Living with Mr. Phan Chau Trinh, a patriotic deputy who received the death penalty from the French colonialists and the very famous lawyer Phan Van Truong, and, helped by the photographer Khanh Ky, Uncle studied and worked hard to grow up rapidly. Six years in France was the decisive period for Uncle Ho's activities, the beginning of revolution, the long fighting for national independence and reunification. It was in this library that Uncle Ho read the news about the victory of the October Revolution in Russia, opening his mind to new revolutionary perspective.

We would like to mention the house at No. 16 Sainte-Geneviève Street. This was the headquarters of Le Paria newspaper, also the headquarters of the Union of Colonial Countries founded by Uncle Ho. We went to house No. 16, which is now a large, beautiful, and crowded restaurant. I sat down and had a cup of cappuccino while thinking about the days when Uncle worked here. It is a brave and daring heart of him. Right in the middle of the capital of France, during the darkest days, he dared to publish a newspaper in French to state the current situation in Vietnam, and demanded national independence for the country. This is the place where Uncle Ho rang the bell inside people's hearts, the bombs within the capital of France at that time.

On the occasion when I came back to Paris in 2010 with Ms. Nguyen Thi Binh - former Vice President of Vietnam, a diplomat whose name has been associated with Paris, with history, we met again the French friends who devoted themselves to support Vietnam. Among those people was Mr. Raymond Aubrac, who was 96 years old, but so cheerful and smiling when seeing Vietnamese friends. He reminded me of special memories of President Ho Chi Minh.

After becoming the President, in 1946, Uncle Ho made an official visit to France, and during his stay in Paris, Uncle decided to leave the castle arranged by the French government to return to Mr.

Aubrac's house. Mr. Aubrac's house had a large garden where Uncle walked every day, read newspapers, and met guests. Comrade Pham Van Dong from the Fontainebleau conference came to meet Uncle Ho in this garden. In those days, there was a very touching personal event that he never forgot. On August 15, when his wife gave birth to their first daughter, Uncle Ho brought flowers to the hospital and accepted to be his daughter's godfather. Mr. Aubrac said: "Since then, on my daughter's birthday, the President always sends gifts or congratulatory letters, even though it was during the war. This is the great honor and loyalty of Uncle Ho."

One hundred years ago, Uncle Ho's revolutionary path was imprinted on every street in Paris, and Paris gave him ideas and opened the way for national liberation. We think about Uncle Ho's difficult days when he was eager to find a way to save the country in Paris, and today in the heart of Paris, in the middle of the history museum of living, Uncle Ho is the embodiment of victory and of compassion and friendship.

3. "Viet Cong" to Paris:

When Vietnam was at war, in the world, besides the official name of the National Front for the Liberation of South Vietnam, which was FNL (Front National de Libération), there was also another name "Viet Cong". This was how the puppet government referred to the revolutionary forces in the South. In France, many people call the government of the Democratic Republic of Vietnam the Vietnamese Communists and the revolutionary forces in the South as Viet Cong. In the period from 1954 to 15 years later, in Paris, besides a large number of overseas Vietnamese who supported the fight of Vietnam against America, there was still a group of Vietnamese who always provoked the revolution in Vietnam. They gathered to protest in uncivilized meetings. The cause of the war in the South, the strong support of the French Communist Party, the French intellectuals, and the majority of overseas Vietnamese had abrased the will of this extremist before the Viet Cong.

In 1968, after the Tet Offensive, we won a big victory at the Khe Sanh front in broad daylight. The National Front for the Liberation of the South opened an information room in Paris to introduce the rightful war of South Vietnam and on October 30, 1968, U.S. President Johnson declared an unconditional cessation of bombing North Vietnam. The Paris Conference between the Democratic Republic of Vietnam and the United States entered a new era; the United States accepted the conference with four parties, of which the National Front for the Liberation of the South was an official party. After the announcement of U.S. President Johnson, in a private meeting between Minister Xuan Thuy (Head of the Vietnamese Delegation) and Harriman (Head of the U.S. Delegation), who was 80 years old. Harriman was honest: "I'm old, so I'm a bit hard of hearing" Mr. Xuan Thuy joked: "No wonder, only one request that the U.S. stop bombing the North takes you six months to hear it."

The new facet of the diplomatic front was opened, and the Southern National Front delegation will arrive in Paris. I was assigned to go to Paris in advance to prepare for the National Liberation Front delegation led by Ms. Nguyen Thi Binh.

I feel it is necessary to say more about the fact that few people know. I think this was the ingenious creation of Uncle Ho and the Politburo. We were the officials of the Government's Unification Committee, also called the Southern Committee, led by Mr. Le Duan, which was known as CP40, later changed to CP72 under the Central Executive Committee. To foreign countries, this was the foreign affairs department of the National Front for the Liberation of the South, until 1969 it was the Ministry of Foreign Affairs of the Provisional Revolutionary Government of the Republic of South Vietnam, with its headquarters located in the South. All foreign affairs officials have two names. The name used in the South was used for traveling abroad, and the birth name was used when traveling to Hanoi. Ms. Nguyen Thi Binh was named Nguyen Thi Chau Sa at home. Mr. Ly Van Sau is also named Nguyen Ba Dan, Mr. Hoang Bich Sown is also known as Ho Lien, Mr. Tran Van Tu as Tran Van Thuc, Ms. Nguyen Thi Thanh Van as Binh Thanh... The officials gradually lost their birth names. My name was chosen by the organization with Phú from Phu Yen, my hometown, and the surname is my mother's surname.

Before going to Paris, we took a photo of Mrs. Binh wearing a scarf and standing under the half-blue, half-red flag with the yellow star of the

National Front for the Liberation of South Vietnam to use as the official photo published in the newspapers. Our organization had various departments in charge of different fields: The Department of State International in charge of the embassies of the National Front for the Liberation of South Vietnam, later of the Provisional Revolutionary Government of the Republic of South Vietnam named Department 1A, Department of People in charge of organizations such as the Front, Youth Union, Trade Union, Women Union named Department 1B and Department of Foreign Culture in charge of foreign affairs of agencies such as Liberation News Agency, Liberation Publishing House, Liberation Photo Newspaper, Liberation Radio 2 and Liberation Film Studio and Sud Vietnam d'études Newspaper... named Department 1C. There were so few people in our organization compared to the load of work, so each person was in charge of multiple tasks. Foreign countries did not know the way we organized the work. They assured us that we would all depart from the South. Before coming to Paris, Ms. Nguyen Thi Binh had traveled to many countries and attended many international conferences on behalf of the National Front for the Liberation of the South. Mr. Tran Van Tu, Ms. Binh Thanh, and Ms. Ngoc Dung have just returned from the 9th World Youth Congress. Ms. Binh Thanh was excellent in French and would be the secretary of Ms. Nguyen Thi Binh.

On the first night of November 1968, we could not sleep. The National Front for the Liberation of the South would arrive in Paris the next day. After researching, I knew that the French Communist Party wholeheartedly supported Vietnam; the Vietnamese Association in France - including the party unit as the center with many famous intellectuals had taken care of the delegation, so as the government of France... We were all happy and excited but also worried and anxious at the same time. French newspapers reported this as an unprecedented special event. Some newspapers were in such a hurry that they had mistaken the photo of female general Nguyen Thi Dinh as Mrs. Nguyen Thi Binh (they could not distinguish between BINH and DINH which was also normal).

That historical moment has come. At 14:00 on November 2, 1968, Paris was cold with a cloudy and gray sky and dim light. Ms. Nguyen Thi Binh and Mr. Duong Dinh Thao, Mr. Tran Van Tu, Ms. Binh Thanh, Mr. Lam Van Kha, and Mr. Nguyen Van Thanh, the member of the

National Front for the Liberation of the South got off the airplane at Bourget airport in the middle of a crowd of welcoming people with the flag of the National Liberation Front and the Democratic Republic of Vietnam in their hands. Ms. Binh wore a pink Ao dai with a light black manteau and a black scarf with polka dots. The group of reporters crowded around her, just like a large colorful raft moving along with the group. The camera flashed continuously. After entering the VIP living room, Ms. Nguyen Thi Binh announced to the press the five-point solution of the National Front for the Liberation of the South. Although she was good at French, Ms. Binh still spoke in Vietnamese, and Ms. Binh Thanh translated it to the surprise and admiration of the journalists; they said to each other, "Viet Cong was so polite", and "Who said that they were from jungle." Mr. Xuan Thuy, Head of the Delegation of the Democratic Republic of Vietnam, came out to greet her and accompanied her to get on the shiny black convoy. The French government has reserved the new D.S. car (Déesse means the queen) from Citroen for the delegation with lights like two eyes that could move back and forth. The flag of the National Liberation Front was plugged in front of the cars, which were escorted by the French police. Overseas Vietnamese and Parisians held flags and flowers standing on both sides of the road to welcome the delegation; there was no presence of extremists throwing rotten eggs and tomatoes as they used to do. We were happily in tears. We were so proud that the historical event raised the position of the National Front for the Liberation of the South, and brought Vietnam glory and a new path to future.

On the same night and the next morning, a series of French and foreign newspapers carried the headlines "Viet Cong arrives in Paris", and "Viet Cong victory." A newspaper wrote: Madame Nguyen Thi Binh was welcomed as Head of state with all official ceremonies and a warm welcome. "Madame Binh shocked Paris and the world", "The wonderful Viet Cong", "The miraculous landing of Viet Cong."

From the first days of November 1968 to January 27, 1973, the four-party conference on Vietnam in Paris lasted nearly five years, the longest one in the history of world diplomacy. During those five years, many happy and sad things happened. I once had lunch with some French journalists at the restaurant L'Etoile Venitienne (the star of Venice) on Kléber Avenue opposite the Kléber International

Convention Center, where the four-party conference on Vietnam was happening. Among them, there was one French journalist Madeleine Riffaud. At this restaurant, there was a dish called Beefsteak rum, in which the beef was sliced thick but cooked tender and sweet. We had red wine while talking to each other; everyone seemed to be very interested in the answer Ms. Nguyen Thi Binh. That time a journalist asked Ms. Binh: "You said the liberated area was occupied mostly in the South. So where is the boundary of your liberated area, madame?" Ms. Binh smiled and replied softly: "Wherever the U.S. forces bomb, that is the land of our liberated area". The journalists looked at each other confused. I asked my French journalist friend: "Don't you think it's right? Does anyone bring bombs to their own land? So wherever the U.S. drops bombs, it's land of Viet Cong, right?" I asserted that in the South, three-quarters of the land was hit by American bombs. I told them that 30km from the Saigon Presidential Palace, there was a land called Cu Chi. It was Viet Cong land… and we, Viet Cong, dug tens of kilometers of underground tunnels to survive and defeat tens of thousands of tons of American bombs being dropped there. They filled their glasses with French red wine and raised their glasses for the excellent explanation of Madame Binh on the question, "which boundary is the land of the Viet Cong." Madeleine Riffaud was a journalist of the French Communist Party who went to the battlefields of the South, wore "bà ba" shirt with a scarf, ate rice balls, and stayed in the basement with the liberation soldiers, we still used to call her by her Vietnamese name, sister Tam. Once, she said to me, "The rightful cause of the Vietnamese war has reached the level that the imperialist cannot match." An American journalist asked Ms. Tam: "Ms. Binh condemned the U.S. for sending troops to invade Vietnam, so if the communists in the North sent troops to the South to fight with the U.S., would they invade the South?" Sister Tam looked at me and replied: "In Vietnam, either the North or the South all speak the same language, we are one big family, the 17th parallel according to the Geneva Agreement is only temporary boundary. With the same family helping each other to fight the enemy who is invading our country, why is it called invasion?" Thank you to Ms. Tam for supporting Vietnam all her life with the deep sense of being a member of the French Communist Party.

***

On January 27, 1973, the International Convention Center was brightly decorated; inside the fence, rows of soldiers, police, and security were arranged to protect the conference; groups of journalists were crowded inside. Outside the fence, crowds of French and overseas Vietnamese were holding flags and flowers – the red flag with a yellow star and the flag of the National Liberation Front with radiant faces. People crowded up from the Arc de Triomphe to the junction of Kléber and Portugais streets and extending beyond the Kléber International Convention Center. When the Democratic Republic of Vietnam delegation led by Minister Nguyen Duy Trinh and Minister Xuan Thuy arrived, all the people cheered. Especially when the delegation of the Provisional Revolutionary Government of the Republic of South Vietnam arrived, the chorus "Ep, En, En" - "Ho, Ho, Ho Chi Minh" echoed again as if in an international festival.

That day, the Kléber Hall was brightly lit. Ms. Nguyen Thi Binh signed 32 documents, each with a different pen. Later, she gave each of these historical pens to her close friends, who were foreign ministers of other countries and famous French communists who had devoted themselves to supporting Vietnam during those 4 years. The UPI news agency of America wrote: "The signing ceremony of the peace agreement in Vietnam was the most magnificent scenery of the 20th century that humans have created."

***

Returning to Paris this time, Ambassador Trinh Ngoc Thai and I revisited Choisy Le Roi City, a small satellite city of Paris located on the two banks of the Seine River, 15 kilometers southwest of Paris. There is a political school of the French Communist Party named after General Secretary Maurice Thorez. This was also the headquarters of the Delegation of the Government of the Democratic Republic of Vietnam during the time of attending the Paris conference on Vietnam in 5 years. I still remember, during the first days when the Vietnamese delegation arrived in Paris, the school was on summer break, so the French Communist Party lent it to the Vietnamese delegation as our headquarters. At the end of the summer vacation, the negotiations process had not achieved any results; it would be unbearably expensive to rent a hotel.

Ambassador Trinh Ngoc Thai, who was the secretary of Minister Xuan Thuy, Head of the Delegation of the Democratic Republic of Vietnam, recalled: "Everyone was shocked when knowing the monthly hotel rental fee. Understanding the difficulties of Vietnam, the French Communist Party moved the political school to another place and let the Vietnamese government delegation use that place as headquarters for five years". Comrade Xuan Thuy and comrade Le Duc Tho were stayed here, and the nearby house at No.11 Darthé Street was the secret meeting place between two advisors Le Duc Tho and H. Kissinger. Today, Choisy Le Roi City has a friendship agreement with Dong Da District of Hanoi. On the occasion of the 40th anniversary of the Paris Agreement on Vietnam, the city has named a square on the banks of the Seine as the square of the Paris Agreement on Vietnam. Hanoi also presented Choisy Le Roi City with a ceramic painting made by a group of Vietnamese artists with the same theme commemorating the Paris conference. Forty years have passed, Ms. Nguyen Thi Binh, a prominent diplomat, and politician, is 87 years old, but her intellectual and emotional enthusiasm is still as vibrant as ever. All the memory is still kept in people's minds, which have forged the friendship between two countries and people.

***

On the occasion of the 40th anniversary of the signing of the Paris Agreement, I met with Mrs. Hélene Luc, President of the Franco-Vietnamese Friendship Association, former French senator and Secretary of the City Party Committee Choisy le Roi of the French Communist Party, during the days of the Paris Conference. She said: "In the city of Choisy le Roi, we had the honor to arrange accommodation for the Democratic Republic of Vietnam Delegation at the Senior Officer Training School. That was the house that the French Communist Party previously granted to former General Secretary Maurice Thorez.

I was then the Secretary of the City Party Committee Choisy le Roi, together with comrades Fernand Dupuy, the mayor of the city, comrade Georges Marchais, General Secretary of the French Communist Party, and all the activists had tried our best to make the Vietnamese government delegation, led by comrades Le Duc Tho and Xuan Thuy, not only have the best working conditions but also feel encouraged and shared. We are more or less like the family of those comrades.

With practical actions, we have actively participated in the development of the movement for peace, contributing to your effort in forcing the Americans to sign the Agreement. The French Communist Party had taken actions anytime and by any means to support the negotiating delegation of the North and the Southern Revolutionary Government led by our dear friend, Mrs. Nguyen Thi Binh as the leader."

The negotiating team of the Democratic Republic of Vietnam arrived in France on May 10, 1968, right at the time when the anti-war campaign was boiling in France (we call it the May 1968 event). At the foot of the Eiffel Tower, many workers and students chanted, "Ho, Ho, Ho Chi Minh." That was the united voice against the wars of aggression.

Every day, many delegations of all religious backgrounds and different parties, such as the Communist Party, the De Gaulle Party, the Socialist Party, etc., have come to meet and discuss with the two negotiating delegations of the North and the Provisional Revolutionary Government of the South.

We launched the fighting campaigns with the participation of Renault car workers, glass factory workers, iron and steel workers, administrative staff of Choisy, Ivry, Vitry, Orly, Villeneuve le Roi, railway staff in Villeneuve Saint Georges, employees of the Galeries Lafayette supermarket system, bank employees, intellectuals across France, oversea Vietnamese in France and many other organizations.

Although overdue, General De Gaulle was aware of the mistakes of the French on Dien Bien Phu battlefield. Therefore, he warned the U.S. President that the U.S. would not be able to win the war. Unfortunately, that warning was not listened to.

However, General De Gaulle, and later Foreign Minister Maurice Schuman, had personal contributions to the efforts of Vietnamese diplomacy, with the idea that France would assist Vietnam by creating favorable conditions for official meetings as well as secret meetings between Le Duc Tho and Kissinger at a modest villa on Darth Street, Choisy le Roi city.

For generations, the image represented the protest against American power, a symbol of radical social change. That day, Xuan Thuy and Harriman, the U.S. ambassador in Paris, shook hands for the first time. That day, May 13, aroused great hope.

In 168, after the Tet Offensive, although forced to sit down for negotiation, the U.S. President still hoped to keep South Vietnam. He bargained with the Vietnamese delegation: "Stop supplying food and weapons to the army in the South; in return, we will stop bombing!" Before that bargain, the representative of the Vietnamese delegation persistently repeated: "Vietnamese people are one; it is necessary to accept that fact!".

During our meetings at Choisy le Roi, Minister Xuan Thuy always assured us that: "We will never give in; the North and the South will be united."

The French Communist Party and the communist youth have always stood on the front lines of the rightful war against the war of aggression by the U.S. imperialists. On February 21, 1968, we organized the anti-colonial struggle day with the participation of 60,000 people in the Latin Quarter, Paris. On February 17 and 18, 1968, as our initiative, young people from 10 European countries participated in the meetings on the streets of Paris. In Italy, Sweden, and Berlin, students associate their struggle movement with the struggle of the Vietnamese people. In Washington, 80,000 Americans protested in front of the White House. The Beatles, Rolling Stones, John Baez, and Jean Ferrat had written many songs to mobilize young people to join the anti-war movement.

The war journalist Madeleine Riffaud of L'Humanité revealed the event of My Lai massacre, which made the anti-war movement in Vietnam even more boiling.

***

The spring is coming, and the big trees on the roadside which shed their leaves in winter are now starting to sprout buds that look like flocks of birds perched on branches. Flowers bloom in parks, roundabouts, roads, and even in balcony windows in all colors. Bright yellow mimosa interspersed with the faithful purple color of French peach blossoms (fleurs de Pêcher), Fleurs de Cerisier flowers, and multicolored tulips has touched the people's hearts. The spring flowers have enhanced the beauty of Paris and of France. The rising sun makes the flowers even more brilliant, and the birds with beautiful feathers are chirping, making us emotionally remember good memories of Paris, of France.

Paris, May 2013

Russia-The Autumn

MEMORY OF RUSSIA

In 1968, when I returned from the Khe Sanh battlefield, I was assigned as delegate of the Southern Liberation Youth to attend the 9th World Congress of Youth and Students in Sophia (Bulgaria). This is the first time the National Front for the Liberation of the South sent such a large delegation, more than 80 people, including the musician ensemble of Liberation Army to attend the international congress. In those years, due to the influence of the Cultural Revolution in China, international railways were not available. The Soviet Union sent a large passenger ship to Hai Phong to welcome three delegations from Laos, the Democratic Republic of Vietnam (the North of Vietnam) and the National Front for the Liberation of the South. All three groups were up to 250 people. We all boarded a white cruise ship called Turmenia. The ship was 3 floors high, has a restaurant and a swimming pool like a 5-star hotel. Two Vietnamese delegations had representatives of youth and students, heroes and warriors of the regions. Among them were heroes: Thai Van A (soldier of Con Co island), Nguyen Thi Kim Hue (Binh Tri Thien), the Southern delegation were mostly those who had fought in the battlefield including heroes, warriors, and young students. Hero of the Liberation Army Huynh Thuc Ba represented the heroes of the Liberation Army. Phu Yen, my hometown, had the first delegates to attend such large congress and there were three delegates, Dang Phi Thuong, the hero of the main army, the poet Lien Nam from Zone 5, and me, from the Khe Sanh battlefield, all three of us were from Phu Yen. Such a rare reunion!

After eight days of crossing the seas of Taiwan, Japan, South Korea and North Korea, the ship docked at the Port of Vladivostok in the easternmost part of the Soviet Union. We set foot in the Soviet country from this city. A train was exclusively designated for the Southern group; all rooms had two-floor beds. The train crossed the Siberia, travelling 9,298 kilometers to bring us back to Moscow. It was beautiful sunny autumn in August. We stopped in many cities such as Khabarovsk, Baikal, Irkutsk, and Novosibirsk... The train also stopped at small stations and even

though it was 2-3 am, there were young and old people at the platform waiting to warmly welcome us and give us flowers. Our delegation had to assign one of us to be on duty and dress up in uniform of the South Vietnamese Liberation Army to come down and answer their welcome. The young people and people of Siberia in general gave us very warm feelings. They gave Vietnamese delegation flowers, colorful scarves, badges and kisses and it was they who made each of us proud to be a soldier of Vietnam, of National Front for the Liberation of the South. One woman told me: "I live far from here, 100 kilometers away, I came here since the afternoon to wait for you, I welcomed you back from the Front." She touched each of us and said, "I am proud that you have defeated the biggest empire in the world." During the days in Khabarovsk, we had chance to visit and bathe in the Amur River. Amur, with its source from the Orion River, is the second longest river in the Soviet Union with nearly 4,500 km before flowing into the Pacific Ocean. Musician Xuan Hong took my hand and said: "I miss the Mekong River in the South so much". When we arrived at Ulan-Ude, it was cold, with freezing wind and rain. Young people from the Komsomol organization welcomed us with the enthusiasm of youth and passionate friendship. They channeled us on their shoulders, sang and danced all night. We did not prepare clothes for the winter, having only light uniforms of the liberation army; so the local youths lit the fireplace for us and gave us bread with butter, cheese, sausages, dried fish from Baikal Lake and horse milk. Our young Soviet friends said that the temperature sometimes drops to minus 45 degree Celsius during the winter; such is the extremely cold and freezing Siberia. The memory of the night with the soldiers of the Soviet Red Army by the Baikal Lake is always with us. Most of them were young soldiers on duty. They asked us about the American army, about how such a powerful army with modern weapons was defeated. In his speech, a major of the Red Army said: "In geography, we are so far from you, but we are always with you, because we know you are fighting for the peace of the world. We are always by your side." The especial passionate friendship of the Soviet friends gave us so much warm. We passionately sang different songs from each other's country. A Red Army soldier was playing an accordion while dancing and singing. We, Vietnam and the Soviet Union together clapped and sang along enthusiastically, which reminded me of the image of a Red Army soldier, Ivan, in several movies about the Soviet Union that I had seen. A very beautiful Siberian girl in a colorful traditional costume sang for us the song "Katyusha". Minh Nguyet and Lan Anh, two girls from the musical ensemble of the Liberation Army stood up to sing along, Russian and Vietnamese lyrics mingled together: *"Flower blooming, the branches playing with the moon in the wind/ the white mist flowing on the river"* and *"Do you know it's Katyusha waiting for you/ Who left for the borderland on that day/ In order to defend our country..."*

After singing, each of the Russian girls came forward to give us a branch of wildflowers. They said: "The Katyushas welcome the warriors back from the battlefield". We listened to the translation, and our hearts were fluttering. Artist Quoc Huong excitedly replied to them with the song "Battalion 307" with heroic sounds that touched people's hearts. We all danced and sang with the feeling of returning soldiers who are embraced in the loving arms of homeland. Those memories still make me emotional whenever I look back at them even after 50 years.

On the next morning, our group stopped at Baikal Lake in southern Siberia. Baikal Lake has lots of "the most": the oldest lake with the depth of 1,600 meters, and being the deepest and largest freshwater lake on the planet; it is calculated that the water of Baikal Lake alone could be sufficient for all mankind in 50 years, accounting for one-fifth of the fresh water on earth. Moreover, Baikal Lake is the home of up to 1,700 species of living animals and plants, including over 1,000 species which cannot be found anywhere on earth. The lake has many islands, but Olkhon is the heart of the island, Olkhon is as big as Singapore and has nearly 1,500 people living by fishing on the lake, most of them are Buryat ethnic people (originally from the Mongol ethnic group), the Buryat people call Baikal Lake the sacred sea of Baikal. Today Olkhon Island is one of the tourist attractions. We visited the hydroelectric power plant that has prevented the Akara River from flowing into Baikal Lake, which is also one of the first large hydroelectric power plants of the Soviet Union. We walked on the shores of Baikal Lake; the mist was like giant chiffon lightly covering the surface of the lake, creating a romantic and poetic

landscape. After a while, the sun gently pushed away the misty to reveal the clear blue lake. The birch forest silhouetted against the lake surface like rows of soldiers ready for battle. Baikal Lake is as clear as crystal, so a traveler on boat can see 40-50 meters deep under water. In the distance, under the birch trees, a few people were fishing. In the winter, the snow cover can be 4 to 5 meters thick. The surface of the lake was covered with a layer of ice, but there were still holes on the surface due to the warmth of the water. People catch fish, then the fish are salted and put in a tunnel under the snow. After one day, the fish were cooked naturally, hung up to be dried with the help of wind, without the need to be exposed to sunlight. This is the famous Astrakhan dried fish. Every Russian enjoys it with vodka or Russian Baltika beer. The fish is cooked due to cold ice and salt, so it can be served just by peeling the skin without the need for grilling, and still the sweet and fatty taste of the fish is not degraded, and the salt makes the fish taste richer. Coming to Baikal Lake, especially to the island village of Olkhon, you will surely be invited vodka or Russian beer with Astrakhan dried fish. Leaving Baikal, we continued our journey to Irkutsk.

We spent three weeks on the special train of great affection, which passed through 87 cities, and 10 longitudes of the globe at the latitude of 50 degrees to the north, near the Arctic Ocean, 25 latitudes higher than Vietnam. The train took us from East to West Siberia with its vast tundra and steppes, passing by birch forests in autumn. We returned to Moscow in the passionate affection of the Soviet people and, from Moscow, the train again brought the Vietnamese delegation to Bulgaria. I was assigned to fly first to Sophia with the ambassador Le Phuong and choreographer Dang Hung to do the survey. My first visit to the Soviet Union left a deep impression in me about the affection of Soviet people for Vietnam. Later I went to the Soviet Union many times, both on assignments and for my studies, stopped in Moscow, and sometimes went back to Dacha to spend the weekend waiting for the team. In our spare time, we wander around Moscow...but the first memories are deep and unforgettable.

Now that the Soviet Union no longer exists, a foreign writer wrote a work called "The sacrifice of Soviet Union". As for me, I still see the image of Soviet Union in the hearts of the Russian people today, especially the elders, who still have the same affection for Vietnam and the will for the great Russia. I know that in the drawer of President V. Putin, the card of the Communist Party of the Soviet Union is still there as the memory of a historical period. President Putin himself signed the decree to make the October Revolutionary day as the day of National Unity. One hundred years have passed, but the October Revolutionary victory is still the burning fire till today, which is the cohesion for people to stand firm and move forward. Because, in the span of three-quarters of a century, Russia had been living and winning by communist ideals. Putin once expressed: "I really like and still like communist and socialist ideals. Those are good ideals." In one press conference (July 2001) journalists asked: "How do you assess the collapse of the Soviet Union?" to which V. I. Putin answered: "Who does not regret the collapse of the Soviet Union has no conscience." Another journalist asked what he would do if given the opportunity, to which V. Putin said: "To prevent the dissolution of the Soviet Union". The road of Russia today might be based on that heroic foundation and noble tradition. I met again comrade V. Glazunov who was Head of the Vietnamese Aid Department of the Central Committee of the Communist Party of the Soviet Union, met again comrade Victor Petrorov, Chairman of the Asia-African Solidarity Committee, later Secretary of the Central Committee of the Communist Party of the Soviet Union… That day I invited these elderly comrades to celebrate the reunion; knowing that Russian Vodka was our favorite, I chose the best silver Beluga. Comrade Glazunov stopped me and said in Vietnamese: "Don't, don't, comrade, it's too expensive". And he said it was unaffordable with our current salaries. I looked at Comrade Victor for help, and he also shook his head slightly. I stood up and said: "Comrades, do you agree with me that the friendship between the Soviet Union and Vietnam is the greatest?" The two elders and those there agreed. I laughed: "Then there is no reason not to drink this fine wine to celebrate our friendship." I whispered to Comrade Glazunov: "Let me do a little payback", I meant to express my gratitude to them. Then we all happily drank the best silver Beluga to celebrate the eternal friendship of our two countries and recalled the days of 30-40 years ago. What did Vietnam need in those days, what did the South need? From short-range guns to high-altitude missiles, tanks, aircrafts, military equipment, medicine, and food... The Soviets were all ready to support Vietnam. The Soviet Union sent many experts to help our troops use modern Soviet weapons. I remembered as I had once come back from Paris and stopped by Moscow, our comrades at home asked us to bring back some small radios for divisional commissars. I met and conveyed this idea to Comrade Glazunov. Three days later, Comrade Glazunov informed me it was ready for the National Front for the Liberation of South Vietnam embassy to receive it and the headsets also. He laughed: Only we can hear, the enemy cannot. I was deeply moved, many times we went to Moscow without planning in order to travel to other countries for business purposes, Comrade Glazunov, nevertheless, was always able to quickly make arrangements for us. It was great devotion and thoughtfulness. The Soviet Union was not only ready to help us on the battlefield and in the diplomatic front, but also to help the North rebuild and develop. The current chairman of the Russia-Vietnam Friendship Association is an electrical expert who has been at Hoa Binh hydroelectric power plant and Uong Bi thermal power plant.

Comrade Glazunov told us in Vietnamese language: "With the foundation from the Soviet Union, I think that Russia and Vietnam will make miracles by comprehensive cooperation. I hope the young people of two countries would understand, preserve and develop this beautiful sentiment."

***

Moscow, The Golden Autumn

Moscow used to be called Mạc-Tư-Khoa by us. I cannot remember the number of times I have been in Moscow. There were times I arrived there in the middle of winter when roofs, cars, and roads were all covered under a thick layer of snow. We stood in the middle of the Red Square with snow that was twenty centimeters thick. I also visited Moscow in springs with blooming oaks and colorful flowers in the parks. But perhaps Moscow in the middle of autumn was the most unforgettable memory for me when birch leaves turned to dark yellow, the "golden autumn" as I called it. In Russia, birch forests, the white-bark trees that stand upright, can be seen in every region of Russia. In fall, the leaves turn yellow and fall, leaving only bare branches to endure the cold winter and bloom again in the spring. On the way to Lenin Hill, birch trees stood quietly with golden leaves fluttering like the musical notes in Tchaikovsky's "Swan Lake" and like in Pushkin's poems. The leaves covered the road with golden color. As I walked leisurely in that golden birch road, I remembered the "Autumn Sound" of my late old friend, the poet Luu Trong Lu: *Don't you hear the autumn?*

Under a lamenting moon

Autumn leaves rustle

a bewildered golden deer

steps on dry yellow leaves"

The autumn wind in Moscow was also gentle as to emphasize the calmness of the golden autumn, gently lifting the yellow leaves; the breeze wind was blowing on the traveler's face like caresses of love. The talented Russian painter I. Levitan has painted a masterpiece "The golden autumn". It seems that the picture was in front of me with yellow leaves scattering, making a golden carpet on the road and on the trees, a three-dimensional picture that raises the human soul. The natural picture of golden autumn on the Lenin hill was magical. Holding golden leaves in hand and gently walking between two rows of birch trees, my heart was lost in the fairyland.

Overlooking the Moscow River from Lenin hill, you can see shops for souvenirs which remind visitors of the Soviet period: national emblems, badges, military badges, clothes, and hats of Red Army soldiers, especially the kind of hat wore by Pavel Korchagin (from the famous novel "How the Steel Was Tempered"). On the shelves are Matryoshka wooden dolls, with 12 to 16 smaller ones inside, pictures of Lenin and Stalin, and even Putin. Walking in the middle of the golden autumn in Moscow and catching the gentle autumn wind was like sitting in the middle of a theater and listen to the symphony of the great Russia, the Soviet Union of the eternal past.

Moscow is one of the largest cities in the world. I have been to all five continents, America, Europe, Asia, Africa, and Australia, and have been to most of the world's famous cities and can say that Moscow is the most beautiful capital. Moscow lies in the junction between Asia and Europe, where the state of Russia originated. In the early 10th century, it was just a town of the Principality of Vladimir. In 1301, Moscow became an independent principality, but later was ruled by the Mongol Empire. It was not until the 16th century that Moscow had a government and military force to govern and develop. Moscow became the capital of the Soviet Union, of Russia, the largest country in the world with an area of 1/9 of the world.

Moscow is beautiful because of the winding Moskva River; the Moskva River is half a thousand kilometers long, flowing through Moscow into the Oka River to merge with the Volga. In 1932, the Soviet government built a 130 kilometers long canal, circling in the heart of the city and connecting with the Moskva River. It is called canal, and yet it's up to 100 m wide and 5-6 m deep, enough space for cruise ships passing. Thanks to this, the city of Moscow connects with five seas: the White sea, the Baltic Sea, the Caspian Sea, the Azov Sea, and the Black Sea. The river system along with the subway system is the ideal traffic circuit of this city. The Moscow Metro system with 170 stations, each with its own style and splendor as magnificent palaces, has created bustling underground life.

In Moscow, when it comes to construction works, many places are worth mentioning, and yet perhaps the first one worth saying is the Kremlin. Today, the Kremlin is still the working place of the President like it was in the old dynasties. On the other hand, however, it is also opened partly for visitors, a great museum of humanity, because it keeps many priceless symbols and memorabilia of the tsarist dynasties, of the Soviet revolution, of Lenin, Stalin, Brezhnev and other Soviet leaders for more than three quarters of a century. The Kremlin with Spasskaya tower which was built in 1491 by architect Pietro Antonio Solari with bronze bells dated back to the 16th century, along with 19 towers creating a majestic palace complex. The Kremlin is recognized by UNESCO as world heritage site. The tallest Spasskaya tower in the Kremlin has a 4-sided shiny clock with yellow numerals elevated by a purple-red marble star which was installed by Stalin himself. The Spasskaya tower has always been the symbol of the brightest stars in the world. In Moscow, there are tall buildings which have upright towers, the top which is called the Stalin's peak. After winning the war over Germany (World War II), Stalin planned to erect 40 buildings for commemoration the victory. Unfortunately, only seven buildings had been built when Stalin died. Those seven buildings still stand majestically today, including the Ukrainian hotel, the headquarters of the Ministry of Foreign Affairs, the Ministry of the Navy, and the most massive of them, the Lomonosov University. Three-quarters of the century has passed, many skyscrapers with modern design have risen up in Moscow, but the tall towers with the purple-red marble stars on top still confirm its strength and champion. Lomonosov University is also a popular historical landmark. Whether in snowy winter or in elegant summer night, the main tower of the university stands majestically, magnificently, reflecting on the lake with brilliant-colored lights, an unforgettable image in the hearts of people from all over the world. I have once walked in the middle of golden autumn on Lenin Hill, looked at the main tower of Lomonosov University and ate sweet and sour green apples picked by the roadside while contemplating the monumental building. Lomonosov University was built in 1755 and was expanded under Stalin and became the largest university of the Soviet Union with a brilliant 5-pointed star on the top of the front of the tower. The school has more than 6,500 classrooms. It is calculated that if a newborn baby lived in different room for every day, he would be an 18-year-old young man at the time of leaving the last room. Many Vietnamese officials have studied and grown from this school. It must be seen that the former Soviet Union and Russia today always emphasize the great importance of education and intellectuals. A writer who becomes member of the Union of Soviet

Writers would receive many benefits. Artists with merit or state awards were given preferential treatment. The offices of scientific, literary and artistic agencies were spacious and splendid. I often see statues and reliefs mounted on the walls of houses that mark the lives of writers and artists. Famous people as Mayakovsky, Pushkin, Gorky, Nikolai Ostrovsky, and Lev Tolstoy have their own statue and square. Lenin highly valued knowledge, he once said: Without books, there is no knowledge; without knowledge, mankind cannot move forward.

Many times, I went to Red Square to visit Lenin, sometimes just standing there to see the mausoleum. The mausoleum is not very big but majestic and contemplative. The mausoleum of Lenin was built in 1930 in the shape of a three-story pyramid after Lenin's death. The mausoleum was designed by architect Alexey Viktorovich Shchusev and was covered with crimson granite interspersed with black stone for sadness and grief. The name of Lenin is also inscribed in red porphyry on a black stone. Along two sides of the Kremlin wall, there is a space that is not too large, but very dignified and quiet, which is the grave of the leaders of the Soviet Union. Some of the revolutionaries have simple and respectful statues on their graves. The graves of Marshal Stalin always had more fresh flowers than other graves. On major holidays, a stand will be built on both sides of the mausoleum of Lenin that can hold up to ten thousand people for meetings and military parades. Thus, on important occasions, the souls of revolutionaries and Soviet marshals such as Lenin, Stalin, Zhukov... are still with generations of Russia today. It is a unique square.

I walked in the middle of the Red Square, visited Lenin's Mausoleum, the eternal flame, visited the graves of Stalin, Marshal Zhukov... The Red Square was built in the 15th century, first it was a commercial square. Today it is a historical and cultural square. The bell on the tower of the Orthodox church of Basil, which is in the shape of giant garlic, rang out and so did the Kremlin bell tower, urging people and reminding us of old memories...

The Kremlin became the heart of Soviet Union from March 12, 1918. Lenin worked here until 1923 when he was under assassinated attempt and wounded. On October 17, 1923, Lenin returned to the Kremlin from the hospital. He entered the meeting room, went to the living room and his office, took a few books, then leisurely walked on the Kremlin courtyard to get to the car, toured the nearby streets of

Moscow in 2 hours... He came to say farewell to the Kremlin, to Moscow. He did not return to the Kremlin forever.

The first Vietnamese setting foot in the Kremlin was our Uncle Ho. In October 1923, Uncle Ho, then Nguyen Ai Quoc, came to Moscow from France to attend the International Peasants Congress and the 5th Communist International Congress. Uncle Ho had a meeting at Andreyevsky Hall in the Kremlin, and then from the Kremlin he returned to Asia to found the Communist Party of Vietnam. The Kremlin has his footsteps imprinted since those days.

In 1968, both of our Vietnamese delegations arriving in Moscow were arranged by the Soviet government to stay at luxurious, four-sided Russia hotel located next to the Red Square from where we would walk everyday along the blue stone pavement to see the star on the top of Kremlin and listen to the bells of the Kremlin clock, visit Lenin as well as the great people and go to GUM department store. GUM still exists till today and is expanded with a high-class supermarket located throughout five underground floors next to the Red Square. This is the first time I went to such a vast 5-storey underground supermarket. And I just understood why in Russia, Moscow and S. Petersburg have metro systems which are hundreds of meters underground, splendid as royal castles.

***

Moscow also reminds me of historical memories to the patriotic Russian people who heroically sacrificed their lives for the victory over the invasion of Napoleon. The commander of that historical victory was General M. L. Kutuzov. That is the Victory square. A monument of Kutuzov is built at the gate of the Borodino Museum, where a 115 m-long circle painting vividly depicts the scenes of Kutuzov's army fighting Napoleon's troops. And it was in this place, the old village of File, on September 13, 1812, that the council of generals had decided to protect Moscow and Russia against the invaders and the decision made from this land had brought them victory. A museum has been built by the Russian people to commemorate the 100th anniversary of the patriotic war (1812-1912). In 1973, a huge monument to the heroes of the war of 1812 was built and today it is embellished to become the magnificent and majestic Victory Square and Park. Under a long line of hanging swords and flags, I walked leisurely while reliving the past. Those flags are, on behalf of the Soviet Union and on behalf of the Russian people, to commemorate tens of millions of people who sacrificed their lives for the victory, for the survival of Russia and for the cause of opening up a new world for mankind.

After the destruction of the Soviet Union, Russia was weakened, but then President Vladimir Putin has determined to restore Russia to its heroic history. It can be seen that despites the change of the political regime, the indomitable tradition of the nation is always preserved by its people, which is invaluable legacy and the cause of all today success and in the future.

In Moscow, there are many beautiful monuments: Museum of Fine Arts, Museum of History, Theaters, Kuskovo Heritage, Ostankino Heritage... and also many parks, squares, monuments, including Lenin Cultural Park and the statue of Uncle Ho which is located at the October Revolution Square.

THE LEGENDARY

The friend who took me to Moscow is a lawyer and also a Russian historian. We met a real-life Stalin impersonator at the Red Square, it costs few hundred rubles to take a picture with "Stalin". I shook hands and took pictures with "Stalin". It was hard to differentiate the fake from the real. Many people from five continents come here to take pictures with Stalin as if to remind of the historical period. I asked my historian friend what he thought of Stalin. He said: "History is history, no one can distort it. Round is still round despites of being distorted. History is about telling the truth and seeing it in the historical context which cannot be put in today circumstances to evaluate."

During this time of the year, in the Red Square, on the occasion of the October Revolution in Russia (November 7) or the day of victory over fascism (May 9), the Russian state still holds military parades to commemorate the tradition and demonstrate the power of the Russian army. One of my Russian friends told me about the military parade on the morning of November 7, 2011 to celebrate the 70th anniversary of the victory of Soviet people against fascism to save the nation. The army parade in 1941 was re-enacted at the Red Square. Twenty-eight veterans in military uniforms who participated in the army parade in 1941 and 2,000 Russian officers and soldiers of Moscow paraded through the stage. The image of tanks T34, T38, T60 and other old legendary vehicles and weapons and costumes of 1941 are reconstructed... All were broadcasted live on Russian national TV channels. In the hearts of the people of Moscow, as well as in the hearts of hundreds of millions of Russians, the heroic achievements and great sacrifices are still imprinted. 27 million Soviet people died, 8.860.000 Red Army soldiers gave their lives for the great victory of the patriotic war and for integrity of the country today and tomorrow.

The mayor of Moscow, in his speech at the ceremony, said: *"Dear people of Russia, I welcome you to the celebration of a historic event that is considered the beginning of the victory of great patriotic war".*

It is remembered that on the morning of November 7, 1941, when the first armies of Germany were only a few dozen kilometers from Moscow, the country was in great danger. Hitler decided to launch his elite force to open the "Typhoon" campaign to destroy the entire Soviet leadership. In the circumstance of being hanged by a thread, it was thought that Stalin would order a withdrawal from the capital. But that were never the case. The Soviet generals, led by Stalin and Zhukov, decided to bravely attack and defend the capital. Stalin decided to organize an army parade to demonstrate the power of their army force and to encourage the Soviet people. The parade took place on the morning of November 7, 1941, at the Red Square (on the 24th anniversary of the October Revolution and the establishment of the Soviet government). On the stage, in the brief summons, Marshal Stalin called on the soldiers: *"The great liberation mission has been given to you", "Under the flag of Lenin, let's bravely move forward and we will win"*. The central political committee and the Soviet Army Command, together with Stalin, solemnly saluted the army of the Soviet people passing through the stage and heading straight to the battle. Just over 30 days later, the armies of Hitler were repelled by the Red Army of the Soviet Union, creating an advantage to liberate Volgagrad, the city of Leningrad and other Eastern European countries from the invasion of Hitler. That victory parade marked "the beginning of the end of Hitler's fascism" (in the words of Sergei Sobyanin). The historic parade lasted only 25 minutes, the shortest parade in Russian history, but it was broadcast to the world to let the whole world know that the Soviet Union did not surrender, and the entire army was fighting for their country. In that parade, there were present of citizens of dozens of countries around the world, including six Vietnamese soldiers who were students of Uncle Ho studying in the Soviet Union.

The talent of Soviet generals headed by Stalin and Marshal Zhukov is illustrated and confirmed by history. The Red Square today still has the marks of those heroic days.

Turning the pages of history, we see the great legend of the military parade on November 7, 1941 in the Red Square.

According to the plan of Hitler, on November 7, 1941, they must destroy the Kremlin, celebrate their victory, and on that same day would execute the leaders of the Soviet Union, execute Stalin, destroy the mausoleum, and burn the body of Lenin...

Hitler deployed both ground and air force with the final goal of capturing Stalin alive. In fact, Hitler had broken through the Soviet defenses and came as close as only 30 km from Moscow. On October 28, Stalin met with the generals and invited Marshal Zhukov to return from the front. The meeting discussed how to fight the invaders and protect Moscow - the situation was very difficult, suddenly Stalin asked the commanders:

- November 7, the 24th anniversary of the October Revolution, is coming, will we hold a military parade?

Hearing his question, the generals looked at each other. Military parade? When the enemy is only 30 km away, and mines have been placed under the bridges over the Moscow River, waiting to stop the movement of enemy?

Stalin still calmly asked for the third time, then the generals understood his thought.

As for Marshal Zhukov, he understood right away, he nodded: "The enemy is heavily attacked by us, winter is coming, they are short of troops, clothing and food, they cannot make any big attack soon, especially to the Moscow, so it is possible for the parade to be organized."

Stalin said solemnly: "We must organize the military parade to boost the morale of the Soviet soldiers and to let the world know that we do not surrender."

The date and time of the parade were kept confidential.

Marshal Zhukov, after returning to the front, sent Stalin an urgent secret message written in chemical pencils confirming that the parade could be performed as the German troops were demoralized and were not able to attack in the near future.

For distraction, Stalin held a party and celebration of the 24th anniversary of the October Revolution on the night of November 6 in a waiting room in the Mayakovskaya metro station. Stalin gave the opening speech.

Hitler watched the news very closely, knowing that Stalin had just finished his speech. However, he did not know that, after the party was over, Stalin informed the central political committee and the commanders about the parade next day.

On the morning of November 7, a few minutes pass 8, Hitler accidentally turned on the radio and heard report about the Soviet military parade. He immediately ordered his generals: "I give you one hour to atone for your failure, to bomb the meeting and destroy Stalin on the stage". When his orders reached his subordinates, the parade became the deployment of troops. Twenty-five planes of Hitler were shot down by the Red Army and buried in the snow that morning.

That great legend is still remembered till today, as a survey of 40 million Russians in 2008 recognized that the military parade in the Red Square on November 7, 1941 is once-in-a-lifetime and a great legendary event. Marshal Stalin was chosen as the third greatest person in Russian history.

The Bridge Of Love

It is impossible not to visit the Moscow River with many bridges once you come to Moscow. Each bridge has its own design, its own memory, and its own beauty. I would like to mention the Luzhkov Bridge over the Vodootvodny Canal at the end of Tverskaya Street connecting with the Red Square. This bridge is not big, just crossing one branch of the Moscow River. There are locks of various sizes tied in long rows to the railings of the bridge. Why? Why are there so many locks? A Vietnamese who teaches at MEI School, the leading Russian energy university, who was awarded the title of Academician of Electrical Engineering of the Russian Federation, Professor Nguyen Quoc Si and has been living in Russia for more than a third of century, explained: that is the symbol of love. When a couple gets married, or after the ceremony at the church, they come here and hook a padlock with their names and their promises engraved, sometimes the lock is decorated with the drawing of two hearts with the initial letters of their names in beautiful colors. Both of them would throw the key into the river as the affirmation of their unbreakable love. From generation to generation, the whole bridge is covered with the padlocks. A row of beautiful metal artificial trees has just been built by the city and been called the tree of love, on these branches there are also countless locks with the couple's names engraved. In the golden autumn, men in suits and women in white dresses and white chiffon scarves have been walking under the falling leaves like butterflies, coming to the bridge of love and the tree of love to put their lock as symbol of their lifelong vow of faithfulness. Unmarried young couples, newly in love, also come here to make their oath. Many elderly couples also come here to find their locks and remind each other of faithfulness. Speaking of the bridge of love in Moscow, I recall other similar bridges of love in other countries. Perhaps the oldest one is in the city of Rome, the capital of Italy, which is the Milvio bridge over the Tiber River built in two hundred BC. When the time passed, the Milvio bridge could not stand the weight of all the locks, so it is prohibited to hook a padlock on Milvio bridge.

In the beautiful Germany, there are also two bridges of love. They are the Eiserner Steg bridge that has crossed the Main River of the city of

Frankfurt in two centuries, and the Hohenzollern bridge connecting the city of Koln with the European countries across the Rhine. People call this the most romantic bridge in the world because of the landscape, the harmonious nature and here, in addition to the love locks, there are also many locks for close friendships.

In St. Pertesburg, in the city of Leningrad, there was the bridge of kiss across the Moika River. Couples come there to make their vow, they don't put a lock on the bridge, but kiss each other like a lasting vow.

In Europe and America, there must be many bridges for love. In Asia, I only know one in S'Nam tower in Korea.

Walking under the beautiful artificial trees with locks of all shapes and colors of the Luzhkov love bridge in Moscow, I said to Professor Nguyen Quoc Si: "Love and faithfulness are the beginning of all life." That love, that loyalty, when multiplied, it becomes the love for country, for the people of Vietnam - the Soviet Union which has transcends space and time and is locked by the faithfulness and affection of two nations and it will be the energy source of boundless power.

Saint Petersburg - Leningrad And The White Nights

The plane from Moscow tilted its wings to prepare for landing at Pulkovo airport in the city of St. Petersburg. Through the window, we had the opportunity to clearly see the second largest city of Russia. The winding rivers are interlaced like the blood vessels in the human body. St. Petersburg is name of the saint who walks on water and conquers all enemies, Peter the Great named the city after Saint Petersburg. In 1703, when discovering this land, Peter the Great clearly realized that this was the river region with over 200 large and small islands with the Neva River in the center, flowing into the Gulf of Finland of the Baltic Sea. It was very beautiful land, and an important gateway to the Northwest of Russia, so he immediately built Peter and Paul fortress as the predestined battlefield on the Zayachy Island. Two bridges were also built to connect to Petrogradsky Island. Later, the Peter and Paul church was constructed, which is also the burial place of the Tsars. The Peter fortress was gradually expanded, including the harbor. In the middle of the monastery, there was a shiny bronze tower, the tallest one in this area like gigantic pen writing on the clouds of Petersburg. On the riverside next to the fortress, it was the military port during that day, where the Dawn battleship was launched to contribute to the protection of this land. The Dawn battleship was recorded in the history as the first fire of the October Revolution of 1917 led by Lenin. Today, the Dawn battleship has become a museum on the premises near the Peter and Paul church and fortress. The battleship is still majestically standing on the banks of the Neva River, with many seagulls flying around as if to adorn the vibrancy of a historical relic.

The Great Peter wanted this city to be like Venice (of Italy) in the North, so only a few bridges were built, transportation was mainly by waterways. Large projects were constructed along the river, tributary canals were dug to connect different rivers, especially between the Neva River and the Moika and Fontanka rivers. Later, the city was developed, and 340 bridges were built with many different designs. Ten large bridges across the Neva River are opened for ships, each bridge is a beautiful landscape. At the two ends of the bridge, there are very artistic monuments.

In 1917, after the October Revolution had succeeded, the city was renamed Lenin City (Leningrad). This is the city of revolution, the city of knowledge, the city of science, the city of history and it is not wrong to call it the city of art. City of St. Petersburg today is the major center of political economy and the number-one tourist city of Russia, voted by mankind as the most beautiful city in the world. It is no mistake that St. Petersburg is chosen by UNESCO as one of the eight most beautiful cities in the world to recognize as the heritage of humanity. It is impossible to not mention one particular event; Uncle Ho, after spending years in France, decided to go to Russia, to the revolutionary country, to the Communist International. Under the alias Chen Vang, Uncle Ho set foot in Russia at the harbor of St. Petersburg on June 30, 1923. Perhaps he was also the first Vietnamese communist to set foot in this revolutionary city.

***

From Morskaya Street, where the famous writer Gogol and the great composer Tchaikovsky lived and died, we went to the square and the church named after Saint Isaac. This is the largest church of the city, built in 1710 to worship Saint Isaac. The church has been uniquely constructed of granite, with 48 monolithic stone pillars, each weighing 114 tons, and over hundreds of other stone pillars built around the church. The church has the largest dome in the world, inlaid with gold. If all of the gold and gold-plated motifs and sculptures of the church are included, it will cost up to 400 kg of gold, a thousand tons of copper and lots of precious stones. The sheer splendor and magnificence of the high, wide and golden arches, therefore, makes people overwhelmed as soon as they enter the church, and opens their mind. The church can accommodate up to 14,000 worshippers. It took more than 40 years to construct this church. Outside the park, where the roundabout lies, is the statue of Nicholas I leisurely riding on horseback.

In the city of St. Petersburg, there are many churches, museums, cemeteries of scientists and talented artists whose names have been recognized by mankind and are worth visiting.

I asked my Russian friends to let me visit the Smolny Palace again. Some tour guide might have forgotten this place, or maybe intentionally forgotten this place. However, for me and my friends from Vietnam, it is unforgettable, because the Smolny Palace was the first landmark of the Revolution, the place where Lenin lived and worked in the early days, the place where Lenin gave his first speech on October Revolution. In 1918, the revolutionary center has been moved to Moscow. Lenin stayed there for just over 350 days, but the palace was remembered in history. Today, Smolny is one of the major universities in Russia. The Revolutionary Manifesto from this white palace has changed the world, the life of slavery has been disappeared in many countries, people have been able to stand up in the truest sense.

I went to Lenin Park near the cluster of monuments commemorating the victory over fascism. Lenin stood there, on the high platform, it was the white fountains on all sides like the rising waves of Lenin's thoughts and feelings for humanity. Statues of Red Army soldiers bravely storming to defeat the fascist enemy. In the city of St. Petersburg, during 872 days under the siege of the fascists, the people and the Red Army soldiers shared a slice of bread everyday, but guns were always in their hands. More than a million people fell, but the people of the Soviet Union, the people of the city St. Petersburg have won.

***

Leaving the center of St. Petersburg for more than thirty kilometers, we visited the Summer Palace, also known as Peterhof. The palace is located at the mouth of the Neva River on the Baltic coast of the Gulf of Finland. Standing on the shore where the boat docks are located and looking up north, you can see the place which had been Lenin's refuge before he returned to St. Petersburg to lead the October Revolution. The Summer Palace is one of the 7 most beautiful wonders of Russia and the top of St. Petersburg. This is a twenty-one-hectare complex built under Tzar Peter Romanov in 1714, with 20 castles built by the famous architect Bartolomeo Rastrelli and master architects in Europe. In the front, it is the immense one thousand hectares Royal Garden connecting the castle with the Gulf of Finland. The forest of birch, oak, and straight pines has created wonderful vegetation. Under the forest canopy are green lawns with field of bright yellow Ramasca wildflowers. The Summer Palace is calm thanks to the carpets of plants, and even more peaceful thanks to the purple color of the flowers in the upper garden, giving people the sense of relaxation, tranquility and excitement.

The Summer Palace is made even more magnificent and brilliant by the great waterfall in front of the palace, including 64 fountains and 150 water towers that are operated by natural mechanical hydraulics without water pumps. They draw water from the natural spring in Ropsha 20 kilometers away. Two hundred and twenty-five statues of the gods of Greek mythology were gilded in gold and sparkled in the water and the sun. Every 11 a.m., the song of the hymn is resounded by the towers and fountains. All the first tsarist dynasties reigned here. It was not until 1783 that the Winter Palace was completed, and the dynasties rotated between two palaces in winter and summer.

Coming to St. Petersburg, it is impossible not to visit the Winter Palace. The entire palace consists of seven hundred rooms with ninety thousand square meters, reflecting day and night into the Neva River. The palace was built of granite imported from Finland and Italy. Similar to Isaac's Cathedral, the ceiling, stairs, and palace motifs are all gilded in gold. It took 2,300 skilled workers nine years to complete the construction. It is said that this was the idea of Queen Elizabeth, but she passed away before the palace was completed.

The Winter Palace is famous for its front square, which is the largest square in the city. Its beauty is enhanced thanks to the arched castle on the other side of the square like two great arms outstretched to welcome victory. On the roof right at the entrance is a monument. This castle with the giant Alexander tower in the middle created a vast square of winter palace and contributed to the majesty of the palace. The square was built in 1834 to commemorate the victory over Napoleon, which has a tower of twenty-five and a half meters high, on top of which is a statue of an angel crushing the enemy under his feet. This is the largest marble tower in the world. Today, major rallies, and festivals in the city are held in this magnificent square.

During the Soviet Union, the Winter Palace was used as the national museum of the Hermitage (literally translated as the place of silence). This is the great museum of the world, which stores three million masterpieces of art (nearly fifteen thousand famous paintings, twelve thousand statues, more than half a million engravings and sketches, millions of reliefs...). Going through all the rooms of the Hermitage Museum is equivalent to walking twenty-two kilometers, and if it only takes two minutes to look at each work, it will take 50 years (8 hours a day) to see the whole museum.

***

In the middle of a night of June, my friends took me and Thanh Huong, editor of the Young Publishing House, also my sister, to visit the bronze knight statue in memory of The Great Peter. Statue of the discoverer of St. Petersburg is set in the middle of a park on the banks of beautiful Neva River. Night in St. Petersburg was very quiet. The sculptor was very successful with this great statue. The four-corner headlights highlight the figure of Peter the Great riding his horse to reach the sky. The base of the statue is a giant monolith stone weighing up to half a million tons which make the levitating posture of the founder of St. Petersburg even more solid and majestic. I read in a Russian novel that there were nights from this statue that Peter rode around the city to observe, contemplate and help the poor. The story is like sacred legend. Watching Peter riding on the bronze horse, I suddenly remembered Saint Gióng, the young saint of Vietnam who rode a horse to fight the invaders from the North with bamboo as his weapon and returning to the heaven after winning the enemy...

The summer night of June by the Neva River, the silver light of the white nights is still chilly. My sister and I had to pull our hats over our ears and passed through the stream of people going to see the open bridge on the Neva River. It was crowded with people from five continents, who all tried to find the best spot to see the bridge open. The clock showed 2 minutes pass one o'clock, and the middle point of the bridges slowly rose up. Boats honked loudly and crossed the bridge to the cheers of the crowd. They took pictures and videos of how the bridge opened. On such white nights, interspersing with ships running across the opened bridge are red sailboats buzzing with lively music and vocals. These red sails recall the love story of Alexander Gin, about the sailor Arthur Gray who made the dream of his beloved Assol come true by thousands of yards of red silk that was spread on the river under the morning sun and in the melodious sound of the organ.

People often try to visit St. Pertesburg in June because of white nights during this time of the year. From June 10, in St. Pertesburg, it seems that the sun never set, the sky is still silvery all night. Especially on June 21 and 26, the night is bright even without the sun. This is phenomenon caused by the refraction of the sun from the other side of the hemisphere during the day, reflecting through the giant snowpack of the Arctic, casting light on the city. It was not sunny, but it was still light and bright. The whole city is awake, the windows are opened, you can still see the flowerpots and flower beds on the balcony of each house without the need for bright lights. People gather in parks, squares, and riverbanks to entertain. They lit a fire to grill shashlyk dishes - a thick cut of lean and fat pork, skewered with fragrant grilled onions. People eat shashlyk, drink beer and vodka and dance. I have met here girls in traditional Russian dress - red sarafan, with a hat decorated with beautiful brim like red peacock's tail with shimmering pearls. The Russians call it the Kokoshirik hat. Russian girls with blue eyes, blonde hair, and little freckles on their faces, wear these clothes while dancing and singing. They sing Russian folk songs that are melodious like walking in the middle of birch forest with falling autumn leaves. A young man wearing a calico like the soldiers Ivan in the novel, playing a harp while dancing with the girls in Sarafan traditional costumes on the grass by the lake, truly moved the heart of people.

Both Russia and European countries have this silver light from 9 to 10 at night. It is exciting to take night photography due to the lights and the soft light of nature. However, white nights can be only seen in St. Petersburg.

***

St. Pertesburg has 221 museums keeping all the great heritages of humanity, Russia and St. Petersburg. Leisurely walking on the streets of St. Pertesburg under the trees, which I used to call Leningrad, I felt like I was seeing the famous scientist Lomonosov, the talented female ballerina M. Kshesinskaya, and the famous painters of Russia: Levitan, Serov, Repin, Surikov, like walking with Gogol, Lermontov, listening to Tchaikovsky's Sixth Symphony. I felt like meeting the great poet Pushkin whose name and work have entered people's hearts. The day when we were on the way to the Summer Palace, we stopped in the city called Pushkin, walking in the colorful flower gardens of the Ekaterina Park, under the birch trees with falling yellow leaves just like gold inlaid on the small road leading to the statue of the great poet Pushkin. A platinum-haired artist passionately plays a flute and poems by Pushkin, who has lived and left part of his life in St. Petersburg. His poem **"Golden Autumn"** is a masterpiece. A Vietnamese translator has translated it, here is an excerpt:

Withered nature suddenly fresh

The forest changes its clothes in the autumn,

The wind breathes through

The sky rippling, a smoky haze.

Dear Pushkin, Russia, despite many changes, even withered, is always green, the birch forest is still standing proudly. Russia - autumn, Russia of love and victory.

The Land Of Roses

Bulgaria, located on the border between Europe and Asia, is a country with a long history. Looking at the map, Bulgaria has the shape of a lioness with the head is the city of Varna and Duran Kulak on the Black Sea coast in the East with many famous golden beaches. The tail reaches to Serbia and almost hitting Romania.

Bulgaria is the country with many mountains, one of which is the Rila range reaching 3,000 meters high. Intermixed with high and low mountain ranges are 540 large and small rivers, the beautiful Danube River flows through many Eastern European countries, with a winding branch in Bulgaria. Interspersed with mountains and rivers are 2,000 lakes, including 260 lakes of snow in the cold winter. The rivers have created calm basins with a mild climate that is very favorable for roses growing. Bulgaria has chosen the rose as its national flower and that is also why people call Bulgaria the land of roses.

The name Bulgaria comes from a tribe of Bulgars with Turkic origin from Central Asia, who were the first inhabitants of this country nearly 2,000 years ago. In the Turkic language, Bulgars means mixing, revolting, rising... In 632, the first independent state was born, named Great Bulgaria. Through many different dynasties, the country of Bulgaria has formed and developed into what it is today. In 1946 the revolutionary state was born. Under General Secretary Todor Zhivkov, Bulgaria was one of the socialist countries who strongly supported Vietnam's struggle against the US imperialists.

Bulgaria has nine UNESCO World Heritage sites, such as Rila Monastery, Ancient Tombs, Pirin National Park, Srebarna Nature Reserve, the Old City of Nesebar, and 13th-century churches carved in rock. What make me particularly impressed is the legacy of the great sculpture "Madara Horseman" which was carved by medieval artisans (in 710), a hundred meters high stone in which a masterpiece of a horseman wielding his sword and gallantly riding forward was carved. From the foot of the horse to the head of the horseman, it is calculated that the sculpture is more than 10 times taller than a real person - 23 meters tall. It's amazing that, 1,500 years ago, the ancient people had been able to produce this unique work of art. The world heritage sites of Bulgaria are a solid demonstration of the civilization of this centuries-old rose land.

Bulgaria was born early, from the 4th century, so its culture has a very strong and unique character which can be seen through the diversification of its traditional folk instruments such as Gudulka, Gaida, Kaval, Tupan, monuments, and its many festivals.

Warm and sincere Bulgaria

Under this title, I wrote a short article for the Liberation Arts (of the Front National Liberation of the South Vietnam) since 1968. Due to the war, the manuscript is no longer available. However, the warmth and depth of emotions that Sofia and Bulgaria showed us in those days are still here, forever.

In 1968, the 9th World Festival of Youth and Students was held in Sofia - the capital of Bulgaria. Youth delegates from 134 countries, amounting up to over 120,000 people, arrived in Sofia. And this was the first time Vietnam had two delegations attending the event with large number of members. The delegation of the Democratic Republic of Vietnam (North Vietnam) consisted of up to 100 people. The delegation of the Front National Liberation of the South were 84 people, including representatives from Binh Tri Thien, Zone 5, Central Highlands, and Southern regions. There were heroes and warriors and a musician ensemble from the Liberation Army led by musician Xuan Hong. Due to the Cultural Revolution in China, the international trains could not run, so the Soviet Union assigned the 5-star Turmenia cruise ship to Hai Phong to welcome two Vietnamese and Lao delegations. I just returned from the Khe Sanh Front and was sent to join the Front National Liberation of the South. As an official of the South's foreign affairs agency, I was sent along with Ambassador Le Phuong and choreographer Dang Hung to fly to Sofia a few days before the event. And so, when two Vietnamese delegations from the Soviet Union arrived by train, I was accompanied by my Bulgarian friends to the platform to welcome the delegation.

In those August days, Sofia was sunny and bright with colors of flags and flowers. There were flowers on the balcony of every house; it seemed that every house had roses. On the streets, in the green park, flowers bloomed; slogans, banners, logos, and congress posters made the streets of Sofia splendidly and majestically on that day.

And even though it was the first time we met, but anywhere, in the Ministry of Foreign Affairs, at the BTA News Agency or at a hotel, in a park, on streets, people treated us with sincere warmth and friendship as soon as they were told we were from the battlefields of Vietnam. People, young as well as old, aware that we were FNL[2] soldiers, hugged us as they did close friends. Bulgarian women normally have a slim figure like that of Asian women, but their skin and face are a mixture of Asian, European and the Middle Eastern features with big black eyes, and their noses is not as high as that of a German and French woman. They always showed us their smiles and friendly gesture. The Bulgarians, in order to show that they share your thinking and feelings, shake their heads, which baffled me at first and made me interpret it as a sign of disagreement. The only thing that convinced me this was not the case was the fact that this head-shaking is accompanied with opened arms and heart-warming smiles.

We had a week in Sofia enjoying the excitement for Vietnam not only from Bulgarians but also from the whole world. They organized white nights to welcome us who they called "Viet Cong", to hear them singing Vietnamese songs. We met again Venezuelan Caracas guerrillas who had captured the American colonel alive in exchange for Nguyen Van Troi. They put all kinds of badges and flags on our chests. My olive-colored hat was "confiscated" many times by international friends as a souvenir, fortunately the group was prepared to bring enough hats for these cases. They would chant "Vietnam, Vietnam" and "FNL" whenever they met us. The day our group interacted with Bulgarian youth was extremely warm. We were welcomed, ate dinner and danced together. Young women wearing traditional Bulgarian costumes with white collars and red and blue decorative embroideries that stood out among hundreds of people. The Bulgarian folk song was also calm, melodious, and gentle like gliding on the fields of flowers.

The opening day of the congress was attended by General Secretary Todor Zhivkov, President of the International Federation of Students and Representatives. One hundred and thirty four delegations from

---

[2] FNL: Front National Liberation

many countries marched through the stadium, passed the stage and proceeded toward to the main streets of Sofia. I attended the event both as a delegate and a journalist of the Front National Liberation (FNL) of South Vietnam, granted an international journalist card that provided me with the right to walk freely around in the stadium. This gave the opportunity to witness the strong sentiments of the whole world in support of the heroic struggle of the Vietnamese nation. That day, I wore a liberation army uniform and an olive-colored hat and stood under the main stage to observe and record images of the delegations. When the Italian delegation saw me, they stopped, perhaps they recognized the FNL soldiers, so they shouted: "Vietnam" and carried me on their shoulders along almost a quarter of the stadium. Immediately the whole stadium was like a wave, resounding with the chorus of "Viva Vietnam, Vietnam - Ho Chi Minh, Vietnam Giap-Giap-Giap, Vietnam FNL."

After the ceremony, many Bulgarian newspapers interviewed me, published photos of me on their channels with many good comments. The Soviet newspaper Komsomol Pravda published the photo with the caption "Welcome the heroes of South Vietnam".

Also at this congress, my photo work titled "Attack, the victory flag" taken in Khe Sanh won a gold medal. During the award ceremony, I gave a speech on behalf of dozens of authors. In my statement that day I said: "I am very honored to be here to receive the Gold Medal, I think that the people who are more deserving than me to receive this gold medal are the those appearing in my work, who are soldiers of the liberation army of South Vietnam, they have been sacrificing their blood to gain independence for the Vietnamese motherland and for the cause of world peace."

A major Bulgarian newspaper published both the photo of mine and the photo of the award with lovely words. The next morning, a Bulgarian mother brought a newspaper to the Vietnamese delegation to meet the leader of the delegation, Tran Van Tu, and asked to see me. The meeting was much unexpected, she hugged me, kissed me for a long time, and in front of everyone she said: "I have a son sacrificed for liberation of Bulgaria. I love Vietnam, I am happy to welcome you back from the battlefield. Today, when I meet you, I feel like meeting my own children." She hugged me again, tears welling up in her eyes. All of us were touched. She said to the leader of the delegation: "Comrade, let me accept this soldier," she hugged me by the shoulder as she said this, "as my Vietnamese child". That is sincere, warm, and heartfelt. Before leaving Sofia, by appointment, I was allowed to visit my Bulgarian mother. The whole family members were there to welcome me, her husband, children, brothers, and grandchildren. That day, my mother gave me homemade traditional wine, low alcohol, very rich liquor, and served me excellent grilled meat made by her. She introduced this as minced meat mixed with onions and spices grilled over charcoal called "Kae-bap che-ta" which is a traditional Bulgarian dish for many generations. I told my mother: "My hometown also has grilled pork skewers". Mother nodded: "We have many things in common", then looking at everyone, she said: "Especially the will for national independence". I hugged my mother gratefully. Farewell, my mother gave me some underwear and said, "I give this to you because I think it will be with you, even when you sleep." I hugged and kissed my mother and then stood up to greet her in the style of a soldier: "Mother, I have returned from the battlefield". She gave me a bunch of red roses freshly from her yard and said chokingly: "You must win." After saying that, she hugged me with tears in her eyes. I returned to the battlefield at the fiercest stage, the war, the bombardment in Truong Son had made it impossible for me to contact my mother. That story was 52 years ago, and still the profound feelings of Sofia's mother, my Bulgarian mother are forever engraved in my memory.

From 2016 to 2019, our Oriental Research Development Institute has cooperated with the global Huesa Institute to research and apply bioenergy for human health. This Institute is run by Professor, Doctor Theresa Nguyen Thu Thuy. Huesa enjoys the participation of up to 5 million people around the world. One of the members of the leadership board is Master Silvana who is a Bulgarian. Silvana was born in 1968, the year I first came to Sofia. Looking at her, I felt like I was reliving the warm days in Bulgaria, I am very happy to tell her about the old memories 50 years ago in her home country. I had thought the story belonged to the past and would not be remembered, and I was surprised to see how it is kept alive till today. When she returned to Bulgaria, Silvana searched the library, the national computer archive… and she found videos of the congress 50 years ago. As she returned to Vietnam, she happily gave me two videos about the 9th Youth and Student Congress, including the scene where Italian friends carried me on their shoulders at the opening ceremony. It was very special and unexpected!

Watching the video, my heart is filled with emotion by the depth and kindness of the young Bulgarian friends, and I deeply admire the way this country meticulously preserves the treasures of the past. Silvana's father was also an official, a Communist Party member during the revolutionary state. Silvana said: "Our class was born by communists, it was a beautiful, golden age. Today, the political system of Bulgaria is different, but the feelings of the Bulgarian people are still strong". Silvana is sincere and so profound as the city of Sofia and the Bulgarians I met half a century ago. Silvana's sincerity and old memories of Sofia and Bulgaria have prompted me to write a memoir about this beautiful land of roses. I cannot forget the people who have left deep impressions on me like Sofia's mother and the writer and journalist Blaga Dimitrova who was very passionate about Vietnam. She had just returned from Vietnam, where she had been welcomed by Uncle Ho and had stayed in Quang Binh fire route for nearly 100 days and nights. She came to meet the Vietnamese delegation and invited us to her house. In her living room there were many memories of Vietnam. She was writing a collection of stories about Vietnam. I was startled to see an iron helmet on her table that we wore in the days of fighting against the sabotage war. I asked her: "You must have used this hat in the days of American bombing in Quang Binh, right?" She shook her head and smiled. After a while, she said two words: "Uncle Ho" in Vietnamese. She said she had visited and greeted Uncle before returning home. That day, on Uncle Ho's table there was a very beautiful vase of roses. Uncle pulled a red rose, a branch with many thorns, gave it to Blaga and said to her in French: "I give a Vietnamese rose to a Bulgarian rose" (He wanted to say Blaga is beautiful, and Bulgaria is the land of roses). The conversation with Uncle was paused because of American planes arriving. The guards took Uncle Ho to the basement next to his stilt house and put an iron helmet on his head. Turning to Blaga and noticing that she did not have a helmet, Uncle Ho took the helmet he was wearing on his head to cover Blaga's head. Blaga asked Uncle Ho to keep him safe. Uncle Ho said very seriously, "This is an order". Blaga wore Uncle Ho's helmet with full of emotions. When the planes went away and they returned to the house, Blaga asked Uncle Ho for a helmet as a souvenir. Uncle Ho asked: "It is a heavy iron helmet and you'll have to travel long distances by plane, is it convenient to carry it?" Blaga said: "But...it belongs to Uncle". Uncle Ho happily gave it to her.

Blaga put the hat on her head and told us "Part of my heart is in Vietnam, for the war in Vietnam". She stood up and walked towards us, warmly hugging each of us... That's it, Sofia was deep inside of us. It is also impossible not to mention the blind prophetess Vanga, whose house is in a town 200 kilometers from Sofia. She is a person with famous predictions. I met her when she was 57 years old, she was wearing simple farmer clothes, with a scarf on her head like an old woman in the countryside of Vietnam. She was blind in both eyes and couldn't understand Vietnamese, but when I stood before her, she said: "Welcome to the soldier from the land of the rising sun, you are doing miracles". "Victory will come in no more than two hands," she predicts. I did not understand that time. That year, the situation in the South was very special, with the general offensive in the Mau Than spring and our victory in Khe Sanh. The United States had to agree to join the peace negotiations in Paris. However, as Uncle Ho said, the war was still difficult and complicated. The assistant of Vanga translated to us: "Two hands have ten fingers, Vietnam would win within two hands, which means the victory would come in no more than 10 years." It was later proved that her prophecy was correct: Seven years later, Vietnam created a miracle by the victory on 30th April 1975, completely liberating the South and reunifying the country. Today, my Bulgarian mother and Vanga have returned to the heaven, but their feelings are still alive. Younger generations of Sofia, like Silvana, are continuing that warmth and sincerity.

Ancient and civilized Sofia

The Bulgarian capital is located at an altitude of 500-600 meters, leaning against the Vitosha mountain. This is the land of the Neolithic inhabitants, there are still traces of the Setdi people settled from 1,700 BC, also known as Setdia land at that time. It was not until the 14th century that the city was named after Saint Sofia (St. Sofia), in Roman, Sofia means "Wise". There is legend about St. Sofia as follows: Sofia is the beautiful princess of an ancient emperor. She had a serious illness. The emperor brought all the royal doctors to treat her, but it could not be cured. An astrologer told the emperor that she would be cured if she lived in a place with mountains and rivers. An entourage was chosen by the king, and they took Princess Sofia to rest at the foot of the Vitosha mountain with beautiful land and fresh air. She was cured and felt happy and healthy after very short time because of positive energy. The king was very happy, he set up a village and built a house by the river for the princess to settle down. The land came to life, the villagers planted, pruned, hunted, and made crafts. Everyone lived in the wealth and love of each other, and the princess became the leader of the region. Sometime later, foreign rebels came to the village, Princess Sofia and the villagers ran away from the land and were killed by the enemy. She disappeared after a thunder and her holy soul was led to the heaven.

The land under Vitosha mountain became wealthier, the air fresher and more energetic. The river next to the princess's house became a mineral spring that cured many diseases. Princess Sofia is canonized. The Church of Saint Sofia was built where the princess ascended to heaven. The name of the Saint was given to the city, which then became the capital of Bulgaria.

Originally, the city of Sofia was built in the Asian style of architecture. Today, in Sofia, there are thousands of ancient black stone streets and low-rise buildings with small vineyards in front, in the small gardens there are roses and fruit trees like many Asian villages. By the time of the Bulgarian empire, Sofia had changed to European urban style with squares, buildings, splendid castles, and churches. In 1968, when I first came to Sofia, I visited Revolution Square where the tomb of G. Dimitrov was located. I once went to the mausoleum to pay tribute to the revolutionary leader of the international communism.

Sofia has a very good ecological environment, with lots of quiet open spaces. I once walked on Sofia Avenue to visit the house of famous Bulgarian writer Ivan Vazov, and, from there, walking toward the Central Park to see the theater named Ivan Vazov located right next to the park, which is the most magnificent theater in Sofia. The Park was magnificent, with green trees and roses, and many other architectural works, ancient and modern monuments interspersed in prime locations. Just like in the Freedom Park near the National Institute of Culture, this park is full of green trees and lakes with swans showing love to their partners. These are living spaces that lift people's souls and give them a lot of positive energy.

From Sofia one can visit Vitosha mountain at an altitude of 2,000 meters, which is vacation paradise even in the hot summer, from July to September, when all the streets of Sofia suffer from the heat. Vitosha has a skiing area, and the spring is the best season to contemplate the landscape and take the most beautiful pictures of snow, blue sky with white clouds, and beautiful sunshine in May... Vitosha has been a tourist attraction from the period of Socialist government. You can reach Vitosha by car or by cable car right on the edge of Sofia. Vitosha is the mountain for Sofia to lean on with a peak of 2,280 meters, a tourist and resort destination for tourists from all over the world and for the people of Sofia themselves.

Arriving in Bulgaria, I saw lots of Russian and Soviet Union stamps here. The Bulgarian scripts share lot of similarities with Russian, albeit with different pronunciation and lexical meanings in the Bulgarian language. In Sofia, there is Tsar Osvoboditel Avenue paved with tiles in the color of ripe rice. From 1877 to 1878, Russian Tsar Osvoboditel led Russian troops to liberate Bulgaria from the domination of the Ottoman Empire after 500 years of domination. All visitors, when visiting Parliament Square, will meditate in front of a large monument dedicated to Russian soldiers who sacrificed their lives for Bulgaria. Nearby is the statue of the Russian Tsar riding leisurely who led his troops to liberate the rose country. Many colorful roses are placed at the foot of the statue to express gratitude and respect. The Bulgarian people built the Alexander Nevsky church to commemorate 200,000 Russian soldiers who sacrificed for Bulgaria. The church was built according to the design of Russian architect Alexander Pomerantsev with the participation of interior architects and artisans from many European countries. The church was built in the typical Russian style of that time, the domes are close to and support each other, painted in blue, and the 52-meter-high bell tower, painted in golden hues, stands magnificently amid the sky. The church has 12 bells and paintings on the wall and splendid golden doors. This is one of the first churches built by the combination of European countries. The lighting and decorative marble are from Munich (Germany), the gates were made in Vienna (Austria), while the intricate mosaics were from the island of love, Venice. And more than 300 colorful marbles and paintings from all regions of Bulgaria are displayed and decorated here. During 30 years of construction, professional workers from Russia, Italy, and Germany... had created the world's largest western-style cathedral. The church was built on the highest piece of land in Sofia with a prominent golden arch roof which can be seen from anywhere, even from the Mount Vitosha. Alexander Church is the pride of the people of Sofia and of Bulgarians in general. It is the symbol of respect and gratitude of the Bulgarian people in memory of the Russians and Bulgarians who had sacrificed their lives to liberate the country.

Right next to Alexander Nevsky Cathedral is the ancient, simple St. Sofia church with rustic red-brown brick walls as quiet as the historical Sofia.

As Silvana told me, today's generation of Bulgaria is descended from the revolutionary generation, or rather, they are descendants of the patriotic communists. The love and respect of Bulgarians for their past can be seen easily because in Sofia, and in Bulgaria in general, there are still many memorials of the Soviet soldiers who sacrificed to liberate Bulgaria in 1946. Still standing in the middle of Sofia is the Lago symbol of 50 years of socialism.

Sofia is a heritage capital that blends both Asian and European characteristics, where the past is well preserved. Sofia has been always treasuring its historical legacy while building itself into a modern city. In the courtyard of the most luxurious five-star Sheraton hotel in Sofia there is the church of Saint George built in the 5th century, and the oldest church of Sofia which has been well-preserved till today.

Sofia has many museums, monumental churches as milestones marking each historical period of one of the oldest cities in Europe. Sofia develops without tearing down its old constructions, but keeping them in perfect harmony, from each of the small, paved roads to the low-rise buildings, the gardens, and the underground ancient works. That is the civilization of a country that is always proud of, and promotes, its long and rich culture.

Valley of the roses

The southern of Bulgaria is a wide valley that has been raised by silt for thousands of years from the Stara Planina mountains and from the alluvium of the two rivers Shiteliema and Dengsa that crisscross the valley. Due to the fertile soil, mild climate, and the salty Black Sea, it is very suitable for rose growing.

After 3 months of winter, Bulgaria seems to be always colorful with roses during the remaining 9 months of the year, not only in Sofia but all over Bulgaria, there are roses in every house, garden with pure white and pink, purple roses blooming throughout three seasons. Bulgarian roses are large, diverse in colors and have beautiful fragrances. Bulgaria has chosen the rose as its national flower. The scientific name of this flower is Rosa and Rose in English. The rose is a symbol of love, victory. The bigger and more beautiful the rose is, the sharper the thorns are, hence the saying "What rose has no thorns? Owing to its thorns, a rose becomes beautiful". Roses appeared in Bulgaria from the 6th century. It is estimated that, of the 2,000 species of roses in the world, approximately 1,500 ones are present in Bulgaria.

From Sofia, travelling to the east 200 km to the city of Plovdiv, we will meet the Kazanlak valley. Kazanlak lies between the Beagan Mountains of the great Balkans in the north as a shelter from the cold monsoons, in the south are the low mountains of Sredna Gora supporting the Dengsa and Shiteliema rivers flowing throughout the Kazanlak valley. There is a folk legend about roses. Once upon a time there was a fairy who, having seen a lot of flowers without her favourite red color, decided to water them with blood, and as a result, there appeared a species of deep red rose with a seductive fragrance that makes people fall in love.

There is another legend. Once upon a time there was a princess who loved the scent of roses. Whenever taking a bath, she always put rose petals in the bath and found out that, floating on the water surface, clinging to her breasts, smoothing her skin, were the tiny drops of oil much like dew drops, giving off a soothing fragrance... It was oil from roses. The princess then distilled it to get the essential oil as a daily fragrance, from which the extraction of rose essential oil was born. In the old days the extraction was completely manual, using earthenware and black copper cauldrons. They distilled it right in the flower fields belonging to each household. Today, the processing technology is very advanced, but people here still think that the quality of the flowers is higher when the roses are preliminarily processed right after being picked, so there is a combination of traditional processing techniques and modern ones. In this rose valley, the Strelcha region is the largest, where most of Bulgaria's modern rose oil production is centered. The Strelcha field is the land that produces the highest quality roses in the country. Along with Turkey, Bulgaria is the world leader in rose production and rose oil production. Although there are thousands of species of roses, but only 4 types can give the oil effectively, the best ones of them being pink roses and, especially, white roses. In Bulgaria it is estimated that it takes 3,000 kilograms of pink petals, equivalent to 1,300 roses, to produce one kilogram of rose oil. If it is a white rose, it takes twice as many petals to extract one kilogram of essential oil. One kilogram of rose oil is worth one and a half kilograms of 24-carat gold, and Bulgaria can earn billions of dollars a year from rose oil. Bulgarian rose oil is an important ingredient for the scent and durability of the production of high-end perfumes and cosmetics. Bulgarian essential oil is supplied to high-end perfume companies in Paris (France), Milan (Italy), and New York (USA)...

Kazanlak valley has long been known as the rose valley. It is the center of the rose country with 173 rose-growing villages. The rose valley stretches over 140 km with an area of 3,300 square kilometers (4,000 square kilometers according to some other sources) including vast and immense fields of Karlovo, Kazanlak, Pavel Banya, and Nova Zagora. It is fairyland where you and your partner can walk hand in hand in the middle of the largest rose field in this world to glance towards the sea of roses. Millions of roses in many colors, rose buds, colorful petals blooming brilliantly like a great flower road stretching to the horizon. Just extend your arms and take a deep breath to enjoy the charming, sweet scented of roses in the gentle breeze under the warm morning sun.

***

Rose harvest season is in May and June when the whole valley is covered by colorful flowers and beautiful fragrance. The rose festival is held for a whole month in many localities and has a history of over 100 years since 1903. From early morning, when the sun has yet to appear, music is played all along the way to the fields where flowers are to be picked. After the flower picking ceremony which lasts until 10 am, there is a festival on the street and in the square. This year 2020, the rose festival in the Strelcha region and in Karlovo is on May 30, the festival in Pavel Banya is on June 14. And in the center of the rose country, the town of Kazanlak, the festival still takes place on the Sunday of the first week of June as usual. The city of Kazanlak is the capital of the rose festival, visitors from all over the world are given roses to wear on their head. The girls of the rose country wear traditional dresses designed with patterns on their chests, hands, and bodies with the image of roses, wearing traditional scarves on their heads and colorful ribbons on their foreheads, their hands holding baskets of rose petals with which to welcome the guests. All the streets were packed with people. Men in traditional costumes play accordions, drums, blow trumpets, while girls dance, sing and wave roses. The atmosphere of excitement is everywhere. In the sky, helicopters spray fragrance, creating a sweet and loving fragrance for the land of rose.

These days, everywhere, from museums to hotels, on clothes, jewelry to food and drinks, we encounter the image of a rose. Not only tourists but farmers here also wear wreaths of roses. During the festival, there is an annual contest to choose the queen of roses. Usually, the queen is chosen from beautiful girls who have graduated from high school. The queen of rose will seat on a palanquin, leading the procession, smiling, and waving to everyone.

At the end of the ceremony there are rituals to chase away evil minded and cold weather, praying for a good harvest of flowers, performed by strong men wearing Kukeri clothes according to the old tradition.

During the rose festival, people and visitors are invited to eat cakes and drink rose-flavored Rakia wine. Visitors are invited to participate in the rose-picking ceremony, so the locals say: Not only are we welcoming you, but also the roses are welcoming you warmly, offering you their heavenly beauty!

Profound Berlin

The Legendary Viet Nam

In 1968, I was selected as an official member of the Delegation of of Youth and Student sent by the National Front for the Liberation of the South to attend the 9th World Festival of Youth and Student in Sofia, Bulgaria. It was the first time the National Front sent such a large delegation of more than 80 persons, many of which were war heroes, regional representatives, and the Liberation Army's troupe as well.

The National Front for the Liberation's team was welcomed and much sought after by other delegations from more than 120 countries in all five continents.

We spent many sleepless nights with Italian, German, Cuban, Venezuelan delegations. They carried our national flags, photos of Uncle Ho, of General Vo Nguyen Giap to meetings and marches, accompanied by thunderous cries of "Viet Nam, Viet Nam, viva Viet Nam," "Ho, Ho, Ho Chi Minh, "Giap, Giap, Giap" and "F, N, L" (the French acronyms of Front National de Liberation).

Everyone supported our fight for national independence. I was at that time both a delegate and a reporter of the National Liberation Front. Wearing an international journalist badge issued by the organizers, I was allowed to roam freely in the stadium in the uniform of the Liberation Army. In an atmosphere bustling with support for Viet Nam, I was welcomed wherever I went and by whomever I met. Among them was a friend from the German Democratic Republic – Miss Eva Fischer.

Also carrying a camera on her shoulder, Eva joined the group of journalists. She was twenty five, young and enthusiastic. I remembered she once told us: "As I arrived from Berlin, I was so excited to meet Vietnamese friends, to meet the delegates of FNL, to shake your hands and to say it loudly, 'We support Viet Nam!'" We were part of a global wave of support for Viet Nam.

At the opening ceremony two huge flags of Viet Nam and of the the National Front for the Liberation of the South (half blue and half red) were flown by the Italian and the Venezuelan delegations. As they marched across the stage, in loud voice they sang the Liberation song of the South, upon which I quickly ran over to capture that striking scene. Recognizing me by my Liberation Army uniform and bucket hat, they rushed to carry me on their shoulders, shouting, "Viet Nam! FNL!"

The whole stadium of more than 100,000 people from over 120 countries raised to their feet and roared slogans to support Viet Nam's victory. Sitting on the shoulders of my Venezuelan friends, I conveyed my gratitude by waving to the world, to the youth from five continents. That historic image was then captured by many journalists, including Eva Fischer.

I kept seeing Eva in press conferences and events during one week of the Festival. And on the day of departure, as fortune had it, I met her again on the platform of Sofia station. We boared the train to Bucharest together and bid our farewell there. Her delegation returned home via Hungary, while we traveled to Modavia to return to Moscow.

After the Festival, we became pen pals and I introduced her to my younger brother, Trinh Tu Kha (Sau Kha), who was studying in Berlin. In 1972, my brother returned to Viet Nam and volunteered to the Southern front. I was also on another the battlefield, and we could not contact each other. Then came the liberation of the South, the fall of the Berlin Wall, followed by the collapse of the German Democratic Republic. Our relation was disrupted by geo-political changes.

However, the fond memories of our friendship, of the sympathy between true comrades remained vivid. Eva and her husband, Peter Fischer, always had a special affection for Viet Nam and for our family. Then our paths crossed again.

The Lunar New Year of 2011, we invited Eva and Peter to visit Viet Nam. We exchanged brothers and sisters' hugs at the Tan Son Nhat International Airport.

After days visiting Ho Chi Minh City, the War Museum, and Cu Chi underground tunnels, Peter, a PhD on German history, often put his hand on his chest and said emotionally, "Here am I, having read so much about Viet Nam and thinking that I understand the country well. But this journey has changed my every thought and imagination. I have simply gone from one surprise to another."

First day of the New Year, we treated Eva and Peter to a siblings' homecoming party. Together over the traditional dinner we relived our good old memories. "Ho Chi Minh City is so gorgeous, so dyanmic, so lively!" said Eva. "Such development and integration can only be made possible in a country of revolutionaries." And she continued, "this visit is an eye-opening experience, which reveals to us your resilience, your ingenuity, your nation's strength. Viet Nam is a legend. A true legend." Recalling his trip to Cu Chi, Peter marveled, "What a miracle! I could not fathom how such a land, devastated by bombs and artillery, where tens of thousands of people fell, still magically prevailed. I'd call it a steel fortress."

Peter handed me a small red flag, whose dimension is 9x12cm. During the war, he and his friends usually organized demonstrations to support Viet Nam, and they had a huge Vietnamese flag for such occasions. When they later handed it over to the Association of Vietnam Supporters in Hanover, it was suggested that the flag be divided into 10,000 smaller ones so that everybody could have one as a souvenir.

Four decades have gone by and they still treasure these flags. Eva, a museum artifact restorer, said, "There's no longer a Communist Party in my country, but the Communist spirit remains alive inside us. And with that sentiment, we always admire the Vietnamese people and the true Communists of Viet Nam."

The reunion after 43 years was so special. We, witnesses of a glorious and sentimental period, shared a cozy traditional Tet holiday together. After his graduation, my brother, Sau Kha, returned from the GDR and volunteered to the battlefront as a soldier of the 5th Infantry Division. He had become the CEO of a travel agency. Eva, Peter and I were in our 70s. Our New Year reunion was also joined by my family and the poet Tran The Tuyen, who fought alongside my brother in the same Division during the war. A mellow glass of wine on our hands, we recounted our memories of Berlin, and of our dear Germany.

Berlin – The Golden Bear

I had been to Berlin many times and through different routes. I once came from Poland in the east, once from the north through Denmark, and I once started from Austria, crossing Switzerland and followed the Romantic Road in the south, then cut across the country through

Frankfurt and Hannover. And there was also another time when I entered Germany from Paris in a car and ran northward to reach Berlin.

My relation with Peter and Eva Fischer was a 45 years old friendship, sometimes intermitted by political changes. Nearly half a century had passed, but our friendship remained unfaded. This time, in Berlin, it was Peter and Eva's turn to take us on a tour. We visited the Museum Island (Museuminsel), surrounded by the Spree River and the Kupfergraben canal. Peter explained to me that there was a time when Berlin was on one side of the river, and the other side was a city named Cölln. It was founded in 1237 and Berlin followed seven years later. At the beginning the two cities shared a town hall and then gradually merged into one bearing the name Berlin. Berlin sounded like Bärlein, which means "little bear." German had chosen the bear as the symbol of their capital.

The Berlin city's emblem was a black bear with red tongue and red claws. The same bear appeared on the city state's flag. And the coat of arms added a golden crown above the bear. The most prestigious award of the Berlin International Film Festival was the Golden Bear. I had encountered this bear in all size and form and materials: the teddy bear, the metallic logo bear, the ceramic bear, the glass bear, and the printed bears. I liked to call Berlin a "golden bear" for the endearing feeling it invoked.

Berlin is growing, the bear has swallowed the satellite cities to become a metropolitan and the capital of Germany. Berlin is now one of the largest cities in Europe, with a population of 4.5 million.

"Without the Brandenburg Gate, the Berlin visit is incomplete," said Eva Fischer. Why? I asked. Because it was Germany's gateway, its most significant architecture, and a symbol of peace. That was right, the Brandenburg Gate on Unter den Linden boulevard, the main street of Berlin. It once was also a gateway that separated the East and West Berlin. It appeared in pictures, stamps, and in German coins.

The Brandenburg Gate was built in 1788 and it took three years to be completed at 26 meters height and 65 meters width, with five passageways. My guess was they might have also believed in feng shui, with the five passageways representing five elements. At the highest position and even more impressive was the bronze statue of the goddess Victoria with angel wings riding a four-horse carriage, holding the bird of peace in one hand and controlling the Quadriga with the other. When it was completed, only the royalties and honored guests were granted acess. After King Wilhelm II's 1918 abdication, the Gate was open to ordinary people, and it became the center of East and West Berlin. Nowadays Unter den Linden is one of the most magnificent Berlin boulevards thanks to the Brandenburg Gate, its numerous water fountains, and the Victory Column further down the road. Every year the Brandenburg Gate is decorated with colorful lights, and hosts thousands of people coming to celebrate the New Year Eve.

The Victory Column is a high rise tower with a gilded statue of the Roman Goddess of Victory on top, which is eight-meter in height and 35 tons in weight.

The winged-goddess wears a long dress that flies with the wind and wears a crown in the shape of a falcon; she holds a scepter in her left hand and a laurel wreath in her highly-raised right hand, which signify victory and glory. The Berliners call this goddess by the dear name of Goldelse or Golden Lizzie.

The statue was originally placed at the Republic Square in front of the German Parliament building, which was situated at the end of Victory Street. In 1939 the Nazi moved it to the current location. The monument commemorates the victory of Germany over the European empire. The inside of this column features many elaborate reliefs, and statues depicting battles in the late 19th century. The 285-step stairway leads to the foot of the statue, where the observatory deck featuring a panoramic view of Berlin is located.

In 2008, Barack Obama, then still a presidential candidate, came here to deliver a speech in front of an audience of 100,000. Some said that it was the Goddess of Victory who brought him to the White House to be the first colored US President.

I looked up with admiration at the glittering goddess in the blue sky and wondered how they managed to place that 35-ton statue on top of that 70-meter collumn. And in a minute of reflection, I thought of our national fight for independence, for which millions of people had fallen so that we could defeat the most powerful enemies in the world. And yet we had not had any monument of this caliber to commemorate their victory, and to educate the younger generations of their ancestors' heroic deeds and traditions.

*∗∗

Berlin is changing day by day and glass skyscrapers are towering over the sky. In no way humbled by the new architecture, the television tower erected since the GDR period is still rising high as the last relic of a golden area. We went to the Alexander Square and climbed up the tower to behold the golden bear, the panoramic Berlin, from above.

Built in 1960, the television tower is 398 meters high, the sphere alone weighs 4,800 tons and features seven floors, with the restaurant revolving at the altitude of 207 meters. It took the elevator 40 seconds to bring us up to the TV-Turm, an elegant and well-known restaurant in Berlin. Savoring a glass of German wine on the rotating platform, we indulged ourselves in the 360⁰ panoramic view of the picturesque city. It was sunny and the white clouds above our head were floating against the blue sky. And Berlin appeared before us, as vivid as a 3D map whose vision could be up to 40 km. It was so elegantly beautiful. This tower held with it the memories of generations, and it represented the will, the strength, and the pride of Berliners. It was Walter Ulbricht, the GDR leader, who authorized its construction. I had the honor to meet him when the Southern Viet Nam was still fighting for independence. Those days, Germans, especially people in the GDR, wholeheartedly assisted our righteous fight for independence with both tangible and intangible support. The red flag that Peter gave me was a beautiful memento of those days.

PROFOUND BERLIN

At the altitude of 200 meters we saw Berlin extending below and beyond us, a vast and quiet city. As I sat here I realized that green still prevailed in such a modern, industrialized city and it was the green that brought Berlin's modernization to a new height. The lake Tegeler and Wannsee are the lifeline of Berlin's vibrant green; and one third of the city is covered by forests, parks, and waters, which make up a massive lung that provide Berlin with its fresh air. The city has 2,800 flower gardens and parks with the total area of 5,500 hectares.

Eva pointed at the dark green area in the middle of the city and said it was the oldest zoo in Germany, established 500 years ago, with an area of 210 hectares. It used to be a city-front natural garden where the Prussian nobility went hunting. Today, this zoo houses up to 14,000 species from five continents. There is even a polar bear whose rescue in

2007 had since then become legendary. The zoo, together with many famous gardens such as the Rose garden, Luisen garden, and English garden have intensified the beauty of Berlin. The city receives over 2.5 million visitors each year. They all marvel at the Berlin wall that used to separate the East and the West, at its squares and flower gardens, its castles, its statues, and the magnificent architectures which captivated the guests and left them with unforgettable memories.

Peter took out a Berlin map, retraced our recent trip and showed it to me from this height. It turned out that from Victory Square we had passed Karl Marx Avenue and crossed the Marx-Engels Bridge, went to the Maxim Gorki Theater, stood in front of the Humboldt University where Marx, Hegel and many other great scholars studied and lectured. I understand the inner thoughts of Peter and Eva. They still treasured the fond memories of the GDR time. I patted Peter on his back: "Things are always changing, but history is forever." Peter was moved, he said solemnly: "That's right. Eva and I dedicated our whole life to history and museums, and we want the world to preserve the good heritage out of history."

Berlin is a city of museums. The Prussian Kings were the first to issue a decree on transforming the residential Museum Island into "a district dedicated to art and science." And in 1999 the Island was designated an UNESCO World Heritage.

Peter held up his two hands and counted the museums with his phalanges, and the 28 of them were simply not enough for the museums in Berlin, big and small. There's the City Museum, the Architecture Museum, the New National Museum, the Art Museum, the Hunting Museum, the Museum of German Separation...

The city already had dozens of famous museums, but Peter still thought that was not enough. I smiled and said, "Among the missing museums, there must be one for the friendship between our countries." Peter and Eva both agreed.

The afternoon on the Berlin TV Tower was strangely quiet under the vivid red sunset. The illuminated city became brilliant, magnificent in the dark. The Republic Palace on the other side of the Spree, lit up by 10,000 high-powered light bulbs, looked like a giant jewel. Berlin was wearing sparkling diamonds. It was the museums and palaces that gave Germany and Berlin its splendor and its unique culture. It was at the same time cosmopolitan and subtle, modern and sacred. It reminds us that no matter how far humankind evolved, their past, their history remains their foundation, their most reliable launch pad. The magical light surrounding those palaces and museum was adding another layer to the shimmering profoundness of Berlin.

August 2014

Visiting Musical Genius W. A. Mozart

The small Airbus from the Air France tilted its wings to greet Saltzburg, a small city in western Austria located at the foot of the Alps the peaks of which are covered with snow all year, an ancient peaceful city like a flower growing in the countryside. Saltzburg Airport is named after Mozart, the musical genius of mankind. We "met" Mozart as soon as we arrived in Saltzburg, the hometown and birthplace of Mozart. The city is extremely beautiful; the main square park was named after Mozart. We placed flowers and bowed in memory of him in front of the quiet bronze statue of Mozart placed in the middle of the square with many other flowers from tourists who came here to visit him. The square is also full of flowers. The city is, as well. We met Mozart on the streets, in shops, on shirts, on hats and even on the balloons in the hands of children... Large number of tourists from all over the world come to visit Mozart's hometown; the city has only half a million people, but every year the number of tourists visiting Mozart's house and Saltzburg is up to a million people.

Mozart was born in this city where he learned his first notes and grew up as a chamber musician, composing and performing at the same time. As a musician, he and his wife, Anna Maria Walburga, lived in the 3rd floor apartment, number 9 Getreidegasse Street, owned by the restaurant owner. Mozart and his wife had been here for decades.

Throughout 200 years the lovely little house has been well preserved; a two-bedroom apartment with a living room, a dining room, a kitchen, and a working room where the musical genius composed his work. More than 600 manuscripts of Mozart are preserved here. There are also handwritten music by Mozart and some pictures of Mozart and his family. With great emotion, everyone watched with their own eyes the violin and clavichord (the piano today) that Mozart had used to play all night long to create heart-wrenching music. From this small room, one still seems to hear the melodious music of Mozart.

***

Leaving the city of Saltzburg that people still call the city of Mozart, we arrived in Vienna - the capital of Austria in a late autumn afternoon. It was cool, sometimes chilly winds blew to our faces, it felt like walking in the middle of Hanoi before the northeast monsoon. The leaves of the trees have turned purple and yellow, ready to fall to endure the harsh winter. On the balconies and in the streets, flowers bloom with many colors like innumerable dots of musical notes covering the beautiful city of Vienna. Just as in Mozart's hometown, in Vienna, we saw him in every part of the city, Mozart statues in restaurants and hotels, Mozart images printed on wine bottles, chocolate boxes and on souvenirs... We see Mozart everywhere. For the first night, the Austrian friends organized for us a music concert with several works by Mozart. Sitting in the theater named after Mozart, in the middle of the capital of Austria, watching the performance of Mozart's "The Magic Flute", it was felt like we were lost in another world. A writer once commented that Mozart's music always embraces fresh, innocent, elegant, liberal, and harmonious emotions. Mozart lived in the eighteenth century, but his music is not academic. Without being restricted, it is always breaking and mixing vividly. Mozart's work was ahead of its time with a new style. His music is magnificent but yet simple and beloved...

The following afternoon, we asked to visit Mozart's final resting place. The Austrian friends were happy to take our request. Mozart rested in the cemetery of Saint Marc - a cemetery for the poor in the 18th century. Today it has been renovated spaciously and become a forest full of trees right in the center of Vienna. The gently sloping stone path brought us to the grave of the musical genius. On both sides of the road there were many wild trees the leaves of which had turned dark purple or bright yellow. An iron board with golden words engraved on a red background "MOZART" and an arrow led us to Mozart's resting place. His grave is unlike any other in the world. A stone pillar bears the inscription "W. A. Mozart 1756-1791" and, next to it, the statue of a prodigy with wings on his back; the grave is a field of bloody red flowers, in an upper corner of which, close to Mozart's statue, is a cluster of yellow flowers. There are no built grave, no tomb, only flowers... Our first impression is that Mozart has left the world with the most beautiful "flowers" embodied by his wonderful works. And now standing in front of his grave, I find myself amid a field full of real flowers. Mozart gave both his soul and his body to life on earth. So sacred, so beautiful, so legendary! That poor musician struggled with poverty, severe illness and yet never stopped composing and creating art. He overcame all struggles to reach the pinnacle of musical world (especially symphonies and operas). During his short life, the genial Mozart composed 626 works, including 24 operas and 52 symphonies. Just think of it: such a colossal legacy as result of a 35-year long life! It is said that Mozart started composing music at the age of 6. The renowned Russian musician Tchaikovsky called Mozart "a luminous genius."

Wolfgang Amadeus Mozart was born in the ancient city of Saltzburg and lived and worked in the capital Vienna in the last years of his life. He passed away at midnight on December 5, 1791, after a long illness. A few days earlier, Mozart was still diligently reading to his pupil the notes that were dancing in his head for the song "Requiem". And, at his request, friends had rehearsed in his hospital room the draft of "Requiem", a piece of music Mozart wrote on the request of a courtier. Mozart listened and shed tears of emotion. He instructed the student with the ideas to complete the music exactly as he wanted. Mozart said to those closest to him: "Perhaps this Requiem I wrote for myself." Yes, this is the last work by Mozart and, several hundred years later, people still see Mozart's soul in this sacred sad music. On the last day, Mozart asked the conductor to play on the piano "The Love Song of the Farmer Papa Guéno", a song Mozart had composed at his peak. Mozart felt asleep ... and took his last breath amid the joyful and gentle music...

***

More than two centuries since then, many works have been written about Mozart, praising him as musical legends. It is said that when the car brought Mozart's coffin out of the estuary of the Stubentor River in Vienna, a fierce snowstorm came and the wind roared, throwing snow to the face of everyone. Not a single relative could take Mozart to his final resting place. Burial men rushed to bury him quickly in the snowstorm at the cemetery of Saint Marc today. When the storm was over, the whole cemetery was covered in snow. By the end of the winter, no one had found his grave and today no one knows exactly where he was buried.

Perhaps that is the reason why his grave was not constructed; instead it has a simple but cozy "flower tray" planted on it. The red and yellow petals are brilliant like musical book dedicated to life and the statue of Mozart, with the wings of an angel - the angel Mozart, the prodigy Mozart, the musical genius of humankind. I stood silently in front of

Mozart's grave and suddenly heard the melodious and mesmerizing music of Mozart; I felt like Mozart was still around, leisurely wandering in the garden and continuing to offer profound love songs to the world.

Spring 2003 - 2013.

The Western Corners

*I*n this memoir, I want to write about five special small countries that I had the opportunity to visit. These are the Vatican City, the Principality of Monaco, the Principality of Andorra, the Principality of Liechtenstein, and the Grand Duchy of Luxembourg. There are many small but beautiful and rich countries in the world. Right in the heart of Italy in Europe, there was one of the oldest countries in the world with only 300,000 inhabitants and an area of 61 square kilometers, which is the "Great Peaceful Republic," San Marino, stretching on the slopes of Mount Titano in eastern Italy. Unfortunately, I have not been able to visit this peaceful country.

THE GRAND DUCHY OF LUXEMBOURG

Luxembourg is the only grand duchy country in the world. Established in 1839 and in 1867, it was declared and recognized as an independent country under permanent neutrality at the international congress in London. However, in 1948, Luxembourg abandoned its neutral regime and became the Grand Duchy under a constitutional monarchy with the Grand Duke as its head of state and the Prime Minister running the Government. Located at the confluence of the Alzette and Petrusse rivers and sharing borders with Belgium, Germany, and France, it has developed heavy industry, especially the steel industry. In addition, the banking system of the country, due to its open mechanism, has become the focus of European and international enterprises and billionaires, yet this Grand Duchy has a population of only 437,400 people.

Luxembourg is at an average altitude of 330m above sea level; the capital city is also named Luxembourg which was founded in 903 and located on the riverside; at the beginning, the city started with only one castle and few trading points and population of several thousand people. The capital was developed along the riverbanks, then gradually expanded to the right and left banks of the river. The Luxembourg River is very deep and divides into two areas called upper and lower areas. That is why some people call it the Upper City and the Lower City. The Lower area is the economic center with many banks and busy commercial shops, far in the suburbs are the industrial parks... The Upper area has many monuments built in the 11th century located in the Kirchberg area, and many ancient palaces and castles built in the 15th century and also the immense forests... Later, the Upper City was expanded; more theaters and television stations were built, and the two cities were connected by long, high and beautiful bridges, bringing a charming and majestic feeling to the capital. Luxembourg has up to 110 bridges connecting the lower area and upper area; many people know Luxembourg as the city of bridges.

Despite the population of less than half a million people, they have their own language of Luxembourgers; however, they also speak both French and German. Street signs and billboards are mostly in French.

Luxembourg is small but located in the heart of the European community, on the road from the north to the south. And it houses many European Union's important agencies, such as the Audit Office, the European Investment Bank, and the European Court. Moreover, as a developed industrial and service country, especially in banking services, the GDP per capita of Luxembourg reaches 81,000 USD, the highest number in the world. Obviously, the country is small in area and population, but with the GDP of a giant. Luxembourg declares itself the grand duchy for these reasons.

We were standing at the foot of the sparkling statue of Princess Charlotte on top of a tower, looking down the river that flows through the city at a depth of 100 meters. Normally, this would be a rocky cliff, but Luxembourg has turned it into hanging gardens on the cliffs. The flower fields, fruit gardens, and roads crossing the riverbank have created a romantic village scene. In this Alzette valley, according to historians, there is an underground 23-kilometer tunnel built in 963, which is still intact. This is also a tourist attraction; on the world tourist map, the attraction called "The Hanging Garden" is this unique ecological area. Across the hill are magnificent ancient castles, and on the right lies the bridge named Grand Duke Adolphe, which is nearly 90 meters high from the river water surface. This was also the tallest and longest iron cable-stayed bridge in the world in the 20th century. The bridge is elegantly designed as if it wants to lift up the human soul to a new level.

Although Luxembourg is a small country, compared to other principalities, it is the largest country because of its larger land area and population and modern industry and services. The capital of Luxembourg gives visitors a sense of softness and a gentle impression of the deep river flowing through the city. Standing in the middle of the city, it is still able to see the high-class ecological area. And more than anywhere else, the Lion Luxembourg restaurant served delicious Moules dish. In Vietnam it looks like mussels in the river estuary. Moules in Luxembourg have golden fatty, and sweet meat dipped in chili sauce or mustard and served with French fries to create a special flavor. Eating Luxembourg Moules with German beer is such an interesting flavor. The Moules dish is especially delicious not only due to the processing method and being caught at the mouth of this river but also because of where it is served, in the middle of the city by the deep river with the tall grand duke bridge. I once stood on the bridge with my back towards the upper mountainside to look at the busy lower part of the city where there is also a fish market, one of the tourist destinations, suddenly realizing its magnificent development despite being such a small country in terms of geography and population. This makes perfect sense, if one country knows how to exploit its potential and has a mechanism to attract human resources, it will definitely achieve such magnificent development; and the living of people is also taken care of due to a small population.

***

VATICAN CITY-STATE

After days of visiting Venice and Verona, we stopped in Rome, the capital of Italy, with many relics from the glorious time of the Greco-Roman culture. We had the chance to visit the Vatican and stand in front of the main hall of the main cathedral; this smallest country in the world is located in the middle of the capital Rome, with an area of only 44ha, equal to our Sao Viet eco-tourism area in Phu Yen, but it is the heart of millions of believers all over the world and has a great influence on humanity, including the heads of state in some countries. The Vatican has connections to Catholic cathedrals in hundreds of countries.

Since the 4th century, the Vatican has been a large and prestigious place of the Catholic church, but it was not until 11 February 1929 that the Latéran agreement officially recognized the Vatican as an independent state under the absolute monarchy. The official name is Vatican City-State (Status Civitatis Vaticanae); it is called a City-State because the country is surrounded by stone walls built 100 years ago. The head of the city is the Pope. The Pope appoints the head of state of the Vatican as secretary of state. The whole Vatican City has 87 members of the monitoring agency and the armed forces with no more than 100 people. The main source of revenue of the city is from admission tickets and souvenir sales, but the Vatican is also a rich country thanks to donations from the global Catholic Churches and from the St. Peter's Foundation. It is said that the accumulated real estate value of the Vatican in the United States has reached 40 billion USD, if divided per capita by the population of 1,000 people of this country, each person already has 50 million USD.

The Vatican State is very small in terms of geography, but this is the Holy Land, the capital of Catholic Churches with magnificent and powerful influence not only in appointing cardinals but also in politics. The world today has over one billion Catholics in almost every country in the world, so it can be said that the Vatican is a borderless country, present all over the world; 35 Popes have been canonized. These canonized saints practice worship every day in the Vatican and receive a great welcome when visiting countries everytime.

The Vatican State is located on a hill just 60 meters above sea level. A long time ago, 2,000 years ago, there was a cemetery located in the Mons Vaticanus area. The Vatican State occupied only part of this hill. The Vatican field running to the Tiber River is not part of the Vatican. In the territory of the city, 23 hectares are used for the construction of beautiful and poetic gardens which were built in the renaissance period lifting up the magnificent beauty of the castles. Especially in the morning or evening, the Vatican is covered by fog, making the cathedrals stand out in the blurring garden...

In 326, the first Basilica and Constantine Square were built next to the tomb of Saint Peter. People began to live around the square, and the first priests came here and founded the Cathedrals that later became the Vatican City State nowadays. In the 16th century, the D. Regg Palace was built precisely with the participation of famous architects, painters, and sculptors such as Michelangelo, Raphael... Also, since the time St. Phero Church was built, it is said that it was here where St. Phero was nailed to the cross.

Palaces and Cathedrals are so splendid, magnificent, and majestic due to their ancient designs of Greek culture and sculptures. On the top of huge stone, pillars are marble statues of saints carved by artist Gian

Lorenzo Bernini. The strong attraction of the Vatican is the magic of religion and belief, but it is deepened by these wonderful sculptures. Covering the ceiling of the Sistine Chapel is a famous giant painting by the artist Michelangelo. This is the meeting place of the cardinals and also where the cardinals elect the Pope as the head of state of the Vatican. Every time a new Pope is elected, white smoke rises from the chapel's roof to announce the good news to everyone. According to religious custom, this is also the signal to heaven...

Vatican City was built in the shape of a wine bottle. From the entrance are rows of solid and splendid houses, which is also the bottleneck of the great "wine bottle." Behind the magnificent cathedrals are the residence and living quarters of the priests. Not far from the Vatican is the Palace of Castel Gandolfo, also called the summer residence, which is also considered the land of the Vatican state.

Arriving at the Vatican, the quietness and majesty were exalted by the guards. The Vatican guards are recruited from good-looking young men; they wear uniforms of armor weighing up to 35kg, holding shields and halberds, and wearing iron hats with red feathers like the combs of roosters. The unchanging criteria of this army must be Swiss, Catholic, at least 5 feet 7 tall, and well-trained in martial arts. This army originated from the volunteer of the Alps dating back to 1400, who worked as security guards in the courts. In 1503 this army was officially hired by the Vatican. The soldiers were tall, carrying imposing posture and serious expression on their faces.

When it comes to the Vatican, people think of it as an architectural work of art, as well as a cultural center due to its museums and libraries. The library is keeping one million works, especially, including 60,000 original handwritten works and 100,000 autographs. The library also has 100,000 engravings of maps of countries, especially the first prints of the printing industry in the world.

The Vatican has its political newspaper Osservatore Romano founded in 1861, and a radio station broadcasting in 33 languages worldwide. The Vatican Museums are also unique because it also houses valuable collections of paintings and statue from the renaissance period.

It is because of that unique culture and fine art that in 1984 the Vatican City State was recognized by UNESCO as a world cultural heritage.

Visiting the Vatican, besides feeling the sacredness of spirituality and religion, we will clearly see the splendor of the architectural works and the great preservation of the culture from the ancient renaissance period. These factors create the solemnity and calmness of the Vatican.

***

LIECHTENSTEIN PRINCIPALITY

From Italy, we passed the Alps and crossed Switzerland into Austria to return to Germany. The dim night from the remaining sunset, the wind was strong, and the snow was flying like white silk ribbons in front of the car. Our car drove through the snowy fields. My friend suddenly came up with the idea of visiting Liechtenstein, the most expensive tourist destination in the world. At night, the Rhin River running parallel to the highway was dimmed in snow and fog, and some parts of the river were frozen. We stopped at the capital named after Count Vaduz, who gave birth to this beautiful country. I could not have imagined that in the snowy Alps, there would be such a brilliant city.

While waiting for the restaurant, my German friend and I went for a walk. Ms. Liva, a woman with white hair and a friendly smile and also a travel agent, happily approached us. Even though she knew we were just stopping by, she happily introduced Liechtenstein to us. Liva opened the map to show us our location and enthusiastically introduced this beautiful country.

Liechtenstein, located in the valley of the Alps, was founded in 814 and was not established as a principality until 1719, the smallest German-speaking principality in the world. The whole country has only 35,000 people with an area of 160km^2 – in which more than three-quarters of the country's area is the mountains of the Alps. The Rhin River runs along the border between Switzerland and Liechtenstein, creating green fields surrounding the city.

Liechtenstein is a constitutional monarchy headed by a prince; the country has no military but has diplomatic relations with nearly 100 countries. Tourism is still the largest source of income, contributing 50% of the wealth of this Principality. Looking up at villas and castles on the mountainside, she said: All these properties are for tourists and those villas must be booked 6 months in advance. Those are fairy mansions in a private world. The cost for one night in this villa is up to 4,000 pounds (equal to over 130 million Vietnamese Dong). I imagined sitting on the balcony of that mansion, looking back at the snow-capped Alps, with the fields, winding roads, and the clouds flying around the castle below; it is such fairyland.

A small country located between Austria and Switzerland with a population of only 35,000 people, yet 15,000 foreign companies have invested in this country and exploited the tourism industry. The mountain and skiing tourism service has brought this Principality to the top of the world in terms of income per capita ($54,000/person/year).

In the morning, the sun rises, and the snow is like a giant mirror reflecting the sunlight, making it brighter but not too hot. We stood in the courtyard of the small hotel overlooking the Rhin. This is the upstream of the river. We have seen the Rhin River from Lake Bodensee in three countries: Austria, Switzerland, and Italy. It flows through the high mountains between Switzerland and Austria, then turns north and runs parallel to the highways in this beautiful country. It was cold; even though it was sunny, the snow still did not melt, and the surface of the river was still frozen, making the Rhin look smaller. We drove along the Rhine, heading north to Germany.

Goodbye, little but great Liechtenstein.

***

MONACO PRINCIPALITY

Unlike Liechtenstein, Monaco is a Principality that I have visited many times. Once, my friends and I crossed three tunnels through the mountains to visit the Italian city of Monaco, which was 16 kilometers from Monaco. That time was very fun; the women in our group stopped at an Italian store to buy clothes that were good in quality, beautiful style, and reasonable price; everyone bought 4-5 things like pants, skirts, and shirts as gifts for their relatives at home. When getting back to Monaco, they took a closer look at the goods and saw the label Made in Vietnam. Going halfway around the world, buying gifts back to Vietnam, it turned out that we bought Vietnamese goods according to EU standards. Everyone laughed in tears. Such confusion and yet meaningful surprise when visiting Monaco.

Monaco, looking on the map, is like a walrus lying on the shores of the Mediterranean Sea – with an area less than the size of a commune in my hometown. That's right, Monaco is less than 4 kilometers long and 200 meters wide with a population of 30,000 people, making it the top two smallest countries in the world, along with Vatican – Half of two square kilometers of Monaco area are cliffs, steep rock, and the hill where the Alps reflect itself into the ocean. Monaco lies neatly within France on all three sides: North, East, and West; only the south reaches out to the Mediterranean. Monaco does not have fields or gardens, but on that mountain, there are still green, flowers and fruit. From a long time, Monaco has been famous for centuries for its glorious beauty and is more famous as a gambling paradise. In Monaco, the casino is called Monte Carlo which has become the favorite saying of people for a while. Monte Carlo Casino has palace-style architecture, a bell tower, and sophisticated carvings, creating a dignified and splendid appearance in the style of a French castle. It is the splendor of the castle and the classy services that make it not just an ordinary casino. Casinos account for 75% of the total income of the country, with the rest from tourism. There are many places to visit in Monaco. France is the land of palaces, but Monaco is the place of sifting different types of palace architecture. The Grimaldi is the representation of the jewel on its sifting. Today the Royal Palace Grimaldi is a botanical museum. The palace was built in the 16th century but still retains its reverent majesty, especially the medieval towers. The Principality of Monaco is like a great park on the Mediterranean coast, captivating people's souls. Two rocky hills head out to the sea, forming the main bay of the city, which is home to many most luxurious yachts in the world. The Oceanographic Museum is located on a very steep mountain that can only be reached by elevator. The Duke of Monaco has dedicated his life to building this three-story museum on top of this seaside mountain. In particular, there is an 8-meter-high stone pillar engraved with the names of ocean surveyors whose names have been honored by world history. Monaco is famous for its La Condamine yacht harbor. We can see here hundreds of yachts parked close to each other. Many yachts cost hundreds of millions of dollars. Monaco is brilliantly beautiful thanks to gardens full of flowers, such as the Japanese garden, Rose Princess Grace, Saint Martin Gardens, and Font Vieille Garden. People lined up in front of the palace to watch the guards change, then turned to the small streets at the top of this mountain to buy souvenirs. In Monaco, land has multiple uses as this is where the most expensive land in the world is. Yet, there are up to 23,000 wealthy foreigners (including some overseas Vietnamese) coming to Monaco to buy a weekend house or do business. Monaco has only 5,000 original people. Monaco is also home to annual F1 sports car races and underwater sports competitions. These competitions have contributed to promoting and attracting visitors to Monaco.

It seems that this country is just a gambling paradise and a land of entertainment. But it is not the case; the education system is prioritized by the state, and learning is compulsory. With only 36,000 inhabitants, the country has 10 public schools from kindergarten, elementary to high school, one technology training school, and one hotel vocational school; Monaco also has two international private schools, an international university (IUM), and an English school.

We sat at Le Cafe de Paris restaurant in the center of Monaco to see the Monaco sea and review the best of Monaco. This is the smallest country which has the highest population density, good climate, and highest average life expectancy in the world (90 years old), among the top of highest GDP per capita, has the most expensive land, and lowest percentage of indigenous people (7.2%), is home of many millionaires in the world and openest banking mechanism, also the largest gambling paradise, and finally the most beautiful eco-city in Western Europe.

***

ANDORRA PRINCIPALITY

From the south of France, we entered the country of the world's famous football team Barcelona (Spain), heading to the west and then crossing the mountain to head back to the north to enter Andorra. Climbing from this pass to the other, from the height of less than 10 meters, we gradually reached the height. After 3 hours of driving up, we reached the capital of Andorra, Andorra la Vella, at an altitude of over 2,000 meters. The autumn weather was cool, looking up at the snow-capped peaks; in the summer, the temperature is 18°C during daytime and 8°C at night. Mount Pedrosa is 2,946 meters high, the highest mountain in this country.

It is interesting, located between two big countries, France and Spain, between the high mountains, there is such a small, beautiful and modern country.

According to legend, more than 1,000 years ago, the Moroccan army invaded Spain. The Catalan tribe in the Urgell region bravely fought the invaders and successfully protected the country, so in 805, Charles the

Great gave the privilege of establishing independent Andorra, which was headed by the lord of Urgell. For more than 1,200 years, this country has always been peaceful land without war.

Andorra became an independent sovereign state under a parliamentary democracy but still recognized the French president and the bishop of Seo de Urgell (Spain) as the co-kings. Andorra is a 100% mountainous country, with 7 cities located in valleys at altitudes above 1,500 meters. The Madrid-Claror-Perafita valley in East Andorra is a typical valley with an area of nearly 10% of Andorra's area (42km2), which is a watershed forest, being covered in snow all year round and is a paradise of precious rare wildlife. It is the primeval forest recognized by UNESCO as a world heritage site.

In the capital Andorra la Vella, translated in the language of the Catalan people, Andorra means old woman. Maybe this name was called when the city still had few people and streets, but today this capital city is so interesting, young and modern civilized city. A city with a population of 50% of the country (33,000 people) but there are more than 50 hotels, many of which belong to international hotel brands such as Central, Paris, Ibis, Holiday Inn, Mercure, Novotel, and President. The city has only three major highways running in the north-south direction and several streets crossing the solidly built houses. The city has 10 modern 30-story buildings, especially the new splendid Caldea area with a giant pyramid-shaped glass building where the largest spa and fitness area in Europe is located. The Valira River flows from the high mountain, running down from the east and the northwest and joining before heading to the south of the city, creating the poetic charm of the capital. Valira River flows along the national highway to Spain. Two beautiful bridges crossing Valira add to the beauty of Andorra's capital. The city has only a few dozen traffic police, no prison, and no army, and the city is known as the safest city in the world. In the cold season, you can open a public faucet to wash your hands with hot water when being outside. Andorra tap water, including taps on the roadside, is filtered to pure and drinkable.

Andorra is divided into 7 regions: Saint Julia de Loria, Escaldes-Engordany, Encaup, Carillo, Ordino, La Massana, and the capital Andorra la Vella. In each region, there are large skiing areas with a busy cable car system. Andorra is not only an attractive place for skiing and climbing but also a place for training and winter sports competitions.

In this small Andorra, there are famous resort villages and skiing resorts. It is known to skiers that the Grandvalira sport tourist area was merged from Pas-de-la-Casa and Soldeu to become a giant sports area that is in the top 50 largest ski sports areas in the world with a length of up to 200km.

We also can visit Arinsal village, one of the most attractive tourist villages in Andorra due to its traditional architecture, a civilized and ecological tourist village located in the complex of Vallnord tourist sports area.

There are many such areas in Andorra, and visitors from all over the world come here in both summer and winter for skiing, hiking, and relaxing...

Andorra has a special mechanism: tax-free, visa-free, and secured and confidential banking services with many major bank branches located here. The whole country lives mainly in service and tourism services - the shops in the streets are full of imported goods from other countries at attractive prices. As a result, Andorra attracts many tourists – it is estimated that every day there are almost 30,000 tourists, roughly the same population as the capital. It is calculated that each person in Andorra welcomes 152 tourists annually (ten million visitors per year). Agriculture accounts for only 2%, mainly for flowers and vegetables. One time, I visited an Andorra businessman whose house was halfway up the mountain with an icy road. The villa has luxurious gold-plated handles frames. Every room has a flashy golden appearance. Unlike Monaco, land and housing here are not very expensive, and Andorra is one of the countries with very high income per capita, with an annual average of 38,000 USD per person, ranked among the highest in the world. It is included in the list of developed countries by the IMF. Andorra is a country with a good climate and clean environment, so the average life expectancy is very high, among the top in the world. Currently, the average life expectancy in the world is 67.2 years old. Vietnam ranks 65th with an average life expectancy of 74.2; Japan 82.6; France 80.7; United States 78.3; Monaco reaches 90 years old, while in this Principality, the average life expectancy is 83.52 years (86.59 years for women).

I have met here the gentle people of Andorra, who speak Catalan, French, Spanish, and English. Regardless of the language, they are sincere and hospitable. In the middle of the pass, we met a girl riding a very large black horse; we stopped the car and asked whether we could take a photo of her. She was very happy, riding the horse and standing in the middle of the pass with the vast and majestic mountains behind; she thanked us after taking the picture. We asked her: "We should thank you, why are you thanking us? She said: "Because you came to my country, and you also bring our pictures back to your country, thank you very much".

It is the language of a tourist paradise, green tourism, and civilized tourism.

We left Andorra on a beautiful sunny morning. When coming to Andorra, we climbed the mountain from Spain in the south and left Andorra through the Highway 02 down the mountain to France in the northeast. The road passes through many mountain slopes at an altitude of over 2,000m with clouds floating around, there are many continuous bends and turns, but the road is in very good condition. The waterfalls along the roadside look like the silk ribbons waving goodbye to us. Goodbye, Andorra, a small but very beautiful and civilized country; a country like other small countries is reinforced by the consensus of each person, sometimes that consensus is just a smile or a gentle, elegant handshake... These small countries, despite its difficult geography, have followed the right direction and breakthrough mechanisms, so they have spectacularly achieved extremely unique results.

Goodbye Andorra, goodbye small and beautiful country of the west.

24 June 2014

From Copenhagen To Bodensee

COPENHAGEN AND THE MERMAID

We landed at Kastrup airport in Copenhagen, the capital of the Kingdom of Denmark. Copenhagen is located on three islands connected by sea tunnels and historic bridges. Copenhagen is the land of history, prehistoric people have been here, leaving traces from the Neolithic period, and Copenhagen emerged from a village 1,000 years ago. At that time, it was named "Havn," meaning the dock, because it was just a small seaport for boats to dock. In 1167, Episcop Absalon built a wall around Havn and a fortress. Absalon expanded Havn into a large port named Copenhagen. Originally in ancient Danish, "Kopmannehafin" means "merchants' port," translated into English as Copenhagen. The city is located on the North Sea coast, an important hub connecting the Northern and Central of Europe, and thus becomes the capital of the Kingdom of Denmark. Copenhagen is a busy city and has been the modern industrial center of Denmark since the 20th century. Coming to Copenhagen, besides airplanes, cars, and trains, people also travel by boat. All vehicles and trains have to cross the longest sea-crossing bridge in Europe. One of the top 10 bridges in the world is the Great Belt Bridge, connecting Copenhagen with the island of Sporo and the Danish city of Funen. It runs for 8 kilometers at the altitude of 254 meters, perhaps the most spectacular sea-crossing bridge in the world. Trains from Germany to Copenhagen also have to cross this sea-crossing bridge, and when they arrive, the train gets inside the ship, and the guests just change their means of transport to continue the journey to the North Sea. The Copenhagen Sea is at a higher latitude than London and many cities in Russia. Still, the weather is warmer because of the Gulf stream, so the Copenhagen Sea is always warmer than the seas of the North. Therefore many kinds of birds gather here. Denmark has multi-branched antlers living in the dense forests and mountain slopes, typical of this country. People here prefer to travel by bicycle, by boat, and on foot rather than by car, so they call Copenhagen a green city. My best friend Le Manh Tuan and I have known each other since he worked as a secretary for

Comrade Vo Van Kiet while I worked as an assistant to Lawyer Nguyen Huu Tho. After that, he was promoted to Director General of the International Cooperation Department at the Government's Office. Later on, at the age of sixty, he was appointed as the Ambassador of Viet Nam to Denmark. Mr. Tuan and his wife picked us up at the airport and took us on a tour of Copenhagen. The most interesting to me was the ancient forest in the middle of the capital, and the roads were the tributaries that ran between the streets. The most beautiful scenery is the straight Nytory Canal, with townhouses on both sides. At sunset, the silver light of the Nordic sky elevates all kinds of lights, illuminating the restaurants and shops along the banks. Guests take the boat and stop at each shop; there is also a restaurant on board. This is the street with the oldest houses in Copenhagen. Standing on high buildings, looking down at Copenhagen, you can see the bridges connecting the islands and connecting parts of the country going further, winding, crossing the sea. Mankind is so astonishing: they have turned such a wild sea into a country whose GDP is among the top of the world, a country where people have prosperous and affluent life, a country being called paradise.

Le Manh Tuan and his wife took us to Langilinic port to visit the city's famous mermaid. I imagined a giant statue, but in fact, she was surprisingly small. Near the rocky shore, a mermaid sits modestly in the corner of the port, a shiny bronze statue overlooking the sea. She is only 4 feet 1 but weighs 175 kilograms. In 1913, the statue was inaugurated after four years of construction. This famous statue was made by sculptor Edward Eriksen at the commission of Carl Jacobsen, son of the founder of the famous Carlsberg brewery. Why did Carl Jacobsen order the statue of a mermaid? Le Manh Tuan and I determined to find out. It is said that he was so much in love with the story Little Mermaid by the great Danish writer Hans Christian Andersen, which is loved by millions of children worldwide. Another source was more specific, saying that in 1909 he saw the musical adaptation of Andersen's "Little Mermaid" at the Royal Theater of Copenhagen. The mermaid was played by the famous ballerina Ellen Price. He was so fascinated that he decided to commission a mermaid statue sitting on a rock near the sea as a gift to his hometown. He also asked sculptor Eriksen to invite actress Ellen Price to sit as the model. Unfortunately, she only agreed to model her face. Therefore the statue's features were sculpted after the ballerina, while its body was based on the sculptor's wife, Eline Eriksen.

On August 23, 1913, after nearly 4 years of construction, the bronze statue "The Little Mermaid" was officially inaugurated by the city council in the presence of all distinguished guests. Carl Jacobsen was very satisfied. A year later, he passed away, leaving a legacy for his hometown. Every year more than a million people from five continents visit the Little Mermaid.

In August of 2013, by chance, I watched the 100th anniversary of the "The Little Mermaid" on television, and was impressed to see 100 female athletes in mermaid costumes forming the number 100 in Langilinie seaport. I found myself revisited by fond memories of Copenhagen, of my friend Le Manh Tuan, and of the beautiful and affluent North Sea.

BODENSEE LAKE

To My Hanh handed the wheel over to Nguyen Van Trung, who drove the car through the snowy fields heading to Austria to visit the famous cable car company Doppelmayr. We traveled in the middle of winter, when both sides of the road were full of snow, covering the tops of trees, mountains, and hills that our car passed through. At night, the light was dimly mixed with the white of the snow, creating the cold color of winter. Finally, we arrived at Dornbirn, a small Austrian town located on Bodensee Lake, which is in the territory of three contiguous countries. Friends from Doppelmayr were waiting for us. Knowing that we came from the easternmost part of the world, the hosts welcomed us with the sound of drums and piano. Entering the company's Hall of Fame, we were warmed up by the energetic music and drum beats. The barbecue served with local wine oozed a typically European flavor. The person who welcomed us was a lady from the Doppelmayr family. We were delighted to learn that we were the first Vietnamese to visit Doppelmayr, and the Vietnamese flag would be added to the company's guest list. By 2013 Doppelmayr cable cars had been operating in Vung Tau, Ba Na, Da Nang; and the company was cooperating with Sun Group to construct the longest cable car lines in the world in Phu Quoc, Ha Long, and Fansipan). The host shared with us that we were sitting on the shore of Bodensee Lake, a great lake in Europe. The following day, the host took us through many tunnels through the mountains to take Doppelmayr's cable car to the snowy Alps, the mountain range running across seven countries and considered Europe's roof. In

Austria, you can encounter tunnels going through the mountains everywhere: they build tunnels just like we build bridges. It can be said that tunnels and cable cars are Austria's specialties.

After returning from a skiing resort in the Alps, in the afternoon, we had the chance to visit Bodensee Lake. As vast, peaceful, and quiet as the sea, its shores were still covered with snow. Rows of oak whose branches had been cut to help them survive the winter were standing leisurely in the snow. The lake's surface was calm and covered with a gentle mist. They said the lake accumulated heat in summer and released it in winter, so the climate here was not too harsh. Flocks of wild birds and ducks were still swimming, creating ripples like a masterpiece painting.

Bodensee Lake stretched across three countries Germany, Austria, and Switzerland. The lake's shore ran long in Germany at the north, including across the city of Lindau, a major town in the state of Bavaria. Bodensee Lake is also known as Constance Lake or Baden Lake, depending on which country you are in. The lake is at 395 meters above sea level and is located at the foot of the Alps. It has an average depth of 90 meters, with the deepest point of 254 meters. The lake is part of the upstream of the Rhine River which is 1320 km long and flows across many European countries. Some say that Bodensee Lake flows into the Rhine, while others say the Rhine River flows into Bodensee Lake. But it is more accurate to say that the lake flows into the Rhine during the rainy season, and in the dry season, water from in the reverse direction. Bodensee Lake has an impressive depth among the European lakes, and is also one of the continent's largest lakes with an area of over 570 square kilometers. When the wind is strong, the sound of waves lapping on the shore is just like sea waves. A Vietnamese Buddhist upon visiting the lake wrote this poem:

Waves of Bodensee

Call for a traveler

From the previous century

Whose song stirred the night.

It was winter but sunny at noon with blue sky and white clouds. The clouds were like smoke, breaking and gathering to form extraordinary images.

On the lake there were thousands of boats in many colors - blue, white, and stripes, most of which carried the flags of the three countries. Whether it was a sailing boat or passenger canoe and speedboat, they had their own flags. The nationality of the ship was revealed by the flag. Ships from Germany, Austria and Switzerland sail borderless here. Switzerland is a European country but entering Switzerland requires a visa. We once went from Como Lake in Italy to Germany through Switzerland and had to wait for a few hours at the border to apply for visa. However, in Bodensee Lake, they can travel freely. Many luxury boats, each worth hundreds of thousands of dollars, were gliding on the lake. I found many sailboats similar to those in Central Vietnam.

Bodensee shoreline is hundreds of kilometers long, it ran across the three countries with many big cities such as Bregenz in Austria, Romanshorn in Switzerland, and Lindau, Meersburg, Vonstaz, and Friedrichshafen in Germany, and nearly 50 smaller towns. Each city had its own festivals and activities, contributing to Bodensee Lake's richness and vibrancy. The famous Tuning Car Festival was held regularly in the city of Friedrichshafen, Germany. Thousands of cars from all over the world participated in the festival and there was even a beauty queen vote. Each contest had 500 participants and one would be selected as Miss Tuning Bodensee every year.

AND MAINAU – THE FLOWER ISLAND

Nguyen Van Trung and To My Hanh took us to Mainau Island, which was located on a corner of Bodensee Lake. We boarded an old Austrian steamboat. The ship sailed along the shoreline to the southwest of the lake, gliding along a mountainside filled with vineyards. It took more than an hour to travel 40 kilometers to reach Mainau Island in Konstanz in Baden state. The Bodensee Lake has three large islands, Lindau, Reichenau and Mainau, but only Mainau is hailed as the island of flowers. Nguyen Van Trung said it was the most beautiful flower island in Europe, which I did not believe at first.

When the ship docked, right at the harbor, we saw brilliant flowers, the road leading to the island ran under the canopy of large trees and lined with many wildflowers in a long road across the lake like a bridge. Visitors stopped by the shops to buy souvenirs and tickets. I went near a little boy who was feeding the pigeons with pieces of bread. Hundreds of pigeons immediately gathered for food and the boy found himself surrounded by pigeons and played with them delightfully.

I enterd the Mainau island, a paradise of flowers of all kinds. Flowers in the castle, flowers in the path, flowers in the park and even in toilets. flowers from grass, from tree, from vines, and flowers at the low and high points. Tulips with many vibrant red, pink, purple, and yellow colors. There are chairs placed in the middle of well-planted trees with only one entrance decorated by flowers, just enough space for a couple to sit down and confess their love. The island is located on the southern shore of the lake, near the Rhine River, at an altitude of 425 meters and only 45 hectares wide, but it is the land of flowers. There is park where the flowers are formed into many shapes including ducks, pheasants, and peacocks with their wings spreading. There are waterfalls and also the "waterfalls of flower", flowers flowing from high to low, just like a colorful waterfall from a distance. Some said this is a multicolored pearl, which may be true. On the island of Mainau, there is a tropical greenhouse with thousands of butterflies. I was lost in the world of fairy flowers and suddenly I forgot where I was. What Nguyen Van Trung said was true: it was not only the best in Europe but best of its kind in the world, the most beautiful ecological flower island.

Mainau Island is owned by the Barnadotte family. At the end of the 19th century, the Grand Duke of Baden abandoned his palace and bought this island to live with his lover. He only planted trees on the island and flowers around the house. His grandson, Prince Leunart Barnadotte, was dedicated to turn the island into flower paradise. In 1930, the Mainau flower island was opened to welcome guests. Every year, over a million visitors from everywhere visit the flower paradise, especially in spring, the most colorful season of Mainau island.

Trình Quang Phú

Venice – A Honeymoon Destination

After we left Berlin, Nguyen Van Trung and To My Hanh drove us across Germany, passing Hanover, Frankfurt, Munich. We then traveled southward through the west of Austria, covering over a thousand kilometers to reach Venice, the floating city.

After having lunch in Mestre, we crossed the road bridge Ponte della Libertà to arrive at Venice. This is a city with many names, from "City of Canals" to "Floating City," from "Land of Peace" to "Queen of Adriatic." But perhaps the most popular and precise name is "City of Love." Locating in northeastern Italy, Venice is a floating city with 117 islets connected by over 400 bridges and 150 canals. Tourists have to leave their cars at hotels to travel by foot or by boat in the city. Perhaps this is the uniqueness of this European city and what made Venice the ideal destination for honeymoon couples.

Venice was established in the fifth century, a city built by people who were resilient against foreign invaders. The earliest houses in Venice were built by driving stakes deep into the mud. Santa Maria Della Salette Church was built on the foundation of more than one million one hundred thousand wooden stakes plugged four-meter long into the ground. We wondered what happened to the stakes when the wood became rotten? How could it serve as the foundation of the houses? An expert explained: When the stakes were immersed in the mud and water, it would not be exposed to oxygen and would not be affected by organisms and bacteria. The saltwater turned the wood into hard stone. From the earliest houses, they proceeded to build mansions, castles and connecting islands to one another to establish this beautiful and unique city on the Mediterranean Sea.

We stayed at the four-star Rialto hotel on the banks of the Canad River, a renovated old building with a lot of furniture in the old Venetian style. It even had a canoe that transported us directly to Venice's Marco Polo airport and other places in this floating city. Four kilometers in length, the Grand Canal is the main street of Venice. It was a wide river boulevard that was voted to be the most beautiful in the world. As I stood upstairs and looked along the canal, I found out that the night light in this European city was not dark but silver, even though its was already 10 PM.

The fairy and beautiful streets of Venice were twinkling with colorful lights along the canals. The most remarkable building was a golden mansion (some called it the golden house) built of granite, its gilded patterns sparkling in the sunset. Nearby was the famous Rialto bridge for couples who came to confess their love. Cruise ships and small boats went back and forth as smoothly as if floating. Nguyen Van Trung ordered an antique Venetian boat to take us to dinner. This type of boat, known locally as gondola, was very popular in Venice. It seemed to float on the quiet river, passing under bridges and into small canals, where on both sides were streets and shops with the entrance facing the river. We climbed up and entered an Italian restaurant, ordered spaghetti and Italian seafood pizza. The owner revealed that the seafood was fresh from the sea. After a long journey across Europe, this was the first time I could enjoy seafood as fresh as my hometown Phu Yen. After dinner, we rode on the gondola to shop along the river.

In the gondola floating next to ours, there was a cuddling couple, the boatman wearing a Mexican wide-brimmed hat and a red scarf, crooning Italian folk songs in a low voice. His gentle lyrics were flying across the river full of lights. Venice was known as the major fashion and shopping center of Italy, offering everything from luxury brands to local souvenirs.

Our local friend said the annual carnival in February, after the New Year, was the city's biggest event, attracting many tourists worldwide. Everybody would wear colorful costumes and carnival masks, happily joining the stream of people on the streets and in the gondolas, as music resonated from street to street.

Around midnight, we returned to the ancient church Saint Mark, located in the same name square, the tourist center of Venice. It is said that the Church of St. Mark is one of the holiest places in the world. The square was crowded and full of pigeons. Professor Ngo Dat Tam and I stood still and held out our hands for the pigeons to sit on our shoulders and our arms, while casually calling their friends. I found my heart throbbing at peace thanks to serenity and holiness of St. Mark Square.

Venice is one of the most attractive city to tourists, with more than 80,000 daily visitors from all over the world. With 30 million annual visitors, while the population is only 270,000, each local receives 110 tourists per year. Following the statistic number, everyear the Italia tourism received over 150 billion Euro (equivalent 180 billion USD) in which the small city Venice contributed the amount of 100 billion USD per year.

What do visitors like? Entering old buildings and buying gifts that had stories so interesting that everyone wanted to bring them home as souvenirs. Goods from both local and big brands were available, along with many attractions, historical sites, and religious monuments. Spirituality and romance are cleverly exploited to attract tourists. It was expensive here, but tourists were satisfied. Friendly people and excellent service were among the factors that drew tourists here and persuaded them to return. Venice is a worldwide favorite destination and it was truly a city of love and the honeymoon destination of newlyweds.

As I walked in Venice at high tide, when the water rose to the road, I thought about the rivers and seas in my hometown. Vietnam has thousands of kilometers of coastline, many beautiful lagoons and bays and many islands. The archipelagos in Ha Long, Kien Giang, the big islands like Phu Quoc, Con Dao, Phu Quy, Ly Son, Cu Lao Cham... and the Hon Ngu, Hon Nua, Hon Mat, Con Co, Hon Chua, Hon Nua in my hometown. Venice was a valuable lesson for us to envision the future picture of Viet Nam's sea and island tourism in the 21st century, as well as to cope with climate change.

Verona, The City Of Love

As we left Venice, the islands of lovers, Nguyen Van Trung drove us to the northwest to Verona, then back to Como, from where we would cross the snow-white Alps to enter Switzerland and reach Germany.

The Verona stop was not long but its memories were unforgettable.

Verona is located in the north of Italy, where the river Adige runs from the Alps across the city and meets the sea southward. The Adige, with fifteen bridges connecting its eastern and western banks, brings the city's narrow streets and old villas a unique tranquility. The residents like to paint their houses in pastel pink and hang baskets of violet flowers on the balcony, which makes those buildings even more charming in an old-fashioned way. The serene river flows quietly, serving as an excellent background for Verona's antique and friendliness.

The Venetians are always amicable, they greet us with delight and say goodbye with nostalgically. I encounter their smiles everywhere in the city; it reflects the city's millennia of civilization. The Venetians' civility, the antiquity of the bell towers, the streets and the riverside trees all carry with them the ancient Roman and Medieval Renaissance civilizations, both well preserved in this city. Probably that was Shakespeare found here the inspiration for many of his plays, including the famous tragedy *Romeo and Juliet*.

We stopped at the Roman arena in the center of the city. I had been to Rome's millennia-old Colosseum, but I was still astonished by Verona's old arena. It can accommodate tens of thousands of people like a modern stadium. It was built in the first century AD, which means it is already 2000 years old. The roman Empire built many arenas for sports, bull flights, horse races, and other entertainments. As we stood there, it gave us a better understanding of the Roman civilization, and it surprised us even further that a two-thousand-year-old architecture is still being preserved and in operation.

The arena was built in pink marble at 140 meters in height. It has 64 entrances at three stories, the highest of which collapsed in the earthquake a thousand years ago. The other two remain intact and can house 30,000 people. It has been used as a theater for nearly a hundred years, with outdoor performances all year round. My local friends said the best season for the theater is between June and August. Operas, concerts, rock and pop shows by famous artists such as Pink Floyd, Whitney Houston, Sting, and Bjork usually occur here.

Verona usually hosts music festivals, many of which adopt love themes to further promote the city's reputation as "the City of Love." Tickets are sold months in advance and bought by many couples.

Verona also has many other worth-visiting destinations such as the old castle Castelvecchio, the basilica San Zeno Maggiore, and the garden Giardino Giusti with caves full of extraordinary stalactite. And one cannot forget the Piazza delle Erbe, one of Italy's most magnificent Roman squares. Therefore Verona has long been recognized by UNESCO as a World Heritage with great culture and tourist attractions.

At noon, the sun rose above our head, pouring the honey-like light all over the city, chasing away the gentle mist covering the city since early morning. This Alps plateau offered us unique sunlight, warm but not hot, like an invisible massaging hand, bringing a pleasant feeling to our skin. The golden sunshine made the dews on flower petals glitter like diamonds. The sunlight also made the favorite pastel pink of the Venetian walls brighter and warmer.

We had lunch in a riverside restaurant overlooking the river surface covered with sunlight. The gondolas typical of North Italy glided smoothly on the river, half-hidden in the lingering mist. Lovers were holding hands and listening to the boatman's love song, whose notes of present love were flying in the air. The riverside offered the best view of the city's ancient Greek architecture. My Hanh ordered traditional Italian dishes, such as seasoned Adriatic fresh mussels mixed with minced pork grilled on charcoal. The next dish was polpette – bread covered with sauteed eggplant with butter and mustard. Then came polenta, a cake made from minced baby corn mixed with cheese and Italian spices. The golden grilled polenta was served with an Italian soup. We skipped the famous Italian pizza and paired these dishes with a glass of Venetian wine. Dessert was a local treat offered by the owner: the pandoro, a must-have cake during Christmas and New Year.

Asked about Verona's number one specialty, the owner recommended dishes made from horse meat, a local favorite. He even advised us to avoid dishes whose names ended with *caval* or *Cavallo* because they may have a strange taste.

We thanked him and greeted him a Venetian farewell to visit Juliet's home, for which Verona has been known by the whole world as the Land of Love.

***

When I was studying literature at the university, I got to know about Shakespeare. In those days *Hamlet* and *Romeo & Juliet* had yet to be translated into Vietnamese. We had to listen to oral translations from French. Young as we were, we were deeply saddened by their tragedy. Here's the main plot: in Verona, there were two families whose rivalry had been passed over many generations, Romeo's Montague and Juliet's Capulet. It was destined that Romeo and Juliet fell in love with each other. They eloped to the basilica San Zeno to be secretly married by Priest Laurence. Then came an incident where Juliet's cousin Tybalt killed Romeo's closest friend Mercutio. Enraged, Romeo took Tybalt's life for revenge and was banished from Verona. Meanwhile, Juliet's parents forced her to marry Count Paris. The desperate Juliet came to Priest Laurence for help, and he suggested that she take a potion to fake her death, then wait for Romeo to come back and rescue her.

After learning of Juliet's death, Romeo secretly returned to Verona. When he arrived at the basilica Sanzeno, Juliet was still in a coma. Assuming that she was actually dead, the heartbroken Romeo committed suicide by poison. When Juliet woke up and saw Romeo's body, she also took her own life.

The Montague and Capulet families were reconciled by their children's death. They recognized them as husband and wife and co-organized their funeral. Since then many generations have been deeply moved by the star-crossed lovers' immortal tragedy.

That was the plot of Shakespeare's *Romeo and Juliet* tragedy, written in 1595, four centuries before our time. The story was set in the ancient city of Verona and based on a true story in an earlier narrative poem by Arthur Brooke.

Nowadays, in Verona, there is a world-famous building visited by millions, known as Juliet's house in English and Casa di Giulietta in Italian. Located on Via Cappello street, the house originally belonged to the Cappello family, who built it 700 years ago. In the early 1900s, the municipal government decided to purchase the house, which remained in excellent condition and turned it into a museum. In 1935, the movie Romeo and Juliet was screened, followed by many other adaptions, which increased the story's global publicity even further. Every tourist asked about Romeo and Juliet when they visited Verona. Upon noticing the similarity between Cappello and Capulet, the city decided to restore this 700-year-old building and named it Juliet's house.

We had no difficulty finding Juliet's house because direction posts were available everywhere. It was very crowded at the gate. I entered a small garden with pebble paths and full of green vines, where stood the statue of Juliet waiting for Romeo. She was the work of Nereo Costantini, who depicted her figure and costume as a typical Northern Italian beauty. She was five feet seven, absolutely charming in a long dress. The whole statue was in bronze with scattering green patinas, except her right youthful breast, which was golden and shiny, thanks to millions of touches by tourists worldwide. Nobody knows when this ritual started, but legend had it that Juliet was the God of Love, and if you touched her breast, your love would be blessed. We saw many couples, even some with grey hair, queuing and praying for everlasting love before faithfully touching Juliet's breast. They did believe in it, those followers of Love. They held hands, closed their eyes and prayed, gently touch Juliet's right breast, then wrote their wish on a piece of paper and pinned it on the wall. There was also a Well of Love nearby, where they put a lock with their names on it on an iron gate, then threw the key into the well. There's a famous quote written here, taken from Romeo's words in the play Shakespeare. "There is no world without Verona walls, Heaven is here, where Juliet lives." It meant to say the walls of Verona were everything to Romeo, and this place was heaven to her because Juliet lived there.

In the play, Romeo stood in the garden and confessed his love to Juliet above the window. But during the third renovation of this building, the city decided to build a two-meter balcony to suggest that Romeo had climbed up to kiss the girl, and they had sworn their eternal love to each other here.

Romeo and Juliet had four movie director: 1935, 1968, 1996 and 2013. Each time a film was made, it enhanced Verona's attraction even further. Verona adopted the slogan "City of Love" from this very house, from the tragedy of Romeo and Juliet. They came up with many creative ways to attract tourists from all over the world, which are worth learning and studying.

In the house, they hang antique paintings and furnished it with Juliet-era artifacts, such as beds, cupboards, tables and chairs. There was even a wardrobe containing Juliet's clothes and an original Medieval bed in Juliet's bedroom. Everything was absolutely fictional, but the followers of Love believed they were real, one hundred percent real.

In the 2020 Love Festival, the mayor of Verona said, "Juliet's house is a museum of great importance, which attracts millions of tourists each year. We are promoting the Shakespearean spirit and the legendary love of Romeo and Juliet in our unique, unprecedented ways. It makes the world understand Verona better and love it even more."

In the annual Love Festival, the luckiest chosen couple will be invited to spend one night in this house and have an ancient-style dinner. Many lovers are willing to pay to visit this ancient nine-room house of Juliet and end their tour by eternally sealing themselves with a kiss on the legendary balcony.

Verona invented many love-related activities. They chose 16 September as Juliet's birthday to breathe a new life into the city. And Valentine's Day of 14 February was of course very lively, with the festival lasting for days. It was called the Warm Valentine Season, although February was quite a cold month. The event was like a magic magnet that attracted people from all over the world to Verona. The city even organized a writing contest themed "Write for Love." This contest took little time to evolve into an annual international award for the best-written works on love. The prize would be awarded either on Valentine's Day or Juliet's birthday.

At Juliet's House, they established the Juliet Club with young volunteers who conducted various activities to promote the Romeo and Juliet legacy. The club even had a team called "Juliet's Secretaries," who, on behalf of Juliet, replied to thousands of letters sent to her from everywhere in the world in the last seventy years. Many of them were so beautifully written that they were selected for the collection "Letters to Juliet."

Each year, during the Love Festival, they presented awards to the authors of the best letters right at Juliet's House. In 2010 Hollywood even made a movie, *Letters of Juliet*, which told the story of an American tourist who visited Juliet's House and found a letter hidden under the floor, leading her through a journey full of romance and surprise. The movie gave Juliet's House and Verona a boost in attracting global tourists.

***

After leaving Juliet's house and throughout the way back crossing the Alps, I was deep in thought. Italy's annual income from tourism was 180 billion USD. The total population of Verona and Venice was only half a million, but at 130 billion they accounted for three-quarters of the country's tourism revenue. Which meant each person contributed 260,000 USD.

Viet Nam has a lot of mangrove forests, such as the historical Sac forest in Can Gio, which is very close to the center of Ho Chi Minh city. If a coastal tourism city could be developed there, it would be able to rival Venice. It is impossible to attract tourists and encourage spending without a long-term vision and a well-planned investment.

Having been to many countries, I have come to realize that Verona is not the only place that exploits the attraction of love. Venice is also called the islands of love. I have encountered trees of love and bridges of love in the former Soviet Union and Korea. Those places are always full of couples. They are unique destinations that foster and nurture love, not simply love for your lover but also for your hometown and your country.

I remember couples once came to a small tower near Hoan Kiem lake in Hanoi to leave their signatures or messages of love, but they were accused of vandalism. Why is there no statue of love or park of love in Viet Nam? In our country's great war, many lovers bid farewell to their other half to join the fight for national independence but did not return.

What if we build statues of love near the tunnels of Cu Chi? Or a park of love in Hanoi? It will promote our nation's legendary narrative, our larger-than-life story because the great sacrifice for love by many generations of Vietnamese youth certainly cannot be rivaled.

Once those statues are erected and those parks built, the Vietnamese youth will come, and the global youth will come. Millions and millions of tourists will come since such places always possess a magic appeal. Love will foster the endeavors in youth, while literature and cinema will give birth to new legends of love. The Vietnamese legends of love based on real stories in our great war will be beautiful, passionate, and heroic, thanks to the courageous sacrifice of our youth. Such sacrifice will sanctify the architectures, turning them into spiritual places for the younger generation to worship. We will be able to develop tourism and, at the same time, promote the education of traditions and foster love and loyalty in our youth. A faithful personal love will be a good foundation for a greater, divine common love for your country.

Ten Days In Cali

SAN FRANCISCO, THE CITY OF MIST

Vietnamese people living in the United States often call California Cali, as well as Los Angeles the city of Los and San Francisco the city of Sanfan. In this article, I also use the way the Vietnamese in the United States call these cities.

We arrived in Cali on a beautiful sunny morning in May. There was no direct flight by Vietnam Airlines; we had to transit in Taiwan in order to take Eva Air to fly to the country at 97th longitude of the Western hemisphere, 14 hours gap from Vietnam, which means that when Vietnam is daytime, Cali is at night.

We landed at the San Francisco airport at dawn. The fog was still covering the foothills of the mountains, painting fanciful and poetic strokes to the sky. San Francisco Bay is as calm as the lake. Sanfan Airport, located right on the shore of the bay is reclaimed land and also the largest airport in the Pacific region of the United States, welcoming up to 33 million passengers annually. Consul General of Vietnam in San Francisco, Le Quoc Hung and his wife, Do Nam Lien, and other officials of the Consulate General came to the plane to welcome us. Our nephew and niece, son and daughter of our cousin living in Cali, Xuan Thanh, Lam, and her husband Phan Ngoc, went to the airport to pick us up. It was so emotional that we felt warm in the chilly weather.

Le Quoc Hung and I were formerly diplomats at the Ministry of Foreign Affairs of the Revolutionary Government of the South; on this occasion, I was assigned by the Central Fatherland Front to Cali to meet with the Vietnamese community. Le Quoc Hung helped me understand more about this country on the other side of the hemisphere.

The city of San Francisco is located on the bay, with 50 hills with steep slopes, within the Sanfan Bay, creating the majestic landscape of this tourist city. San Francisco is smaller than Los city in the south, smaller than nearby San Jose and even San Diego. Still, Sanfan is the number one tourist city in Cali and in the United States.

In 1769, when the first Spaniards came to this land, they met the small villages of the Ohlone people. According to archaeological sites, humans resided in this land 3,000 years ago. Seven years later, the Spanish colonists invaded and built a military trope at the Golden Gate. It was not until 73 years later that the city began to be built, and then it became the largest city on the West Coast of the United States at that time. San in Spanish means Saint; this city was named after Saint Francisco from that day. At the beginning of the last century (1906), three-quarters of the city was burned down and destroyed in a terrible earthquake followed by a great fire. Nine years later, the new San Francisco was restored to be bigger and more beautiful than the old city, and opened the Panama-Pacific International Fair.

Sanfan has a cool climate thanks to the cold currents from the Pacific Ocean flowing into Sanfan Bay and three sides of the city adjacent to the sea; the cold and hot currents have created dense fog covering Sanfan. There are up to 100 foggy days a year, and clouds covering the mountain, creating poetic scenery. The whole peninsula is continuous steep hills; nature and people have created here an ecological region with great attractive landscapes. Therefore, Sanfan is the best tourist city and has strong attractions, ranked 35th in the top 100 cities with the most tourists in the world. In 2012, it welcomed 16.5 million tourists, earning 9 billion dollars.

Sanfan city has a strange architecture, both modern and friendly to nature, and is a very gentle, elegant, and peaceful city. Americans call it the Paris of the West Coast, and international visitors call Sanfan "The City of Mist" and "The City by the Bay. "Sanfan is a city suitable for people who enjoy walking. On the small streets, there are many restaurants, cafes and convenient shops. Many of them are open all night. Sanfan has the oldest and largest Chinatown in North America. There are also many Vietnamese restaurants here and many shops selling everything from small goods to high-end goods.

From Russian Hill with many skyscrapers, we went to Lombard Street. The road is only 400m long but at a steep slope of 27 degrees, the road zigzags back and forth, and cars only run at 5km/h and in only one direction of going down. The car runs slowly not only for safety reasons but also to enjoy the scenery of flowers. The roadside is full of colorful flowers and neatly green trees like in a Vietnamese village. From above,

Lombard Road looks like a giant python slithering between the flower hills. Visitors to Sanfan are curious to visit this Lombard Road.

Sanfan City has a long coastline running from the Pacific Ocean through the city center. Market Street is located right on the beach leading to Union Square, the financial center and shopping center of Sanfan. And next is the Fisherman's Wharf where there are specialty restaurants with seafood dishes such as big oysters in oil and famous Dungeness crab. From this coast, the cable car takes guests to the top of Mount Nob, formerly the living area of the rich, and then takes guests through the national park... Electric cable cars are the only means of transportation which are being allowed here. Sanfan beach is so buzzed with surfers. Baker beach is a quiet hiding place, an ecological area by the natural saltwater lagoon. Next to the Pacific coast is Golden Gate Park, one of the 220 parks of Sanfan. There are many large trees imported from five continents and also a zoo with more than 250 species of rare animals. The Marced freshwater lake is located in the middle of the park, creating a peaceful and ecological feature of the park.

At night we crossed the Bay Bridge on Sanfan Bay to go to the city of Oakland. The bridge is up to 14 km long - 58 to 67 meters high above sea level, which is a 2-story cable-stayed bridge (5 lanes on each floor). The car kept running. That night we met many people in the Vietnamese community and Sanfan officials who came to bid farewell to Consul General Le Quoc Hung, who was about to return to Vietnam. Sitting in the water house in the port of Oakland, in the gentle waltz music, looking at San Francisco over the bay, Sanfan clearly shows itself as an attractive peninsula. The city of Sanfan is illuminated by the lights, reflecting on the calm sea. The houses with all kinds of colored lights show themselves on the sea. I wish that peace would be forever for mankind, no war, no natural disasters, and for people to join hands to build and protect their beloved earth.

The next morning, we were taken to visit the Golden Gate Bridge. The bridge starts from the shores of Sanfan Bay to the Pacific Ocean. The bridge was built in 1937 by architect Joseph B. Trans and was the longest cable-stayed bridge in the world in the 30 – 40 years of the 20th century. It is calculated that the total length of all cables of the bridge is 128,000km. The bridge is painted in dark tangerine yellow - Americans call it International Orange. The bridge connecting the two peaks creates a grandeur and monumental landscape and becomes more lyrical because of the fog; sometimes, it looks like a white silk wrapping around the bridge. Visitors walking across the bridge at this moment are like being in a fairyland. Americans voted this bridge as one of the seven wonders of the modern world, and the Golden Gate Bridge was selected as one of the 14 most beautiful bridges in the world.

We went to the other side of the bridge, stood at the monument to commemorate the people who built this bridge and looked at the Golden Gate to see the whole city lying on the bay. Sanfan city in the morning sun stands out in pure white color, the deep blue sea, the white sails gliding and the speeding canoes drawing waves on the surface of the bay. I suddenly remembered the comment of writer Henry: "East is East and West is... San Francisco".

***

SAN JOSE, THE CAPITAL OF SILICON VALLEY

Phan Ngoc, my nephew-in-law, drove a Jeep to bring us to San Jose and will be the guide to take us to visit Southern California.

This was the first capital of California, founded by the Spaniards in 1777.

An area, or rather a valley in the south of the San Francisco Bay named after Saint Jose, it also has another name, the City of Yellow Flowers, because, during spring and early summer, the whole area from the mountains to the fields is brightly colored in the yellow of wild sunflowers, wildflowers and beet flowers, colza flowers which is made into cooking oil. The climate here is mild, with little rain and little humidity. It is a dry area, with up to 300 days of mild sunshine a year. Perhaps due to the suitable climate and terrain, since the 1970s, high-tech businessmen in the fields of electronics and information technology (IT) came here to set up factories. And very quickly, an area stretched from the southernmost tip of the San Francisco Bay to San Jose and later to the Scotts of Santa Cruz County, there are 20 cities in the IT development zone. An American journalist, Mr. Don Hoefler, in a series of reports on the IT boom, called this valley "Silicon Valley USA. "In the past, silicone was used in beauty salons for women's beauty purposes. Now the word silicon has become the word for this smart technology industry, common in the language of Americans and San Jose has a new name, "Silicon Valley."There are thousands of IT technology corporations in this valley, and many of them are at the top of information technology and electronics, such as IBM, Dell, Cisco, Google, Intel, Yahoo, Fry's Electronics, Hewlett Packard, and Apple Computer. The headquarters of the IT industry are located in San Jose, so the city of San Jose is called the Capital of Silicon Valley.

I had the opportunity to meet Russian-American billionaire Mr. Arthur Rock, who has persevered for 50 years in the pursuit and development of semiconductor technology as a pioneer. Formerly, his company cooperated with Davis (called Davis & Rock Company), then he opened his own company called Arthur Rock & Co., the leading semiconductor company in San Jose. He has the ability to recognize and forecast the feasibility of the market and make investment decisions very quickly. Asking him about the secret of success, he said: "The first is to have the will to overcome difficulties, the second is to understand the market, the third is the technology, and that technology must keep up with the times."

During the meeting with the Vietnamese businessman, I also had the opportunity to meet Cao Kim Vu, a beautiful, gentle and very sociable under 30 years old woman who is enthusiastic about community and charity work. She works as the assistant to the Vice President of Finance at Technology Credit Union (Tech CU) in San Jose, which is the leading financial company in Cali. She worked excellently, the President of Tech CU has commented on her as a brave, creative and flexible woman, and she was also selected as one of the 40 stars in this Silicon Valley. She told me: "Vietnamese people are diligent and smart. They have IT heads; therefore, Vietnam must be a place to develop IT" she wishes to have Silicon Valley in Vietnam.

San Jose city does not have many tall buildings but many trees, surrounded by mountains. Because it is the capital of Silicon Valley, the income per capita here is 96,000 USD/year, twice the GDP of the United States. San Jose is home to 100,000 Vietnamese people. There is one Vietnamese commercial center designated by the City Council as Little Saigon San Jose. Silicon Valley is a large area; the IT companies such as Google and Yahoo that we visited are located on the hillside full of green trees. The house of our nephew is also very open, with a small flower garden in front. San Jose also has the title of the safest major city in the United States.

I really like the San Jose ecoregions, but perhaps what I like more is that there are prestigious universities here, of which San Jose's Stanford

University is as famous as Harvard and Yale. Stanford University has trained more than 30 billionaires in the United States, including two co-founders of Google. The previous US Secretary of State, Dr. Condoleezza Rice, was a teacher and principal of this university for 6 years.

I deeply understand that: Without good people, there is no high technology. Machines and technology are just means for human.

LAS VEGAS - "THE ENTERTAINMENT CAPITAL OF THE WORLD"

We left San Jose in the early morning and headed south. Phan Ngoc drove the car while introducing our places along the way. The car drove through fields of the olive fruit. My favorite is the tangerines fields, ripe fruits are bright red and make the whole field bright. From afar, it looks like blooming flowers. The road to Las Vegas must run to the southeast, passing the Tahachabi pass, which can be called the forest of windmills. Thousands of windmills are located close together; from the foot of the mountain to the top, the wind blows the windmills. We got out of the car to take pictures and suddenly thought about our hometown. Vietnam, according to the World Bank, has 8.6% of its territory with wind power potential and with a capacity of 500,000 megawatts each year. It is calculated that 1 megawatt of hydroelectricity will take away 10 hectares of forest. If hydroelectricity is replaced by wind power, that half a million megawatts will save 5 million hectares of forest. My thoughts quickly brought me to Las Vegas, the capital of Clark County. This was originally a desert area; in the past, there was only a small train station as the stop for passing trains; later, people opened casinos, and in the early 20th century, there were only 2,000 people. The temperature here is quite fierce. In summer, the day is hot, with the temperature up to 45º; in the evening, it is cool at 21^0-25^0. But in winter, it is cool during the daytime and below zero degrees during nighttime, as cold as in the North Sea.

This land is in the state of Nevada, very close to the state of Arizona. I remember that in between these two states, there was the legendary Colorado River cutting through the rocky peaks that brought water from Lake Mead to the Hoover Dam hydroelectric power station. Standing in the middle of the Hoover Dam, on the left is the land of the state of Nevada, and one step further is to the land of the state of Arizona, so only one step makes the clock differ by 1 hour, due to the time zone of each state.

People call Las Vegas the entertainment capital of the world. That nickname called by the Americans is so true because the whole city is a city of tourism, entertainment, and gambling. Hotels are built close together from 4 to 5, even 6-stars accommodations. There are hotels like the pyramids of ancient Egypt, and others like walking in the middle of a tropical island. If tourists want to find the feeling of being in New York or in the US capital, there are hotels with such characteristics.

The Fortune 500, the world leader in casinos, has a large market share in Las Vegas. They built complexes of hotels, restaurants, shopping centers and casinos - each area has its own different way of entertainment and dining. Besides, there are villas, apartments and high-rise buildings. Each year, up to 25,000 new apartments are sold, which are for tens of thousands of employees working in Las Vegas. Villas are bought as weekend residences by rich people all over the United States... Each hotel and casino here is a miniature city that always provides food, accommodation and shopping services. Any kind of service is more expensive than in other places. Las Vegas was selected as one of the 10 best culinary cities in the world because it imported many culinary arts of mankind.

The casino also has its own nuances, such as Casino Luxor having the same architecture as the Pyramids in Egypt. Casino Wym has a water stage, where 50-60 acrobats perform in the air and in the water every night. Casino Paris has the Eiffel Tower and street musicians. Casino Venice is very unique because of its artificial river like the one in Venice. Hostels, restaurants and shops are located along these two small riverbanks. On the river, there are also Venetian-style curved gondolas carrying tourists. The ferryman also wears an old Italian-style wide-brimmed hat with a red scarf while rowing and singing Italian folk songs. Walking in Las Vegas on a summer night is interesting because of the cool weather and bright lights. Perhaps few cities have as many bright and colorful lights as here. Lights on the street, lights in hotels, lights on the roofs of high-rise buildings, lights on the goddess Venus, on the pyramids, on the Eiffel Tower...such the entertainment capital of the world. Mid-class and rich people come here to the cities and go shopping; the richest people come to gamble all night. Banks operate all night for gambling services. Many small planes of millionaire land at the

Las Vegas airport. They come here to gamble. Many people lost their fortune because of this gambling game. Las Vegas is also known as "Lost Wages," which means the city of "lost all wages" and "the land of no money." If it is a game of luck, then it is mostly bad luck, but people are still attracted by it and become addicted and burn themselves in gambling (!).

A FEW THOUGHTS ON CAM COUNTY

Leaving the capital of gambling, we returned to Cam County where there is a large Vietnamese community. The United States has over one and a half million Vietnamese or Vietnamese-origin people, and Cam County accounts for over 12%, which is the county with the largest number of Vietnamese and Vietnamese Americans in the United States. The Vietnamese have changed the face of this land. Restaurants, shops, and hotels written in Vietnamese with "pho," "hu tieu," "Quang noodles" can be seen everywhere across the streets... In the Saigon sub-area in Cam County, there are many commercial shopping centers, but the largest and most famous one is Phuoc Loc Tho area. In Cali, there are many strange things about buying and selling things that the women in our group are very interested in. For example, a pair of shoes of any brand bought in San Jose can be exchanged anywhere, in Cam County or in Los, as long as for the same brand. They even refund the difference in price in case you buy the goods at a high price and find them on sale after a few days. Also, I heard that some people take advantage of this policy, so they can buy the clothes, wear a few times and then exchange them for another type. Shoppers might love to shop in the US because of that.

I met many Vietnamese people here, some came to the US by crossing the border, and some went under the H.O category (the US Government sponsors people working under the regime of the Republic of Vietnam). Many people have returned to Vietnam and understand their homeland, but there are also some who have not returned to their homeland and lack information about Vietnam.

Mr. Trieu Phat, an American millionaire and owner of Phuoc Loc Tho in Cam County, is a Chinese-Vietnamese; he speaks Vietnamese like the locals, and he once joined as one of the leaders of the Republican Party. He understands Vietnam very well and is impatient about some stagnant mechanisms in Vietnam and is confused about education. He said: "The country has to take into account the next few generations; education and training are crucial matters because the children will be the masters in the future. With a good education, the people who serve the country will also be good." He has a daughter who is his assistant and takes care of the educational cooperation. He told me: "In this field, we will wholeheartedly support you."

I met Mr. Lanh, and Mr. Phuc, officers of the Republic of Vietnam who went under a re-education program and was sponsored by the US government to settle their living in Cam County. We got to know each other in Vietnam. I ask them why some Vietnamese people do not understand and support the country. They said: "Because they are not willing to understand."

Once my visit to a weekly Vietnamese newspaper, the Vietweekly, the chief editor invited representatives from some anti-communist newspapers and televisions in the community. The atmosphere was quite tense when we first met.

One said:

We used to be enemies; how can we talk?

I looked him straight in the eye and said:

I do not think there are any bigger enemies than the United States and Vietnam, during so many years of bombardment and fighting, it seems that there would be a lot of hatred. But as you see, the two countries have put aside the past and cooperated for development. You are Vietnamese; even if you have American citizenship, you are still of Vietnamese origin, speaking the same Vietnamese language, and you share the same root with us; there is no reason why we cannot talk to each other.

Then, we talked and shared our thoughts with an open mind, what they heard about Vietnam was mostly false and misleading information, such as the story of selling nylon instant noodles in Vietnam. We must explain in detail with sincerity. I asked a former commander under the government of the Republic of Vietnam, now the owner of a television company in Cam County:

- Do you think why some Vietnamese like you oppose the current political regime in Vietnam?

- Because the communists are not martyrs, forcing us to go to re-education.

- After liberation, if we do not request you to be gathered, will the people whose families are killed by you let you live? Did you know that people in the Central region executed some of your officers themselves? Gathering you first is to protect your lives, avoiding bloody execution. Unfortunately, at that time, the economy was difficult, and your life was not good.

- If an enemy like us returns to the country, will you ensure our safety?

- As Consul General Le Quoc Hung said when seeing you before. We ensure your safety when you visit your hometown and do not provoke politics.

Back and forth, at the end of the meeting, he shook my hand: "We have not returned to the country, so we lack information."

I ask him:

When President Nguyen Minh Triet visited Cam County, he met and had a conversation with overseas Vietnamese. Were you there?

He smiled honestly.

- I'm anti-communist, but I read about his talk with overseas Vietnamese in Cam County.

I laughed: Probably reading to fight us, right?

He laughed: Mr. Triet said, "The motherland is a kind mother."

- Yes, it is good that you remember that. The Mother always loves her children, right? I shook his hand.

A few months later, he returned to Vietnam and now his television company has provided a lot of truthful information about Vietnam.

The reason why many people do not understand Vietnam is partly because they are not willing to understand, but also partly because the country has not helped them understand properly. They lack information.

I am walking on a land where people deliberately do not want to understand the country and are ready to fight against their homeland. My heart is sad. In the evening, an overseas Vietnamese took us to visit Long Beach. The car ran along the long beach. In the flickering electric lights stretching over the waves, he talked about his boredom and dissatisfaction with his homeland. He talked about Vietnam today with many thoughts. Listening to my explanation, he finally lowered his voice: "Falling leaves return to their roots."

The war was over. I hope it has gone forever and there are no longer invasions or wars that cause unjust and meaningless deaths so that people can truly love each other, for nearly 5 million overseas Vietnamese to remember their dear motherland, their loved country, as the sweet star fruit of each expatriate.

... AND IN "THE CITY OF ANGELS"

The next day, our group arrived in Los Angeles, the largest city in the state of California. Los Angeles, in Spanish, is the city of "Angels."Los Angeles is also named "the diamond city of the gold coast."Like other cities we have visited, Los Angeles was the land of native Americans who lived thousands of years ago. The Spanish colonial invasion drove them out of the city. Currently, Los Angeles has people from 10 countries coming for business. Los Angeles is famous for Hollywood, the cinema center of the world. Standing in the center looking to the north, on the mountain of Cahuenga Passe, the words "Hollywood" are clearly visible on the green background of the mountains. Around 1883, a young couple who had to sit in a wheelchair determined to explore the new land and build an ideal residential area because there were lakes, mountains, streams, and beaches presenting there. A land of 50 hectares was built and named Hollywood. In 1910, a famous director D. Griffith came here to make the first movie. After that, many directors came to film the movie and after the movie "Nightscape in New York" was released, Hollywood quickly became the center of cinema. The biggest and most modern studios are here. If San Jose is called Silicon Valley, then Hollywood is really a cinema valley, the cinema center of the world. In the evening, Phan Ngoc took us to visit and have dinner at the Hollywood Walk of Fame. On the right sidewalk along this avenue, people carved more than 2,000 five-pointed stars in honor of famous stars in the entertainment industry, such as Marlon Brando, Marilyn Monroe, Charlie Chaplin, Michael Jackson, Gary Cooper, Bob Hope... The boulevard is not big but busy and long, running from East to West of Gower Street to La Brea and from North to South of Vine Street to Yucca Street. Each rose stone star has a prominent bronze border. The name of the honoree is also engraved in bronze. Visitors coming here will choose their favorite person to take pictures with the star. Our team, too, Kim Huong, Thu Nguyet, and Minh Dao chose 3 famous actresses, and Ambassador Trinh Ngoc Thai and I chose male characters. We sat, resting our hands on the star with admiration. There are still many, many unnamed stars for today and future generations.

On this boulevard, there are many Thai, Mexican, Chinese and Vietnamese restaurants. Los Angeles has many places to visit, eat and shop. There are days when celebrities are at major shopping stores ready to take photos or sign guestbooks with fans.

I walked on the boulevard of fame in the city of "Angels" and thought about America, the world's biggest economic and political country. America is the United States of America because it is the land of all ethnic groups from five continents. The United States was established only after the Spanish colonial invasion 350 years ago. Scientists and billionaires are mostly from five continents. It is reported that the number of Jews in the United States accounts for only 2.5% of the population, but the most powerful and richest Jews in the United States make up 51 of the top 100. What the union of stars and excellency from many nations. Unfortunately, America lacks an indigenous culture, the national culture of thousands of years ago. Walking on the Walk of Fame of the city of angels in the Western hemisphere, thinking about the modern culture of America, I think more deeply and proudly about Xoan singing, Dặm singing, and Folk songs. Quan Họ, Bài Chòi, Cải Lương, Đờn ca tài tử and Gong Culture, further to the Stone musical instrument, Kèn đá... of Vietnam with the history dating back several thousand years.

December 2013

From Sydney To Gold Coast

A 12-seater high-speed canoe was gliding the Homebush Bay in Sydney. The sea was azure in the morning, illuminated by the slanting rays of the sun that pierced through the misty air. Seagulls, shrieking their mating cry, rocketed in the mist and swooped down to greet us from time to time.

From the sea Sydney looked like mystique watercolor painting, an effect created by the thin layer of impalpable mist covering the bustling buildings. Sydney Opera House, the unique symbol of Australia, was magnificently visible in front of us. The entire theater was located on a large area of ocean reclamation. To build this theater, a contest was held and 233 designs were submitted. The winner was the Danish architect Jorn Utzon. They had to plant 580 concrete pillars into the seabed and used a special tile imported from Sweden for the roof. It required a million of white granite, self-cleaning tile to fully cover the theater's roof. It was truly a miracle, since the seashell roofing alone cost them ten years.

The theater had five performance halls, the smallest could host 350 guests, and the largest hall could accommodate an audience of 2679 persons, and was also home to the world's largest organ.

From the sea, one could clearly see six facets of the three roofs that resembled three huge sails. The architect's concept was three sails full of wind flying in the bay. But somehow he chose to depict a docking boat. It would have made more sense if the three sails were flying seaward. The building was known to many Vietnamese as the "Shell Theater" because the roof's resemblance to a seashell. It was a perfect architecture, hailed as Australia's largest art performance complex, and also one of the world's largest theater, where the country's most elite artists come to perform. In 2007, when the theater was granted the World Heritage title, UNESCO said "it was not only one of the masterpieces of the twentieth century but also of human history."

Our Australian friend said, "Sydney Opera House is not only the pride of our arts and culture but also our world-famous monument." From the bay I could see, right behind the theater, the Sydney Harbor Bridge, the world's tallest arc bridge. The bridge looked like a rising arc attempting to elevate the theater even higher, but it also served as the frame for this marvelous Opera House "picture." We had the chance to visit the bridge during sunset.

In the north of Sydney lies the Horu area where mountain reaches the height of 400 meters and closes to the sea, while in the south is the beautiful Cumberland plain. The north and the south are separated by a bay and also connected by the Harbor Bridge, which completes the splendid seaside Sydney.

Sydney Harbor Bridge is 139 meter tall at the highest arc, 1,149 meters long and 49 meters wide. It offers eight lanes for cars and two for pedestrian. The main arch alone is half a kilometer long. Being the world's longest, widest and tallest single-arch bridge, it is also considered a world heritage. The bridge also has a special observation deck at its highest point, which offers a spectacular view of the city.

The Bridge was not simply the stage for monthly cultural events, it was also a place to come for lovers. Although the night had not yet fallen, the lights were already on, the theater's sails were reflected in the glittering surface of the bay. The bridge was illuminated by the ever-changing color lights. The reflections of both the bridge and the theater in the stillness of the ocean invoked a sense of magic and modernity. Every New Year's Eve or in a major festival, the beauty of the bridge, the theater, and the Port Jackson were intensified by the spectacle of the colorful fireworks.

Sydney is the capital of the state of New South Wales. With four and a half million in population, it is Australia's largest, oldest, and most famous city. With 70 natural beaches, Homebush Bay has gifted Sydney an unique charm made up by the ever-sunny sand, and turned Port Jackson into one of the world's largest seaports. With that advantage, Sydney has quickly transformed itself from an isolated prison island into a global economic center, and also a tourism and service powerhouse. The city has only 4 million inhabitants but it has 4,000 hotels. It even has areas for tourist campervans along the beaches. At the city's back lies a national park, a wild-life park, and especially the Blue Mountain range, a famous destination for tourists. It is the sea and the mountain that give Sydney its unique beauty. The air is fresh and pure. In the suburbs I visited each house had a green lawn without any fence or gate. Unlike America's "democracy," Australia's gun control policy is very tight, and it seems to me that there is almost no crime and no shooting incidents. Life is peaceful here. Probably that is why Sydney ranks among the world's top five most livable cities.

***

The next day I headed north to visit the Gold Coast. The journey was quite long but it was green everywhere we passed, be it cities or villages. There was almost no barren landscape along the way. The trip was a good chance for me to observe and meditate on this land, a country that equals a continent.

The name Australia was coined in 1606, when the Dutch first discovered this continent. It derived from the Latin word Australis, which means the south, or the globe's southern land. It was not until 1 January 1901 that the federal state known as the "Commonwealth of Australia" was established. The spring here is from September to November, and October is the most beautiful month, when hundreds of flowers bloom. Australians celebrate spring first and New Year later. Australia and New Zealand are among the earliest countries to welcome the New Year.

The aboriginals have been in Australia for 40,000 years and a research on their origins claimed that they came from Southeast Asia, as tribes of hunters and gatherers. Then the Western colonization and migration followed. Consequently, Australia nowadays has 260 communities with 200 different languages. It is a multi-racial, multi-cultural nation whose land is a vast plain formed from the earth's oldest continental crust. It has an impressive biodiversity, buts its soil is not fertile due to the large area of deserts.

Australia is big in size but small in population. At 7.5 million square kilometers, it is the sixth largest country in the world, while its population is only 23 million, which means on average there is only less than three persons in one square kilometer.

Thanks to its developed economy, Australia's GDP per capita is even higher than the those of the United States, United Kingdom, Germany and France. Its human development index also ranks among the top of the world. Australia has a prolific education system, where public schools are free. It is also the nation with most names in the world's top

100 universities. We traveled with an Australian researcher. He said, "Without good education, the next generation will not be intellectually capable to realize the country's development goals." It seems that human resource is always the key element for a country's prosperity.

We stopped at the northernmost town of the state New South Wales. This hilly area is covered by tropical rain forest and is considered a world heritage. In both northern New South Wales and southern Queensland there are a number of national parks famous for their biodiversity and for being the origin of three rivers: Nerang, Coomera, and Albert.

The mountains here are numerous and craggy, the legacy of volcanic eruption 20 million years ago. The Warning looms highest, like a giant crouching elephant with a crown of clouds. Warning in Aboriginal means mountain of clouds. At its feet nests a beautiful valley, which according to locals used to be a sacred ground for indigenous people conducted their religious rituals.

Dr. Theresa Nguyen Thu Thuy, the President of Huesa Global Institute, teacher to millions of people in fifty countries, called me her brother. According to her, the Warning Valley, stretching from the west to the center of the east coast, was sacred and full of energy. She chose the Tweed valley in this vast area to house the Huesa headquarters and to serve as its place of gathering and teaching. Huesa was a method to assist people to absorb the energy from nature for health, self-healing and self-improvement, to become a better, more confident and friendlier person. "Love among people is the most universal and sacred language," said Dr. Theresa. Many Vietnamese had come here to be her students.

Our car had entered the state of Queensland, a land with many scenic spots, beautiful seas, vast coral reefs, primeval forests and charming waterfalls. Queensland has unique world heritages, including fossils of ancient animals in Riversleigh, national parks and tropical rain forests. It is one of the most developed states in Australia. Its education system is also highly respected, with many prestigious universities. Among them, the University of Queensland has been the cradle of many Vietnamese doctors and masters, including our son. The state is probably most well-known all over the world for its Gold Coast.

***

Part of Australia' eastern coast, the Gold Coast extends as far as the eye can see. Its golden sand beaches run curvingly for 70 kilometers from Beenleigh to the south, where it meets the mountain range known as the Great Dividing, separating it with the neighboring state of New South Wales. Two hundred and fifty years ago, in the beautiful morning of May, the Lieutenant James Cook sailed the yacht along the East coach of South area, he discovered this pretty land. He landed and wrote in his naval journal, "An endless beach, with glittering golden sand and crystal-clear blue sea, probably the most beautiful beach in the world."

Later on, when the map of Australia was completed, this was named The South Coast, due to its location at the south of Brisbane. Since the early twentieth century, this beach had attracted visitors and streets started to emerge along the coast. People came to build holiday houses, to open shops selling food and groceries, and to provide services for tourists. Since 1958 it carried the name Gold Coast, and quickly became the city of Gold Coast.

The city saw rapid development and a boom of tourism. Its population soon reached 600 thousand, making it the fastest growing city in Australia. In the last few decades it was Surfers beach that witnessed development at neck-breaking speed. The three kilometers long beach has become a vibrant town, with bustling high-rise buildings resembling a forest of skyscrapers. Are they trying to bring the golden sand to the sky?

The golden sand, the azure sea, and those gently lapping waves under the blue sky with scattering white clouds makes it the fair background for those soaring, proud buildings. There are all kinds of services here: shopping malls, amusement parks, restaurants, coffee shops, casinos, bars and night clubs. On Wednesdays, Fridays, and Sundays, there is even a market with hundreds of bustling stalls. Therefore the three kilometers of coastline gets the name *Surfers Paradise*. Its Cavill Avenue is the number one destination for shopping and entertainment – it is a pedestrian street with great outdoor eateries.

Any cool place here always has the word Paradise in its name. Sky Point Surfers building, the area's highest tower, at 270 meters, is also called Sky Point Surfers Paradise. It has a hotel, offices and apartments for rent, as well as a casino and other entertainment, shopping, and dining services. The 77th floor is particularly special for its panoramic view of the whole Gold Coast.

One cannot find any unexploited spot along the seventy kilometers of this coast. It is fully occupied by famous resorts and hotels, and offers the best beaches and surfing areas in both Australia and the world, such as the Split, Duranbah, Main Beach, Burleigh Head, and Stradbroke. The waves here are not the fiercest but high and quick, therefore excellent for thrill-seekers. Tourists can also board a sail boat to see whales and, if you are lucky, dancing dolphins.

Gold Coast has many fairy beaches with pleasantly flat shore, crystal clear water, and silky golden sand. Gold Coast has 300 sunny days a year, whose sunshine is always as sweet and mellow as honey. There are dozens of beautiful beaches such as Mermaid, Nobby, Miami, Rainbow Bay, Duranbah, all of which carry the word Paradise in their names.

At night, the coast is splendidly illuminated by a color lighting system. Sitting in my room overlooking the indistinct beach being gently lapped by the waves, I suddenly recalled a line in Xuan Dieu's poem, "If I were the waves, forever kissing the golden sand you." The sea was falling upon the sand, under the gentle but passionate haziness of the light, giving the Gold Coast a mysterious and incredible charm.

Bathing, surfing, and shopping in pedestrian streets are not the only things that Gold Coats can offer you. Seafood is also a heavenly treat. Crabs and lobsters are extraordinarily big here, one claw is already enough for one person. An average crab or lobster can weight up to 3-4 kilograms, that makes the seafood here so special.

At one end of the city lies the Lamington National Park, listed as a World Heritage thanks to its tropical primeval rain forests. There are lots of gorgeous waterfalls nesting between cliffs which are connected by hanging bridges. Australian tropical forest *has up to 250,000 species of plants and many unique animals which can only be found in this country such as kangaroo, koala, vombatidae, dingo wolf, ostrich, red-head crane, bandicoot...*

I saw a few groups of kangaroos approaching houses to find food, they seemed gentle and friendly, some even carried babies in their pouch, which made them really adorable. Those kangaroos can be that friendly and fearless because local people have been educated to protect the nature and they do not hunt wild animals.

One could still find aboriginal people in this city. They came from remote villages to perform their music and dance in town. They played wooden lutes whose sound was as resonating as Vietnamese t'rưng.

They also demonstrate how to make fire from wooden tools and sell their popular forest specialties.

The federal government and the state of Queensland also organize festivals for ethnic groups such as the Dreaming festival in June, where aboriginal artists collaborate with world artists. The Ord Valley festival of the Miriwoong tribe is held in May, where they dance around the fire and conclude it with a unique barbecue. The Laura festival, whose location is forty minutes away from Gold Coast, is also extremely bustling with indigenous people wearing their colorful traditional costumes and dancing all night.

Visiting Gold Coast can be seen as a double discovery: enjoying the sea and exploring the forest. Both are unique in their own ways. More than ever, if humankind know how to preserve and enrich the legacy of nature and of their ancestors, their sea and their forest will forever be gold.

April 2021.

About the Author

Dr. Trình Quang Phú

Professor Dr. Trình Quang Phú was born in 1940, in Phu Yen province (the South Central of Vietnam). He is a member of the Vietnam Writers' Association. He has the privilege to visit many countries around the world. "A Journal of Faraway Lands" records his journeys to 25 countries all over five continents. He is also the author and co-author of 50 Works since 1961.

www.ingramcontent.com/pod-product-compliance
Lightning Source LLC
LaVergne TN
LVHW041659070526
838199LV00045B/1122